Interpreting Artefact Scatters:
contributions to ploughzone archaeology

Edited by A. J. Schofield

This book is available direct from
Oxbow Books, Park End Place, Oxford OX1 1HN
(Phone: 0865-241249; Fax: 0865-794449).
Payment can be made by credit card

Oxbow Monograph 4
1991

Published by
Oxbow Books, Park End Place, Oxford OX1 1HN

© Oxbow Books and the individual authors 1991

ISBN 0 946897 25 5

This book is available direct from
Oxbow Books, Park End Place, Oxford, OX1 1HN
(Phone: 0-865-241249; Fax: 0-865-794449)
Payment may be made by credit card

Printed by
The Short Run Press, Exeter

CONTENTS

LIST OF CONTRIBUTORS

Allen M J, Wessex Archaeology, Portway House, Portway Estate, Old Sarum, Salisbury, Wiltshire.

Bintliff J, Department of Archaeology, University of Durham, 46 Saddler Street, Durham.

Boismier W A, Department of Archaeology, University of Cambridge, Downing Street, Cambridge.

Bowden M C B, RCHM, Line Building, Haymarket Lane, The University, Newcastle upon Tyne.

Clark R H, The Archaeology Service, The Planning Department, Bedfordshire County Council, County Hall, Bedford.

Ford S, Thames Valley Archaeological Services, 78 Watlington Street, Reading, Berkshire.

Gaffney V L, Department of Archaeology, Univerza Edvarda Kardelja, Ljubljana, Yugoslavia and Undergraduate School of Studies in Archaeological Sciences, Bradford, West Yorkshire.

Hayes P P, Heritage Lincolnshire, 51 Newland, Lincoln.

Healy F, Wessex Archaeology Portway House, Portway Estate, Old Sarum, Salisbury, Wiltshire.

Keay S J, Department of Archaeology, University of Southampton, Highfield, Southampton.

Millett M, Department of Archaeology, University of Durham, 46 Saddler Street, Durham.

Schofield A J, English Heritage, 23 Savile Row, London.

Slapsak B, Department of Archaeology, Univerza Edvarda Kardelja, Ljubljana, Yugoslavia.

Stoddart S K F, Department of Classics and Archaeology, 11 Woodland Road, Bristol.

Tingle M, Tudor Cottage, Ham, Hungerford, Berkshire.

Wagstaff J M, Department of Geography, University of Southampton, Highfield, Southampton.

Whitehead N, 73 Watling Street, London.

PREFACE

Much of what appears in this volume was originally presented as a session at the Theoretical Archaeology Group conference, University College, London in December 1986. Other contributions stem either from additional conference papers or were written specifically with this volume in mind. The session, organised jointly by myself and Simon Keay, was intended as a theoretical and frank discussion of the way survey data is perceived largely in terms of specific places or foci, with little concern for the use and exploitation of space. That theme is maintained for the present volume.

Under the general heading "Interpreting Artefact Scatters", discussion is focused on four specific questions or problem areas. These are presented as individual sections each of which is preceded by a short introduction. Within each section the aim has been to present a range of environmental and cultural perspectives in an attempt to present the pro's and con's within specific sets of data. The level of interpretation appropriate to prehistoric flint collections and Roman ceramics is a case in point.

The sections are therefore thematic. The first is largely an introduction and considers the problems of definition, scale and the need for clearly established research priorities. The second involves post-depositional disturbance and the significant role played by both environmental and cultural processes in determining the structure of surface distributions. Section 3 considers the case for integrating the results of surface collection with those from excavation, controlled experiments and the use of theoretical land-use models. Like section 2 the papers appear largely as cautionary tales, warning against the use of artefact distributions without a proper understanding of what they represent. Finally section 4 demonstrates the range of human activity which may occur within the landscape and various ways of presenting such data without necessarily resorting to the "dots-on-maps" approach, often favoured in the past.

All the papers therefore represent variations on a theme, discussing in both quantitative and qualitative terms what artefact distributions represent. When the idea for a TAG session was originally discussed we felt there was a need to debate the role of specific places or "sites" in field survey, what they represented and how they might be defined. Although this volume concerns a rather more general discussion than the site/off-site issue, the underlying principle is the same.

Publication would not have been possible without the original TAG session and for that I must thank the contributors and discussants, first for agreeing to participate and second for contributing to a lively and, I hope, constructive debate. I must also thank Simon Keay for his help in organising the original session and for advice on its publication.

Aspects of the volume were also discussed with Clive Gamble, Mike Allen and Royston Clark while my wife gave invaluable editorial assistance at all stages of the preparation. To all I am most grateful.

[It should be stressed that opinions expressed in the various papers are those of the individual authors and do not necessarily reflect those of the editor].

A J Schofield
Southampton
July 1988

Section 1
The Background to Interpretation:
Method, Theory and Research Design

The papers in this section stand as an introduction to the volume and consider some of the underlying principles and assumptions that have caused confusion in the past.

In introducing the volume Schofield describes the various interpretations of "site" upon which so much debate has hinged as well as providing examples from the ethnographic and archaeological record to suggest that (1) a high density of artefacts does not necessarily represent occupation, and (2) that often occupation will be manifested through surface collection by a blank collection unit. The solution is simple. Rather than looking for only one type of activity and assuming that sub-surface remains will be manifested in plough zone collections, we must appreciate the extent of post-depositional disturbance (Section 2) and the range of human activities which occur (Sections 3 and 4).

Wagstaff's paper is the first of two "geographical contributions" within the volume and expresses clearly the nature of the problem which archaeologists face. Sites do, of course, exist in the real world although their identification and interpretation is by no means simple. Wagstaff's paper offers suggestions rather than solutions and draws on the experience of geography in exploring the concept of space and spatial relationships to illustrate them. Scale, for example, is an all-important aspect in determining what is and what is not a site. At a scale of 1:50,000 clustered settlements will be relatively simple to recognise, while collection by metre units may produce a less obvious distinction.

We should also be aware of the means by which the term site is defined. To talk in terms of sites may involve a number of variables and conditions, location for example, or function (the archaeological correlate for the settlement unit). Whichever the case, the geographical perspective offered by Wagstaff's paper highlights the problem of definition encountered in the interpretation of surface distributions, a problem brought about largely by the ambiguity and over-use of a specific term. As Wagstaff's paper suggests, an appropriate definition depends more on the nature of the questions raised and specific problems rather than on the opinion of individuals.

Specific questions and problem domains is an area explored more critically in Boismier's contribution. In this, the role of research design is assessed in terms of fieldwork at Broom Hill, Hampshire. As Boismier suggests, research design is not an academic disease imported from the America of the 1960s, nor is it something only prehistorians need to understand. Rather it is an essential element in any fieldwork project and is necessary for guiding research in the direction of those questions considered most worthy of attention. To understand the distribution of artefacts across an area, one cannot just "go out and walk", expecting the results to produce some structure and meaning. Questions must be established to determine the various processes responsible for producing a distribution (ie the potential for pattern recognition) long before the question of interpretation may be addressed.

Both Wagstaff and Boismier, therefore, make the point central to the remainder of the volume, that a crucial first step in understanding surface distributions is to appreciate the background, both agricultural, environmental and cultural, as well as the problems being tackled and the questions being raised. Only then can interpretation begin to take shape.

Chapter 1
Interpreting Artefact Scatters:
an Introduction

A J Schofield

"Let us not waste our time in idle discourse. Let us do something,
while we have the chance!"
Samuel Beckett: "Waiting for Godot"

Surface collection has, for a variety of reasons, gained prominence in recent years. A number of conferences and conference sessions have dealt with questions of methodology, analysis and interpretation, resulting in such volumes as *Field survey in Britain and Abroad* (Macready and Thompson 1985), *Archaeology from the ploughsoil* (Haselgrove, Millett and Smith 1985) and *La prospection archéologique: paysage et peuplement* (Ferdiére and Zadora Rio 1986). Monographs have also had a major impact on the development and acceptance of regional survey. Foley's (1981) work in eastern Africa and Shennan's (1985) East Hampshire survey, for example, are widely quoted in the present volume, while *The Cannon Reservoir human ecology project* (O'Brien, Warren and Lewarch 1982) and papers in *Lithic analysis in later British prehistory* (Brown and Edmonds 1987), *Archaeological survey in the Mediterranean* (Keller and Rupp 1983) and in volume 4:1 of the *Archaeological Review from Cambridge* have contributed much to the current debate on survey methodology and the understanding of regional artefact distributions.

Why, therefore, another conference session to debate the issue (TAG 1986 at University College, London, organised by myself and Simon Keay) and, perhaps more pertinent in this context, why another collection of papers debating a specific field technique which has surely received its fair share of attention in recent years?

The answer is the same now as it was four years ago when the idea for a TAG session first arose. Understanding what artefact scatters represent is not so much a methodological issue as a theoretical one. Obviously collection strategies will determine the quality of information recovered as well as the nature of any given distribution. To understand what the distribution means, however, one must understand the behaviour responsible for generating patterns of human activity as well as the various post-depositional processes which obscure any order which may previously have been apparent within a

distribution. Despite the tendency for both field-related and theoretical conference sessions to debate the issue, this remains an area of some confusion. Although ethnographic studies (eg Binford 1980;1982), technological investigations, for example into tool use (eg Hayden 1979) and production cycles (eg Zvelebil *et al* 1987,17-18), the logistics of settlement location and land-use (eg Chisholm 1962,102-107; Trigger 1968; Hamond 1980) and the nature of cultural deposition (eg Okpoko 1987,453) and post-depositional processes (eg Schiffer 1987) have seen considerable advance, their application to the interpretation of artefact distributions has been varied. Much has been made, for example, of the distribution of natural resources in the landscape. My own work in the middle Avon valley (Schofield 1987a) and investigations into the Roman settlement of north west Essex (Williamson 1984) are examples of this. Yet despite the detailed discussions concerning post-depositional processes, their value in terms of analysis and interpretation has been limited (but *cf* Boismier and Reilly 1988).

The aim of this volume is not to produce any all-embracing solution to ploughzone archaeology, but rather to define, through various case studies, what the problems are and how they vary between environmental contexts and depend on the nature of the evidence. At the original TAG session, from which several of the papers derive, the question was really one of definition and whether the "site", whatever that implied, was an appropriate unit for investigation and subsequent analysis. The areas of research described above suggest that something rather more flexible should be employed, and which would allow the full range of human behaviour to be identified. Let us consider this question in more detail.

A question of definition

"Site" has meant a variety of things to various authors. Anderson (1984), for example, described a site, as represented through surface collection, as two or more artefacts in close association. Warren (1982) on the other hand described it as, "any isolable aggregate of five or more artefacts having a spatial midpoint that occurs inside a spatial quadrat". Jones (1985) regarded site as any area characterised by a contiguous and continuous scatter of stone or other archaeological debris, while Ammerman (1985) defined it as a "spatially discrete surface scatter". The term most widely used in describing surface distributions, therefore, appears to mean something different to the majority of people responsible for their interpretation. It is a term which is largely descriptive, is rarely justified through quantification and is invariably taken for granted. As Plog, Plog and Wait (1978,387) have suggested, "the rigid application of density-based definitions may result in a systematic exclusion from analysis of significant components of the archaeological record". Gamble (1982,529) makes a similar point: "flint scatters are considered poor data unless a tent or a hut can be resurrected from among the chippings". The same could be said of all surface data in the present climate.

Definition is often made, therefore, in terms of high density "patches" in contrast to surrounding low density scatters or "background noise". This is an argument, however, with serious complications. First, that in the ethnographic literature we are told repeatedly that discard tends to occur more frequently *away* from habitation areas (eg Binford 1978; Simms 1988; Gould 1967) and that high density and extensive artefact distributions will often represent other activities, flint mining (eg Torrence 1986) or manuring (eg Wilkinson 1982) for example. Indeed Gould (1980) has observed that only 1% of the lithic material of Aborigines from the western Desert of Australia is discarded at the settlement, while Wood (1978), analysing locational strategies in the Rio-Grande valley of New Mexico, suggested that secondary "sites" contained higher artefact densities than base camps. Another example is Robertshaw's analysis of artefact density on a recently abandoned pastoralist settlement in Numaqualand (1978). In this case the mean density of finds across the settlement was 0.163 per square metre.

A second point concerns the general low density of specific artefact groups. The question of middle and late Saxon remains is a case in point. In the East Hampshire survey, for example, only a single chaff-tempered sherd and two other sherds probably of late Saxon date were recovered (Oake and Shennan 1985,89). If this is the off-site material, where are the settlements which we know existed? The solution may lie in the poor quality of the pottery, although it is perhaps significant that pottery only appears in small quantities from excavated contexts. At Maxey, for example, the excavation of a Saxon settlement produced only 270 sherds (Addyman 1964,47), while at Cowdery's Down, Hampshire, excavation of the Saxon phase produced only 146 abraded and chronologically undiagnostic Saxon sherds (Millett and James 1983). Bearing in mind the generally low quantity of ceramics on excavated sites of this period, do we interpret every sherd of Saxon pottery recovered by surface collection as evidence for settlement activity, or is it indicative of off-site activity such as manuring? Furthermore, how should high density pottery scatters be interpreted on the rare occasions when they do occur. At Hay Green, Norfolk, for example, a spread of Ipswich-type ware was located, covering at least seven hectares (Rogerson and Silvester 1986) and concentrated on the distribution of roddons, silt-channels dominating the landscape and standing to a height of around 2m. Around 1,000 sherds were recovered, often associated with spreads of animal bone, both of which appear in far greater frequency than on the majority of contemporary middle Saxon settlements. Indeed comparable figures from elsewhere in Norfolk make interesting reading: Around 200 sherds of Ipswich ware were encountered in a survey of the Launditch Hundred (Wade-Martins 1980), 134 in the survey of Hales, Heckingham and Loddon and 28 in the parish of Witton (Lawson 1983,70).

Density in this case may reflect a number of factors, most of which are relevant to all classes of surface material. The first is surface visibility, rejected in the case of Hay Green as no other pottery types occurred with similar frequency. A second is that high density represents a large population or continued occupation. This is logical but for the fact that even on excavated settlements, pottery occurs in much smaller quantities (above). A third factor, however, and one not discussed so far is that of differential access. Pottery will occur with greater frequency in areas where access to supply zones is available. Although this does not account for the enormous density in relation to the majority of excavated units, it is one factor which must be taken into account in the analysis of regional density variations.

Where low quantities of a specific artefact group are the norm, the high density patches cannot possibly be regarded as sites at the expense of the background scatter. Through simple comparisons with sites such as Cowdery's Down, it is apparent that only one or two sherds may represent habitation areas. Against this we must attempt to distinguish the settlement discard from the similarly low densities produced through manuring. Density alone, therefore, is not a reliable measure by which to study those variations. Instead the composition or structure of pottery distributions needs to be considered in more detail (*cf* Cogbill and Lane) and compared with the types of discard regime that the two types of behaviour may produce (Hayes this volume). Against this background and all the confusions within it, relative changes in artefact density, considered by Plog, Plog and Wait (1978,387) and Gallant (1986) as the most appropriate measure of "site" versus "background noise", are insufficient. Such is the problem we face.

Thus the suggestion is that although "sites", understood in the sense of being discrete locations distinct from their surroundings, may occur under certain circumstances, their value to regional interpretation is limited unless we know precisely what form a settlement system should take. The terms "site" and "settlement" are not synonymous, while such units are only considered of value where quantitative statements regarding their frequency through time, internal patterning and the extent of their distribution in relation to environmental variables, can be assessed. Rarely will this be the case. To define a site for the prehistoric period would involve first drawing a boundary which distinguished the on-site material from "background-noise". As numerous authors have implied, this is not so much an observation as a decision, and one which will inevitably vary between individuals. The second level of observation is to confirm that all the material within the site is representative of a single episode. This, for lithics at least, is virtually impossible, unless found in association with ceramics or with bounded units of either discoloured soil (Cherry *et al* 1988,164) or soil "islands" (Healy this volume). Flint artefacts may be considered broadly contemporary on the basis of some chronological distinctions (Ford 1987), but that does not prove that artefacts found together were used together.

For a Roman or medieval site post-depositional disturbance may be less marked and the artefacts recovered all the more diagnostic while integration with documentary sources may provide a clue as to where the rural settlements were located, the size and intensity of occupation and the total number present within a specific area at a particular time. As Hughes (1984,70) has observed for Hampshire, the results of surface collection and excavation combined have produced evidence for only 8% of rural settlements recorded in late Saxon charters and the Domesday Book. Regarding chronology, in the area around Wharram Percy, survey has produced evidence for Roman occupation, with ceramics providing a chronological range for a variety of locations (Hayfield 1987,177). Another example is the case of Roman Silchester, where the site boundary remains and the distribution of artefacts associated with known occupation episodes can be established (Corney 1984). In this case survey revealed evidence for ribbon development in areas to the east and

west of Silchester, based not on "precision dating" but on broad chronological brackets. Further examples are apparent from survey in the Mediterranean where the internal arrangement of urban areas has been investigated through the distribution of artefacts (eg Bintliff and Snodgrass 1988). The internal structure of known sites, whether urban areas or field monuments (eg Bradley 1987), offers a challenge to surface collection, not only for the development of an appropriate methodology but also for analysis of the distribution and association of artefact groups. Appropriate methods may include straightforward statistical investigations, for example correlation and regression analyses, depending on the aims and questions raised (Millett 1979). Alternatively more detailed quantitative analyses may be used, such as those described by Berry, Meilke and Kvamme (1984), Whallon (1984) and Cogbill and Lane (1985).

The wider context of collection

Although high density scatters do, therefore, occur and undoubtedly represent repeated occupation and the accumulation of discard in specific locations, a more perceptive approach to their interpretation is required. At one level, "site" tends to imply "settlement", while on another, to describe all high density scatters as sites, implies that all performed a similar function. As Binford has suggested, this is a static view of what, in reality, was a dynamic landscape (1983). Surface collection can do so much more than simply produce "figures in a landscape". Most types of human behaviour, for whatever period, should be visible through surface collection. Signatures, in the form of artefact scatters, will occur, the one proviso being that material remains were the end product of a given aspect of human behaviour. So long as those remains have survived the passage of time, the patterns should be there. The onus is on us to interpret those patterns and to understand precisely what it is that they represent, whether settlement activity, quarrying or manuring.

The belief that artefact density will reflect not only cultural but environmental processes has already been stressed on numerous occasions, most recently by Schiffer (1987). To look at collection in a wider context, for example between regions, in relation to the more detailed excavation records or in terms of contemporary land-use in a specific region, one needs to look for an aspect of the collection which may be considered more representative of the activities which created it. One possibility is the structure of an artefact collection, looking, for example, at its content in terms of artefact diversity as well as the quantity of items and the intensity of their distribution. One example has been Hayfield's investigation into Roman settlement in the parish of Wharram Percy. To study the range or hierarchy of the settlement system, the artefact collections were divided into two major categories (1987,176): villas and farmsteads. He suggested that the former would be represented by large artefact-rich areas including debris from mosaic floors, tiled roofs and plastered walls as well as containing a high class of pottery. Farmsteads, however, would be smaller but, more significantly, would be less artefact-rich. The pottery would be of poorer quality and although some traces of ceramic roof tile would probably be found, it is unlikely that many buildings would have had tiled roofs. Although such distinctions may also be the result of differential access, for example to fine wares, or differential preservation, the possibility of investigating structural differences between artefact collections can aid in their interpretation.

A more objective approach to the same problem may involve comparison between scatters on the basis of correlation between aspects of the collection. In the upper Meon valley survey of south-east Hampshire, for example, domestic and industrial zones were distinguished on the basis of correlation between specific artefact groups (Schofield this volume). High proportions of retouched artefacts, for example, were considered a feature of domestic contexts while high density, low proportions of retouch and high proportions of primary waste material were a feature of industrial zones. The strength of correlation within, for example the industrial zone, indicates the extent to which industrial activity overlaps with other aspects of human behaviour. The strength of correlation between zones, in other words indicates the extent to which they remained distinct through time.

A final example is the Maddle Villa Project, described in part in Chapter 9, in which the Roman villa was investigated not as a site, but as one part of the archaeological landscape and as just one of a variety of archaeological "signatures" present in the area (Scott and Gaffney 1987; Gaffney, Gaffney and Tingle 1985). Pottery distributions, for example, were interpreted both in terms of settlement-based manuring episodes, carried out to maintain soil fertility (Scott and Gaffney 1987,87), and in relation to a possible settlement hierarchy in which the presence/absence of tiles represented a distinction between high and low status settlement units. Such approaches to the examination of surface distributions are not new and are certainly not confined to Britain, as these examples might imply. Work in the Mediterranean, for example, often makes the distinction between types of activity on the basis of either the function of ceramics, for example storage jars, cooking wares, or the structure of the vessels, for example coarse wares, fine wares (*cf* papers in Keller and Rupp 1983). Through such investigations

it may be possible to consider the relative status of contemporary settlements (eg Upham, Lightfoot and Feinman 1981) or the internal structure and zoning within settlements recorded either from upstanding remains, air survey or geophysical prospection. Either way, this dynamic approach to surface distributions has much to offer, especially when combined with appropriate quantitative analyses.

The papers presented in this volume continue this theme and constitute a further attempt to investigate the range of activities which surface distributions represent. Integration of surface distributions with, for example, the results of excavation (eg Millett 1985), geophysical prospection (eg Gaffney and Gaffney 1986; Richards and Entwistle 1987) and environmental evidence (Schofield 1987b) have much to contribute, as do models of behaviour adapted from human geography. It is important to stress, however, that no simple solution will emerge. The complexity of the agricultural regime, combined with natural processes and the suitability of the data for chronological investigations will determine the outcome of any regional survey. It is that point above all else with which the papers in this volume are concerned.

One final cautionary tale on which to end: Excavations by Richard Gould in several areas around Aboriginal settlements which had produced surface remains, failed to reveal any underlying structures. The explanation offered by his Aboriginal informant does much to invalidate "site-based" collection, at least where sites are considered correlates for the settlement unit, and is a lesson to all those with a vested interest in the interpretation of artefact distributions:

"...them old timers never put their houses in the garbage dump...they don't like to live in their garbage any more than you would" (Gould 1966,43).

Acknowledgements
I am grateful to Simon Keay and Clive Gamble for commenting on an earlier draft of this paper.

References

Addyman P.V., 1964. A Dark Age settlement at Maxey, Northamptonshire. *Medieval Archaeology* 8, 20-73.

Ammerman A.J., 1985. Ploughzone experiments in Calabria, Italy. *Journal of Field Archaeology* 12, 33-40.

Anderson J., 1984. *Between plateau and plain: flexible responses to varied environments in south-western Australia.* Canberra University, Occasional papers in prehistory, 4.

Berry K.J., Mielke P.W. and Kvamme K.L., 1984. Efficient permutation procedures for analysis of artefact distributions, in Hietala H.J., editor, *Intrasite Spatial*

Analysis in Archaeology, 54-74. Cambridge University Press, Cambridge.

Binford L.R., 1978. Dimensional analysis of behaviour and site structure from an Eskimo hunting stand. *American Antiquity* 43, 330-361.

Binford L.R., 1980. Willow smoke and dogs tails: hunter-gatherer settlement systems and archaeological site formation. *American Antiquity* 45, 4-20.

Binford L.R., 1982. The archaeology of place. *Journal of anthropological archaeology* 1, 5-31.

Binford L.R., 1983. *In pursuit of the past.* Thames and Hudson. London.

Bintliff J. and Snodgrass A., 1988. Mediterranean survey and the city. *Antiquity* 62, 57-71.

Boismier W.A. and Reilly P., 1988. Expanding the role of computer graphics in the analysis of survey data, in Ruggles C.L.N. and Rahtz S.P.Q., editors, *Computer and quantitative methods in archaeology 1987,* 221-225. BAR (International Series) 393. Oxford.

Bradley R.J., 1987. A field method for investigating the spatial structure of lithic scatters, in Brown A.G. and Edmonds M.R., editors, *Lithic analysis in later British prehistory,* 39-48. BAR (British Series) 162. Oxford.

Cherry J.F., Davis J.L., Demitrack A., Mantzourani E., Strasser T.F. and Talalay L.E., 1988. Archaeological survey in an artefact-rich landscape: a Middle Neolithic example from Nemea, Greece. *American Journal of Archaeology* 92, 159-176.

Chisholm M., 1962. *Rural settlement and land-use: an essay in location.* Hutchinson. London.

Cogbill S. and Lane P., 1985. Spatial analysis of Roman pottery from the East Field ploughsoil, in Pryor F. and French C., editors, The Fenland Project No.1: The lower Welland valley, volume 1, 53-58. *East Anglian Archaeology* 27.

Corney M., 1984. A field survey of the extra-mural region of Silchester, in Fulford M., *Silchester: excavations on the defences, 1974-80,* 239-298. Britannia Monograph series, No. 5.

Foley R., 1981. *Off-site archaeology and human adaptation in eastern Africa: an analysis of regional artefact density in the Amboseli, southern Kenya,* BAR (International Series) 97. Oxford.

Ford S., 1987. Chronological and functional aspects of flint assemblages, in Brown A.G. and Edmonds M.R., editors, *Lithic analysis in later British prehistory,* 67-86. BAR (British Series) 162. Oxford.

Gaffney C.F. and Gaffney V.L., 1986. From Boeotia to Berkshire: an integrated approach to geophysics and rural field survey. *Prospezioni Archeologiche* 10, 65-70.

Gaffney C.F., Gaffney V.L. and Tingle M., 1985. Settlement, economy or behaviour? Micro-regional land-use models and the interpretation of surface artefact patterns, in Haselgrove C., Millett M. and Smith I., editors, *Archaeology from the ploughsoil: studies in the collection and interpretation of field survey data,* 95-108. University of Sheffield.

Gallant T.W., 1986. "Background noise" and site definition: a contribution to survey methodology. *Journal of Field Archaeology* 13, 403-418.

Gamble C., 1982. Review of Foley 1981. *Proceedings of the Prehistoric Society* 48, 529-530.

Gould R.A., 1966. *Archaeology of the Point St George and Tolowa prehistory.* University of California, Publications in Anthropology, 4.

Gould R.A., 1980. *Living Archaeology.* Cambridge University Press.

Hamond F.W., 1980. The interpretation of archaeological distribution maps: biases inherent in archaeological fieldwork. *Archaeo-Physika* 7, 193-216.

Hayden B., editor, 1979. *Lithic use-wear analysis.* Academic Press. London.

Hayfield C., 1987. *An archaeological survey of the parish of Wharram Percy, East Yorkshire. 1: The evolution of the Roman landscape.* BAR (British Series) 172. Oxford.

Hughes M.F., 1984. Rural settlement and landscape in late Saxon Hampshire, in Faull M.L., editor, *Studies in late Anglo-Saxon settlement,* 65-79. Oxford University Department of extra-mural studies. Oxford.

Jones R., 1985. *Archaeological research in the Kakadu National Park.* Australian National Parks and Wildlife Services, 13.

Keller D.R. and Rupp D.W., editors, 1983. *Archaeological survey in the Mediterranean area.* BAR (International Series) 155. Oxford.

Lawson A.J., 1983. The Archaeology of Witton near North Walsham, Norfolk. *East Anglian Archaeology* 18.

Millett M., 1979. How much pottery?, in Millett M., editor, *Pottery and the archaeologist,* 77-80. Institute of Archaeology, Occasional Publication No.4.

Millett M., 1985. Field survey calibration: a contribution, in Haselgrove C., Millett M. and Smith I, editors, *Archaeology from the ploughsoil: studies in the collection and interpretation of field survey data,* 31-38. University of Sheffield.

Millett M. and James S., 1983. Excavations at Cowdery's Down, Hampshire 1978-1981. *Archaeological Journal* 140, 151-279.

Oake M. and Shennan S.J., 1985. The Saxon and Medieval periods, in Shennan S.J., *Experiments in the collection and analysis of archaeological survey data: the East Hampshire survey,* 89-104. Sheffield University Press.

Okpoko A.I., 1987. Pottery making in Igboland, eastern Nigeria: an ethno-archaeological study. *Proceedings of the Prehistoric Society* 53, 445-456.

Plog S., Plog F. and Wait K., 1978. Decision making in modern survey, in Schiffer M.B., editor, *Advances in Archaeological Method and Theory* 1, 384-420.

Richards J. and Entwistle R., 1987. The geochemical and geophysical properties of lithic scatters, in Brown A.G. and Edmonds M.R., editors, *Lithic analysis in later British prehistory,* 19-38. BAR (British Series) 162. Oxford.

Robertshaw P.T., 1978. The archaeology of an abandoned pastoralist campsite. *South African Journal of Science* 74, 29-31.

Rogerson A. and Silvester R.J., 1986. Middle Saxon occupation at Hay Green, Terrington St Clement. *Norfolk Archaeology* 39, 320-322.

Schiffer M., 1987. *Formation processes of the archaeological record*. University of New Mexico Press. Albuquerque.

Schofield A.J., 1987a. Putting lithics to the test: non-site analysis and the Neolithic settlement of southern England. *Oxford Journal of Archaeology* 6, 269-286.

Schofield A.J., 1987b. The role of palaeoecology in understanding variations in regional survey data. *Circaea* 5, 33-42.

Scott E. and Gaffney V.L., 1987. Romano-British villas: practical lessons for tactical fieldwork, in Gaffney C.F. and Gaffney V.L., editors, *Pragmatic Archaeology: theory in crisis?*, 83-88. BAR (British Series) 167. Oxford.

Shennan S.J., 1985. *Experiments in the collection and analysis of archaeological survey data: the East Hampshire survey*. Sheffield University Press.

Simms S.R., 1988. The archaeological structure of a bedouin camp. *Journal of Archaeological Science* 15, 197-211.

Torrence R., 1986. *Production and exchange of stone tools: prehistoric obsidian in the Aegean*. Cambridge University Press.

Trigger B., 1965. The determinants of settlement patterns, in Chang K.C., editor, *Settlement Archaeology*, 53-78. California National Press.

Upham S., Lightfoot K. and Feinman G., 1981. Explaining socially determined ceramic distributions in the prehistoric plateau south-west. *American Antiquity* 46, 822-833.

Wade-Martins P., 1980. Fieldwork and excavation on village sites in Launditch Hundred, Norfolk. *East Anglian Archaeology* 10.

Warren R.E., 1982. Prehistoric settlement patterns, in O'Brien M.J., Warren R.E. and Lewarch D.E., editors, *The Cannon Reservoir human ecology project: an archaeological study of cultural adaptations in the southern Prairie peninsular*, 337-368. Academic press, New York.

Whallon R., 1984. Unconstrained clustering for the analysis of spatial distributions in archaeology, in Hietala H.J., editor, *Intra-site spatial analysis in archaeology*, 242-277. Cambridge University Press.

Wilkinson T.J., 1982. The definition of ancient manured zones by means of extensive sherd sampling techniques. *Journal of Field Archaeology* 9, 323-333.

Williamson T.M., 1984. The Roman countryside: settlement and agriculture in NW Essex. *Britannia* 15, 225-230.

Wood J.J., 1978. Optimal location in settlement space: a model for describing settlement strategies. *American Antiquity* 43, 258-270.

Zvelebil M., Moore J., Green S. and Henson D., 1987. Regional survey and the analysis of lithic scatters: a case study from south-east Ireland, in Rowley Conwy P., Zvelebil M. and Blankholm H.P., editors, *Mesolithic north-west Europe: recent trends* 9-32. Sheffield University Press.

Chapter 2

The Archaeological "Site" from a Geographical Perspective

M Wagstaff

For geographers a *site* is fundamentally a place or location where something is found – certain physical properties perhaps, or a settlement or activity area of some kind. Each site is in some sense recognisable and discrete. In settlement studies *site* is frequently used with *situation,* that is the wider context of location. Whilst situation is perhaps functional in its application and recognises change over time, *site* implies a fixed, formal entity. It is surprising, therefore, given the apparently basic function of the term, that there appears to be no discussion in the geographical literature as to how a site might be recognised, defined or delimited, let alone how it might be applied in the context of archaeological discovery. When these questions have arisen, they have been answered pragmatically. There seems to have been no need for a theoretical literature to emerge. For example, the classic early work, *Principles of Human Geography* by Paul Vidal de la Blache (1926), discusses *site* purely in terms of the influences on the distribution of activity centres (*établissements humaines*), whilst Haggett's seminal book, *Locational Analysis in Human Geography* (1965), does not even index *site.* More recent works seem to assume that the meaning and use of *site* as a concept are known and understood. This, apparently, is not the case.

The lack of any specific literature devoted to the definition and recognition of sites may be attributed to the working practices of many geographers. Habitually, geographers work at a meso or regional scale so that the recognition of centroids or centres of gravity in otherwise continuous fields (Hägerstrand 1957,27) has not been strictly necessary. Until recently, much geographical research was based upon the analysis of topographic maps of 1:50,000 or greater. The limitations of scale have not only filtered out much of the detail, they have also reduced many of the practical problems of defining "centres of gravity" in a continuous landscape. For example, distinctly clustered settlements are easy to recognise at 1:50,000 and easy to locate as particular units in the physical landscape. It is more difficult to process and interpret frequency data collected metre by metre across a continuous surface, even when a distinction between presence and absence of material (for example sherds) has been adequately defined. This is rarely the case and illustrates clearly a major problem faced by archaeologists.

To provide a geographical perspective on the archaeological *site,* it is necessary to look first at the practice and assumptions of geographers. I do this with reference to my own experience and my attempts to study various aspects of human geography, chiefly rural settlements. Like many geographical problems, the question of site is scale-dependent. Discussion in this paper will begin on a regional scale and move to the level of the individual site.

A regional perspective

On a regional scale geographers seem to use the term *site* to refer to individual places with specific attributes and which, collectively, make up a spatial pattern. Settlements are often reduced to geometrical points so that some form of spatial analysis (nearest neighbour or quadrat analysis for example) can be carried out; they may also be classified, however, according to size, function or form. By whichever means, each settlement or *site* is recognised as a centroid; it is by this method alone that position can be defined within a regional system. Without it, mapping and spatial analysis are impossible. Identification of the centroid requires some measure of discrimination or clustering. Appropriate measures might include density frequencies and spacing thresholds.

Density frequencies allow variations in the number of characteristics per unit area to be measured and seen in the context of other adjacent units. When modern settlement patterns are studied relevant characteristics might be confined to structures, whilst in an archaeological context they would include the debris resulting from occupation, for example the number of sherds or flint artefacts in a sampling quadrat. The data thus collected might be used to measure either the central tendency or the *degree of dispersion* (Haggett *et al* 1977, 312-3) within a given area. Spacing thresholds represent distances which appear to be critical to the recognition of discrete groups of elements. Again structures might be appropriate in the context of settlement studies, while the distance metric could be either linear (metres, kilometres) or temporal (minutes, hours). The choice of both areal units and also of threshold (critical distance) is fundamental but, to a large extent, "a matter of judgement". The basis of the judgement, however, should be explained, a requirement seldom met hitherto. Different sized units and different thresholds will alter the results obtained in any statistical analysis. Each must be adjusted, therefore, to the size of the region considered appropriate for the problems concerned.

This may all be very well in theory. However, unless data are collected under controlled conditions, as through the systematic analysis of a map, approximations may have to be used to locate relevant information. Thus, if population data are available only for a generalised area, then attempts to attach them to actual places must depend upon being able to use other criteria for recognising settlements and discriminating between them. Whilst the nature of the places occupied by settlements may not be strictly relevant to purely geometrical or topological styles of analysis (where configuration, continuity and connectivity may be important), they are basic to other types of study. These might include social patterns across a region or the organisation of settlement plans. Classification might then be important.

Settlement sites have often been classified in terms of elevation (hill-top or valley-bottom sites), possible function (defensive) and their relationship to a vital resource (spring-line). The attempt to develop these types of classification requires the making of some *a priori* assumptions. The most basic is that discrete entities can be recognised in some consistent fashion - defensive hills, spring-lines, valley-bottoms. Operational criteria then become important. Proximity, for example, has to be defined in terms of distance and threshold for spring-line villages, while the angles and properties of slopes, as well as relative elevation, may be required to identify defensive sites. Relative elevation and relative position need specification to distinguish valley-bottom sites. Once a classification has been devised and applied, the results of the study allow the exploration of correlations and the comparison of distributions. In both exercises presence and absence are equally important.

The individual site

At the level of the individual site, definition becomes crucial. What is appropriate, however, depends upon the nature of the problem and the questions raised. For certain types of problem centroid definitions of the type already described may be sufficient. In some cases, however, a more precise definition of the site may be required. An example might be the study of settlement plans or the investigation of artefact patterning on an intra-site level (for example various papers in Hietala 1984). Here the relationship between topographic properties and such things as street alignments or the position of buildings will be of interest. If that is so, it will be necessary to specify the limits of the site before proceeding to inventory its properties and look for influences. In operational conditions, the settlement geographer would look for edges or breaks. One might look for the edge of the built-up area and see whether that corresponded with some characteristic of the physical site. Alternatively, the edge of the site might be sought independently by looking for some sharp break in topography - a sudden change of slope, a precipice for example. The search is for something which can be used to delimit the site. Abrupt changes in what would otherwise be regarded as a series of transitions are ideal. In some instances though, sharp breaks may not be apparent, as on a gentle slope or in a loose and scattered pattern of buildings; in such cases a more arbitrary definition might have to be used. This may depend more upon notions of centrality and distance than on purely physical properties.

Conclusion

In conclusion, the best that the geographer can offer the archaeologist in trying to decide what is meant by *site* are one or two concepts and the notion of scale. The concept of the centroid is very useful where edges or discontinuities cannot be recognised. Edges and breaks are important; they do exist in the landscape but are more difficult to recognise on distribution maps if the scale of plotting is inappropriate. It is no good using scales appropriate to making excavation plans for the analysis of data produced by extensive field survey. More thought has to be given to (1) distinguishing an appropriate scale for the intended analyses, and (2) defining the level at which variation in land-use may be "measured" by artefact discard. At the same time, it is important to be clear precisely what problem is being tackled and the questions being asked. If *sites* cannot be distinguished through the mapping of surface scatters, an alternative means of interpretation must be sought.

Acknowledgement
The author is grateful to Dr S J Shennan for his helpful comments on an earlier draft of this paper.

References
Hägerstrand, T., 1957. Migration and area: survey of a sample of Swedish migration fields and hypothetical considerations on their genesis. *Lund Studies in Geography, Series B, Human Geography* 13, 27-158.

Haggett P., 1965. *Locational Analysis in Human Geography*. Edward Arnold, London.

Haggett P., Cliff A.D. and Frey A., 1977. *Locational Analysis in Human Geography,* 2nd edition. Edward Arnold, London.

Hietala H.J., editor, 1984. *Intrasite Spatial Analysis in Archaeology*. Cambridge University Press, Cambridge.

Vidal de la Blache, T, 1926. *Principles of Human Geography*. Constable, London.

Chapter 3

The Role of Research Design in Surface Collection: an Example from Broom Hill, Braishfield, Hampshire

W A Boismier

As emphasis on the use of surface remains for both research and management purposes increases, so too does the need to determine what information surface data contain. While there has been a growing awareness of the pattern recognition problems posed by surface artefact distributions, due to the destruction or alteration of accompanying contextual information by ploughing, very few substantive results have been reported in the literature. Published investigations have been largely characterised by a poor fit between archaeological theory, method and the resource base. Middle Range Theory, that is the problems, hypotheses and attendant techniques that operate in-between general concepts and empirical facts, has remained underdeveloped and largely intuitive (cf Haselgrove 1985; Brown and Edmonds 1987). Techniques of data collection and analysis have been frequently used with little or no justification other than that they have been applied elsewhere and allow for standardised comparison (cf Richards 1985; Bradley 1987; Ford 1987). A technique's appropriateness for investigating the particular pattern recognition problems posed by surface artefact distributions has rarely, if ever, been questioned. Analytical techniques for the description, classification and quantitative analysis of surface data remain poorly developed and have often been incorrectly used or only partially interpreted (cf Tingle 1987; Gaffney et al 1985). These and a number of other methodological shortcomings and ambiguities highlight the need for some consideration to be given to the role of problem orientation and research design in addressing the methodological, technical and theoretical problems posed by surface artefact distributions.

In this paper I will be concerned with the application of problem orientation and research design in the investigation and interpretation of artefact scatters. My discussion will focus on what constitutes a research design, what its essential elements are and the advantages it provides for data collection and analysis through the integration of method and theory. These aspects of research design are first discussed and then illustrated using an example provided by the surface collection project undertaken at Broom Hill, Braishfield, Hampshire. My purpose is not to present any substantive results, but rather to look at the underlying issues and principles involved in data collection, analysis and interpretation, and the guidelines provided by research design. What I hope to demonstrate is that problem orientation, involving the use of explicit research designs, provides an objective procedure by which methodological approaches and interpretative frameworks for surface data can be developed, applied and evaluated for their effectiveness in addressing substantive archaeological problems.

Research design

While discussions of problem orientation and research design are not new to the literature (Binford 1964; Hill 1972; Redman 1973; Goodyear et al 1978; see also the contributions in Schiffer and Gumerman 1977), there still seems to be some confusion as to what actually constitutes a research design.

One misconception is that a research design is simply a kind of mechanical procedure by which questions or problems of interest are tacked onto a standardised methodology for data collection and analysis. Archaeologists often overlook the fact that the way in which data are collected and analysed determines whether a question can be meaningfully investigated (Gaffney and Tingle 1984). Standardised methodologies for data collection and analysis have a tendency to force data into predetermined descriptive frameworks that are largely unrelated to any particular problems or concerns. Such methodologies are generally not designed to meet any specific data requirements and have the potential for obscuring or missing the patterning relevant to the questions being addressed. Another misconception is the equation of a research design with a description of how the fieldwork is to be undertaken. Designs that simply concentrate on descriptions of fieldwork and the presentation of budgets, lists of equipment and work schedules, largely fail to integrate methods with substantive problems and are relatively inefficient in their use of archaeological resources. A research proposal attached to a grant application is also often misconceived as a research design. Research proposals are primarily descriptive summaries of the questions or problems the research seeks to solve and how it plans to accomplish it. They are largely written with the audience of the awarding committee in mind and are rarely explicit in content. Their purpose is not to integrate the conceptual and empirical components of an investigation but rather to provide a description of the research for which funding is sought.

Additional misconceptions include the equation of research design with research priorities and lists of questions or unresolved problems and the notion that research design is largely an academic exercise and unnecessary for resource management fieldwork. Specified research priorities and lists of research questions and unresolved problems focus attention on areas of potential research. Other than serving as a starting point in the design process, they are of limited utility in planning field studies. The idea that a research design is somehow "academic" in character is based on a limited interpretation of management information needs and how this information is acquired. It is tacitly assumed that only the lowest level of archaeological information, and often expertise, is needed to effectively manage the resource base and that this information can be obtained through the use of either uncontrolled "grab samples" or standardised methodologies. As increasing emphasis is being placed on the use of surface remains in acquiring information on the nature, extent and significance of the resource base, the need to determine what information surface data contain is becoming increasingly essential for effective management. Clearly, before archaeologists can decide what surface data have to tell them, they must determine what kinds of patterning can be detected in these data. Explicit research designs offer one potential way of determining this through the integration of management and research goals.

A research design is an explicit plan for investigating a problem or set of related problems. This plan specifies what problems the investigation aims to solve and how it is to be accomplished. Essential elements of a research design include the objectives of the investigation in the form of specified problems or hypotheses, relevant analytical variables, and a specification of the data that will allow empirical testing. The design must also set out the methods and techniques for acquiring and analysing the data. A research design is not, as I have emphasised, some sort of standardised or prepackaged approach by which problems and methods are pieced together with little forethought. The diversity of archaeological questions and problems that are currently being addressed with surface data largely precludes the possibility of any one approach or set of techniques being applicable to all problems. A research design is instead a flexible application of archaeological method to the problem at hand, where methods and techniques are "finely-tuned" to the data requirements of specified problems or hypotheses.

Design development requires some knowledge of archaeological method and theory, a familiarity with previous work on the problem and a clear understanding of the physical characteristics of the resource base to which the problems are addressed. Problem definition and the selection of data collection methods and analytical techniques are largely dependent upon an investigator's understanding of these areas of expertise. A poor or partial understanding may result in the definition of problems and the selection of methods and techniques which are unrelated to the properties of the resource base under investigation. The result of this in an investigation is often one of "cautionary tales" concerning the limitations of the resource base and polemic regarding the development of appropriate methodological frameworks.

Explicit problem definition and hypothesis formulation in research design directs attention to the kinds of data necessary for their investigation, indicate how this data should be collected and provide a framework for data analysis. The patterning to be investigated and the role of the various kinds of data in an investigation are made explicit in advance and, therefore, subject to conscious control during collection and analysis. Problems and hypotheses function as a bridge between the conceptual and empirical components of an investigation by linking abstract general concepts or theories with the more or less directly observable or measurable aspects of the resource base. Artefact attributes and class groups are selected in relation to the data requirements of specific problems or hypotheses and provide the basis for classifications relevant to particular analyses. Observational data to be recorded in the field are specified and their relationships to artefactual data clearly defined. Data collection methods are selected in terms of specified data requirements and evaluated for their effectiveness and efficiency in acquiring these data, given the time and means available for fieldwork. Decisions such as those concerning sample size and fraction, unit size and shape and sampling scheme can only be made with reference to particular problems or hypotheses. Critics of probability sampling (*cf* Hall 1985; Gaffney and Tingle 1985) have largely overlooked the essential role of problem orientation in sample design. Likewise, the choice between unit or point provenance collection strategies can only be made with reference to the data requirements of specified problems or hypotheses.

Data analysis also becomes more clearly defined and integrated into the plan of an investigation. Analytical techniques for the description, classification and qualitative and quantitative analysis of the data are selected in relation to a techniques ability to accurately and adequately address particular problems or hypotheses.

The problems and hypotheses set out in a research design also serve as a starting point in the investigation process by providing a basis for generating new and more specific questions. In archaeological research the discovery of new, often unexpected, data is frequently the case. One widely held misconception about research design is that an explicit design forces an investigator to ignore or destroy new or important data that were not considered in the design. As the investigation of particular problems or hypotheses requires the systematic examination of data for meaningful patterning, this process often reveals more specific insights about the patterning under investigation or new, totally unexpected, data. New problems or hypotheses can then be developed and either investigated within the framework of the initial research design or provide the basis for developing a new design more directly related to the investigation of these new problems and hypotheses. In the absence of initial problems or hypotheses, new data often yield less information than might have been possible if there had been more effective guidance from the outset. This analytical feedback process of problem or hypothesis definition, investigation and evaluation allows existing research objectives to be continually re-evaluated in the light of new information and provides a framework by which archaeological investigations, even small projects, can more effectively learn from the resource base.

Explicitly written research designs offer one major methodological advantage over implicit or unstructured approaches, that of increased research efficiency. Without problem orientation as defined by clearly stated problems or hypotheses, it is more difficult to objectively evaluate the effectiveness of a particular approach in acquiring and analysing archaeological data. Problem definition and hypothesis formulation establish the criteria for determining relevant data and for assessing the adequacy of inferences drawn from it. An explicit design increases efficiency through its ability to co-ordinate data collection and analysis with specific problems and hypotheses. With problems and hypotheses set out prior to the start of fieldwork, it is more likely that the data relevant to their investigation will be collected and subsequently analysed in a meaningful way. Research biases are made relatively clear through problem and hypothesis specification and the results of the investigation more objectively evaluated. In the development of analytical and interpretative frameworks for surface data, an explicit design provides a structured procedure by which methods and techniques for data collection and analysis can be selected or developed, applied and evaluated for their effectiveness in solving particular problems or hypotheses related to surface data. It is my view that the structured procedure of research design offers one way of systematically investigating surface artefact distributions for meaningful patterning.

An example of research design

During August and September 1982 a programme of systematic intensive surface collection was undertaken at the multi-period site of Broom Hill, Braishfield, Hampshire, to investigate the effects of natural processes, ploughing and unsystematic artefact collecting on intrasite structure. The research design discussed in the following pages was written prior to the start of fieldwork. It was initially prepared during the summer of 1982 and discussed a number of issues and problems that were of importance to pattern recognition in surface artefact distributions from the site. While aspects of the discussion are slightly dated and in scale it is limited to the investigation of a single site, the general and preliminary nature of the design provides an example that may be of some utility to other archaeologists at a similar stage in planning fieldwork.

Physical description of the site

Broom Hill (NGR SU 384260) is located in the parish of Braishfield and is situated 1.2 km north-east of the village at the southern end of a region of high ground forming the watershed between the rivers Test and Itchen. In elevation the site area ranges from approximately 76.20 to 91.40 metres above mean sea level and is dominated topographically by the end of a spur extending to the south-west. Geologically it occurs on an outlier of the Tertiary Reading Beds with concentric beds of flint gravel intermixed with sand exposed on the surface around the summit of the spur. Approximately 7.32 hectares of the site's area are under cultivation with the lower slopes on the north-west and south-east covered in deciduous woodland. A number of springs and solution holes are located in these woodlands.

History of archaeological work

In the early 1930s Neolithic and Beaker ceramics were collected from disused pits on the northern part of the spur by the Reverend S.T. Percival who also noted the presence of a Roman building on the eastern slope of the hill (Percival and Piggott 1934).

From 1970 to 1979 approximately 0.22% of the

estimated area of the site under cultivation was excavated by a local amateur, M. O'Malley. This excavation uncovered four pits, numbered from one to four in sequence of discovery, which he attributed a Mesolithic date. Pit three was interpreted by the excavator, on the basis of radiocarbon dates and apparently associated features, to be the remains of a Mesolithic hut (O'Malley and Jacobi 1978). Temporally diagnostic lithic and ceramic artefacts recovered by the excavation and unsystematic surface collecting range in sequence from the Later Upper Palaeolithic to the Roman period.

In 1982 a period of post-excavation work on the site archive and finds from O'Malley's excavation failed to find any supportive evidence for his claims and interpretations regarding the nature of Mesolithic occupation at the site (Boismier nd). This work indicated that the four Mesolithic pits did not exist as recognisable archaeological features, but were instead composites of features from later occupation phases that had either disturbed or destroyed traces of Mesolithic occupation. These had been misinterpreted as belonging to one set of related Mesolithic occupations.

Problem domains

Problem domains are simply project-specific research statements specifying the particular problem or set of interrelated problems and hypotheses that are to be investigated and the data necessary to solve them. Specification of problem domains at the beginning of an investigation allows for a better integration of the conceptual aspects of problem definition and hypothesis formulation to the empirical components of data collection, classification schemes and analytical techniques.

The specification of problem domains begins with the identification of problems that need to be solved. The brief history of archaeological work at the site has revealed that its occupation history extends from the Later Upper Palaeolithic, through succeeding periods, to the Roman. This long sequence of occupation, along with the effects of poor archaeological techniques, pose a number of problems to understanding the nature of prehistoric and early historic occupation at the site. These problems are best presented as a series of questions.

1 Where are the various occupations located on site and to what extent do they overlap spatially?

2 What is the spatial extent of these occupation areas?

3 Is there any patterning manifest in the distribution of artefacts across the surface that reflect the spatial arrangement of activity areas within individual occupations?

4 What distortions have occurred in these patterns as the result of natural processes, ploughing and unsystematic artefact collecting?

With these questions in mind two interrelated problem domains have been developed on the basis of Lewarch and O'Brien's (1981a) discussion of the role of surface data in archaeological research. These problem domains are:

1 Surface formation processes
2 Intrasite structure

Both problem domains are concerned with the question of pattern recognition in surface data. The first with the problems of recognising the effects of natural environmental processes, ploughing and unsystematic artefact collecting on the form and content of artefact distributions. The second with the problems of recognising patterning presented by artefact distributions that reflect the spatial configurations of the different occupation periods present at the site.

Before discussing aspects of the two problem domains in detail, it is necessary to explain how surface artefact distributions are viewed as potential data sources and what kinds of patterning can be detected in them. This view is empirical and is concerned solely with spatial aspects of an artefact assemblage in terms of varying densities of type and size class across the surface and how these density distributions may be used as data sources for investigating the four problems listed earlier.

As potential sources of archaeological data, surface artefact distributions have been viewed in relation to excavation-based interpretative frameworks. This view holds, and rightly so in terms of its data requirements, that due to the destruction or alteration of their accompanying contextual information by ploughing, surface artefact distributions offer little potential as sources of archaeological data. If, on the other hand, these distributions of artefacts are viewed as being more or less continuous across the surface with highly variable density characteristics, then their patterning in terms of spatial configuration and population size becomes a valuable source of archaeological information. As the phrase "highly variable" implies, these distributions are not uniform in either their densities or content across the surface. In some areas surface artefacts are infrequent, widely dispersed and limited to a small set of type and size classes. In other areas they are abundant, highly clustered and contain a wide range of type and size classes. It is these structured spatial patterns of association and disassociation, occurrence and co-occurrence between artefact type and size classes within surface artefact distributions, that serve as data sources for investigating aspects of surface formation processes and intrasite structure at Broom Hill.

These distributions are largely mathematical in character and are relatively unknown in both their form and content. Clearly, before it can be determined what information surface data contain, it is necessary to establish what kinds of patterning can be detected in these data. Exploratory Data Analysis or EDA (Tukey 1977; *cf* Clark 1982) offers a formalised procedure by which it is possible to explore surface artefact distributions for meaningful patterning. It is an alternative approach to data analysis that emphasises systematic pattern-search techniques. It is based on the premise that as much as possible should be learnt about the structure of a data set prior to it being used to evaluate hypothesised relationships. EDA addresses the problem of comprehending the complex network of relationships in a data set by breaking down these relationships into smaller, more manageable, components for investigation. Analysis begins with the examination of individual variables, proceeds to the examination of relationships between two or more variables, and finally, to multivariate analysis. Each level in the analysis is characterised by a set of concepts and techniques that allow for thorough structure searching. The approach compliments, rather than replaces, hypothesis testing and can be integrated into a programme of problem solving and hypothesis testing. Figure 3.1 has been modified from Clark (1982,259 Figure 6.7) and shows the role of EDA within the framework of data analysis for investigating the two problem domains.

In form, surface artefact distributions are most closely approximated by the isopleth or contour map. This map type is based on the assumption that the distribution of the variable being mapped is continuous across its surface. With its congruence to both the underlying theoretical assumptions and empirical characteristics of surface artefact distributions, the contour map provides a basic descriptive analytical model for investigating spatial structure or pattern within surface distributions. The role of existing cartographic programs such as SYMAP (Dougenik and Sheehan 1977) and other forms of computer graphics (*cf* Arnold 1982) in pattern recognition studies concerned with surface artefact distributions has only been partially investigated and forms one of the basic elements in the investigation of the two problem domains.

Surface formation processes

Investigation of the processes which create contemporary recovery contexts is a necessary methodological step if surface-derived data are to be used for quantitative research. The major pattern recognition problem posed by surface artefact distributions is the recognition of post-depositional patterning and to what extent it limits the potential of surface data for answering research and management questions. Three categories of post-depositional processes have been observed or recorded for Broom Hill which have had an impact on artefact distributions.

1 Natural processes
2 Agricultural ploughing
3 Unsystematic artefact collecting

1 Natural processes

The archaeological and geomorphological literature (*cf* Wood and Johnson 1978; Lewarch and O'Brien 1981a; Small 1974) identifies a multitude of natural processes which have the potential to affect surface artefact distributions. These processes can be subdivided on a general level into subtractive and additive regimes. Subtractive or erosional processes are conditioned by situational factors such as slope gradient, duration of surface exposure, climate, and vegetation cover. The most severe of these situational factors on surface artefact distributions being slope gradient (Rick 1976). Additive or depositional processes include aeolian, colluvial and alluvial sedimentation. Colluvial and alluvial deposition are the most serious of these additive processes on surface artefact distributions in temperate environments (*cf* Allen this volume). Acting cyclically, these processes of erosion and deposition operate to form and modify land surfaces and the artefact distributions occurring on them.

The problem of interest in relation to natural processes is the recognition of erosional or depositional patterning in the artefact distributions at Broom Hill and how to distinguish it from other forms of surface patterning. The particular pattern recognition problems posed to the investigation of these processes may be summarised as follows:

1 To what extent do artefact distributions reflect not only erosional or depositional patterning but also other forms of patterning?
2 Can these classes of patterning be analytically distinguished in artefact distributions?
3 What analytical techniques can (a) recognise erosional and/or depositional patterning, and (b) minimise their effect on artefact patterning?

Two general classes of data are required for these problems: (1) the distribution of size or weight classes, and (2) slope gradient. Recognition of erosional and/or depositional patterning requires that the distributions of different size or weight classes be examined for correlations and associations with each other and with local slope conditions. The variables

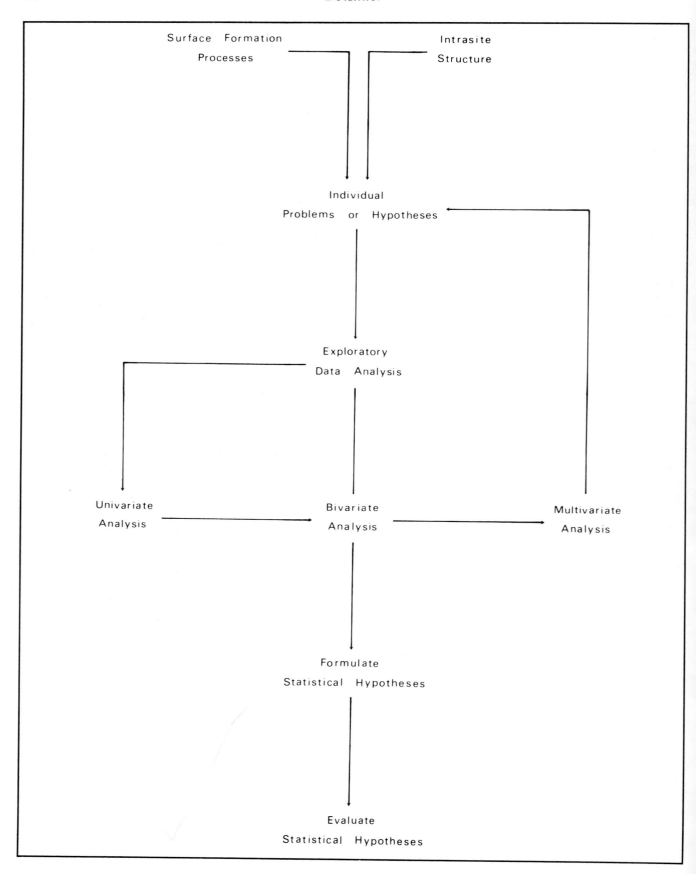

Fig. 3.1 Framework of data analysis for investigating the two problem domains (modified from Clark 1982, Figure 6.7).

will be examined alone and in bivariate and multi-variate combinations in order to recognise any patterning that may be attributable to either erosional or depositional processes. Hypothesised relationships will then be evaluated using a number of analytical techniques including contingency table analysis, least squares regression, partial correlation and various graphic scaling techniques (Dickinson 1981).

2 Agricultural ploughing

Perhaps the most common type of formation process affecting archaeological resources in the countryside is arable ploughing. The problem of interest here is the recognition of plough-induced patterning in artefact distributions at the site and how to distinguish it from behavioural patterning. Contract archaeologists in North America (Lewarch 1979; Lewarch and O'Brien 1981a,b) have shown that for plough zone distributions, five factors must be considered by pattern recognition studies: (1) horizontal displacement, (2) vertical displacement, (3) changes in class frequencies after ploughing, (4) changes in the condition and preservation of artefact assemblages, and (5) destruction or alteration of features and layers. Only factors 1 to 4 will be outlined

here. Factor 5, the destruction or alteration of features and layers, has been discussed by Fasham (1980) and Reynolds and Schadla-Hall (1980).

Archaeological and experimental studies (Roper 1976; Trubowitz 1978; Lewarch 1979; Lewarch and O'Brien 1981b) have shown that the horizontal displacement of artefact patterning is largely related to size, equipment type and slope. In general, these studies have indicated that for all types of equipment, artefacts larger than 4 cm are moved the greatest horizontal distance, with artefacts smaller than 4 cm tending to be subjected to less horizontal displacement. Table 3.1 is taken from Lewarch (1979,112 Table 8) and outlines the kinds of horizontal displacement by equipment types. The greatest overall displacement of objects is by mouldboard ploughs, with displacement of objects by discs and tines lower due to their particular actions on the soil (*cf* Lambrick 1977). Quantitative results of controlled ploughing experiments (Lewarch 1979; Lewarch and O'Brien 1981b) have indicated that, when holding slope and erosion constant, transverse displacement was minimal, with ploughing in alternative directions producing an average longitudinal displacement of around five metres over time (*cf* Clark and Schofield this volume). Variations in this patterning appear to

Table 3.1: Expected magnitude of horizontal displacement by equipment type (source: Lewarch 1979: table 4.8)

EQUIPMENT TYPE	EXPECTED DISPLACEMENT MAGNITUDE			
	TRANSVERSE		LONGITUDINAL	
	SMALL OBJECTS	LARGE OBJECTS	SMALL OBJECTS	LARGE OBJECTS
Moldboard	+	+	+	+
Disk	-/+	-/+	-/+	+
Tine	-/o	o	o	+

+ = Movement in direction of equipment.

o = Negligible effect.

- = Movement away from equipment.

be related to the directionality of ploughing and local slope and erosion conditions (*cf* Rick 1976).

Vertical displacement and the resulting segregation of artefacts by size appears to be a cumulative directional process. Research in agricultural engineering, summarised by Lewarch (1979, 116-122), has shown that tillage implements tend to segregate soil particles, with large objects being displaced to higher soil levels and small objects into lower levels. As the number of equipment passes increases through time, vertical displacement decreases until a state of equilibrium is reached, where further ploughing fails to alter soil structure. The result of vertical segregation on surface artefact distributions is that artefacts greater that 4 cm tend to occur in higher proportions on the surface relative to the total plough zone artefact population. This observation has been termed the "size effect" by Baker (1978).

Changes in artefact class frequency after ploughing is also a product of vertical segregation. If the surface of the plough zone is considered as being only a sample of its total volume, then surface artefacts, in turn, are only a sample of the total artefact population in the plough zone. Results of ploughing experiments (Lewarch 1979; Lewarch and O'Brien 1981b; Clark and Schofield this volume) have indicated that this sample is usually less than 10% of the total population. The most severe frequency changes occur, as has been mentioned previously, among large artefact classes, where the sorting action of implements causes them to be proportionally over-represented on the surface. Segregation effects on small artefacts result in them being either more evenly distributed throughout the plough zone or sorted to lower levels within it. Both result in lower frequencies of small artefact classes on the surface relative to the total plough zone population. Although their frequencies are lower, small artefact classes do tend to reflect their population proportions within the plough zone as a whole.

The final factor to be considered here concerns the changes in condition and preservation of artefacts in the plough zone. Plough-damage is determined mainly by implement weight, object size, and frequency of ploughing, and is particularly serious for its reductive effects on bone, shell and ceramics (*cf* Lambrick 1977, 1980; Lewarch 1979; Lewarch and O'Brien 1981a). For chipped stone alone, Mallouf (1982) has defined seventeen plough-damage attributes and recognised twelve different categories of plough-breakage that need to be considered before assigning functional attributes to individual artefacts. Ploughing loosens and aerates the soil, facilitates the movement of moisture through the soil, and increases soil temperature to promote seed germination. These processes also contribute to an increase in the processes of chemical and organic decay that affect the preservation of ceramics, bone, and shell within the plough zone. More durable artefact classes tend to occur in higher frequencies within the plough zone, while the frequencies of more fragile artefact classes are lower or absent altogether. The effects of differential preservation on ceramic fabrics within surface artefact distributions is relatively well known and needs little additional comment.

Given the previous discussion, it is now possible to specify the problems related to the investigation of plough-induced patterning in the surface artefact distributions at Broom Hill. In general, these problems may be summarised as follows:

1 Although surface artefacts are likely to represent less than 10% of the total plough zone population, to what extent do their density distributions reflect not only plough-induced patterning but also their original behavioural patterning?

2 Can both of these classes of patterning be analytically distinguished in artefact distributions?

3 What analytical techniques can (a) recognise plough-induced patterning, and (b) minimise its effect on artefact patterning?

Three general classes of data are required for these problems: (1) distributions of size classes, (2) direction of ploughing, and (3) plough-damage and preservation of artefact classes. Large artefact classes have been shown by archaeological and experimental studies to be subjected to a greater amount of pattern disturbance and plough damage than smaller artefact classes. The former are more suitable for recognising plough- induced patterning with the latter better indicators of archaeological patterning. Classification of plough-damage to artefacts and the effects of differential preservation on artefact class frequencies involves the development of attribute classifications for different artefact classes. Recognition of plough-induced patterning requires that the distributions of different size classes be examined for associations with each other and with local conditions such as slope and direction of ploughing. Variables will be examined individually and in various bivariate and multivariate combinations in order to identify any patterning attributable to the effects of ploughing. Hypothesised relationships will then be evaluated using contingency table analysis, bivariate and partial correlation, and graphic scaling techniques.

3 Unsystematic artefact collecting

With an increased awareness of archaeological resources by the general public there has been a concomitant increase in the weekend pastime of artefact collecting. While the effects of such vandalism to archaeological resources are well recognised, the more subtle effects of intensive unsystematic artefact collecting on artefact populations in the plough zone are relatively unknown. Quite clearly, intensive unsystematic artefact collecting of one form or another can severely depopulate the plough zone of particular artefact classes and render it useless for answering a number of research and management questions. The selective collection of temporally sensitive artefact types or retouched tools is a case in point.

The site of Broom Hill has been subjected to an intense period of unsystematic artefact collecting from the surface by a local amateur over the last twelve years. The problem of interest with regard to unsystematic collecting is the recognition of collector-induced bias in artefact distributions and its effect on artefact class frequencies. In contrast to natural processes and plough-induced patterning, a number of hypotheses concerning collector bias and its effect on artefact class frequencies can be proposed and tested:

1 That temporally diagnostic and retouched artefact classes will occur in higher proportions relative to other artefact classes in unsystematic collections.

2 That these temporally diagnostic and retouched artefact classes will occur in lower frequencies or be absent altogether from the plough zone at the site.

3 Through time, as temporally diagnostic and retouched artefact classes become rarer, more common artefact classes, such as marginally retouched tools and debitage, will be increasingly collected from the surface.

4 That in unsystematic collections artefact size classes greater than 3 cm will be proportionally over-represented.

Two general classes of data are required for testing these hypotheses: (1) dated unsystematic collections, and (2) frequencies of artefact classes remaining on the surface. With regard to the first data set, a total of thirty-four bags of artefacts, mainly lithic classes, collected from the site have been inventoried by the project. Thirty of these bags possess dates of collection ranging from 1970 to 1980 and allow hypothesis (3) to be tested. Analytical techniques that will be used to evaluate hypothesised relationships include contingency table analysis, difference of proportions and graphic scaling techniques.

Intrasite structure

Intrasite structure refers to the spatial arrangement of occupation and activity areas across the site. This arrangement being a reflection of the way people organised their use of space in relation to other activities and situational factors such as the presence of structures and other man-made and natural features during particular occupation episodes. The occupation area is the largest unit of investigation and refers to the type, number and distribution of activity areas for a particular period. Individual activity areas are the local units of investigation and are classified on the basis of functional differences as reflected in their size, artefact density and artefact content. Activity areas in this context represent concentrations of artefacts produced by activities carried out by people following some form of organisational strategy during a particular occupation. These activities included tool manufacture and repair, cooking, food processing and the disposal of refuse.

Surface finds and small-scale excavation have indicated that the range of occupation at the site extends from the Later Upper Palaeolithic to the Roman period. The problem of interest posed by this long sequence of occupation in relation to intrasite structure is the potential of local patterning present in the distribution of artefact classes across the site to recognise individual occupation areas and their associated activity areas. Three particular pattern recognition problems are posed to the investigation of intrasite structure at Broom Hill. These problems may be summarised as follows:

1 To what extent do artefact class distributions reflect not only large-scale occupational patterning but also small-scale activity area patterning; and can these categories of patterning be distinguished from post-depositional patterning?

2 Can occupation and activity areas be classified on the basis of characteristics such as size, artefact density and artefact content? Do qualitative and quantitative differences in these characteristics reflect differences in their function and duration of use and what effects do preservation and other post-depositional processes have on their content?

3 The relative temporal ordering of occupation and activity areas. How can the chronological ambiguities in surface data be reduced and what effects do multiple or long occupations have on the form and content of occupation and activity areas?

Three kinds of distributional data are required for these problems: (1) temporally diagnostic classes, (2) technological classes, and (3) morphological and functional classes. Recognition of intrasite structure requires that these distributions be examined for the presence of correlations with site topography and with each other which suggest patterns of association and disassociation reflecting local patterning across the site and localised activity-specific assemblages. Variables will be examined individually and in various bivariate and multivariate combinations in order to recognise any local patterning that may reflect intrasite structure. Analytical techniques that will be employed to evaluate hypothesised relationships and classify areas include pairwise associational tests, cluster and factor analysis, quantitative indices of estimated size, artefact density and diversity and graphic scaling techniques.

Sampling design

The area of cultivated surface on Broom Hill covers approximately 7.32 hectares with varying densities of artefacts occurring across it. Both problem domains require a representative coverage of the site's surface area and data on artefact size and class distributions. In addition, several classes of site-specific data such as direction of ploughing, slope gradient and surface conditions are required. A small team size and the period of time when the field is available for collection required the development of a non-probabilistic sampling strategy designed to meet these data requirements. A systematic point sampling design, based on the spatial aspects of surface artefact distributions, has been developed to ensure a representative coverage of the site's cultivated area.

Decision to employ a non-probabilistic sampling design for data collection was based on Asch's (1975) discussion of the use of non-probabilistic reasoning in mapping artefact distributions and the possible effects of collector-induced bias on sample estimates. The mapping of artefact and other item classes on the basis of small dispersed sampling units involves the interpolation of variable values between units. Interpolation between units was based on the assumption that the particular values for the individual units are representative of the area immediately surrounding them. This assumption of unit representativeness involves the use of non-probabilistic reasoning in that, in the absence of total collection, its reliability cannot be systematically evaluated on an objective basis. Unsystematic artefact collecting involves the selective removal of artefact classes from the surface and can have a serious impact on interclass frequencies remaining in the plough zone. The alteration of interclass frequencies through the selective removal of artefacts introduces an indeterminate amount of bias in estimates of population parameters based on extant sampled data and can lead to seriously distorted estimates of population characteristics.

Well designed non-probabilistic sampling strategies have a number of potential applications in archaeological research and are similar in many respects to probabilistic strategies in the selection and dispersal of sampling units. The systematic point sampling design developed for data collection is intended to provide a representative coverage of the site's surface area using a set of small dispersed sampling units. The design of this or any other explicit sampling plan requires that a number of decisions be made as part of the design process. These decisions are similar to those made in the design of probability samples (*cf* Mueller 1974, 1975; Rogge and Fuller 1977) and involve the choice of sampling unit, sample size and sampling scheme.

Decisions regarding the choice of a sampling unit are concerned with the shape and size of the units to be used for data collection. Three alternative choices are available for unit shape: quadrats, transects and circles. The last of these units, the circle, being applicable only to non-probabilistic designs. Choice of unit size involves a balanced consideration of the data requirements for particular problems or hypotheses and logistical factors such as the time available for fieldwork and team size. In this choice the loss of accuracy between the use of a small number of large units must be balanced against the increased cost of dealing with a large number of small units. This balance between size and cost can only be made with reference to specified data requirements and logistical constraints. Unit size, in this context, thus represents a compromise between data requirements and practical considerations. For data collection at Broom Hill circles were chosen as sampling units on the basis of having the lowest ratio of border to area and the need to minimise the amount of time required to set-up and record individual units. A two metre radius circle with an area of 12.57 m^2 was considered the smallest sized unit able to meet the data requirements of the two problem domains and the largest unit that could be set-out, recorded, and collected by one or two individuals within a short period of time.

Sample size refers to the absolute number of individual units included within the sample and is expressed as either a fraction or percentage of the area of selected units divided by the total area of the site. An initial sample of 200 circles was selected as the maximum number of units that could be collected within a four week period by a small team. These circles give a total surface coverage of 2513.27 m^2 or a 3.43% sample of the ploughed area of the site.

A sampling scheme is the particular method by which the sampling units are selected. A variant of systematic sampling was chosen as the sampling scheme for data collection. This involved the selection

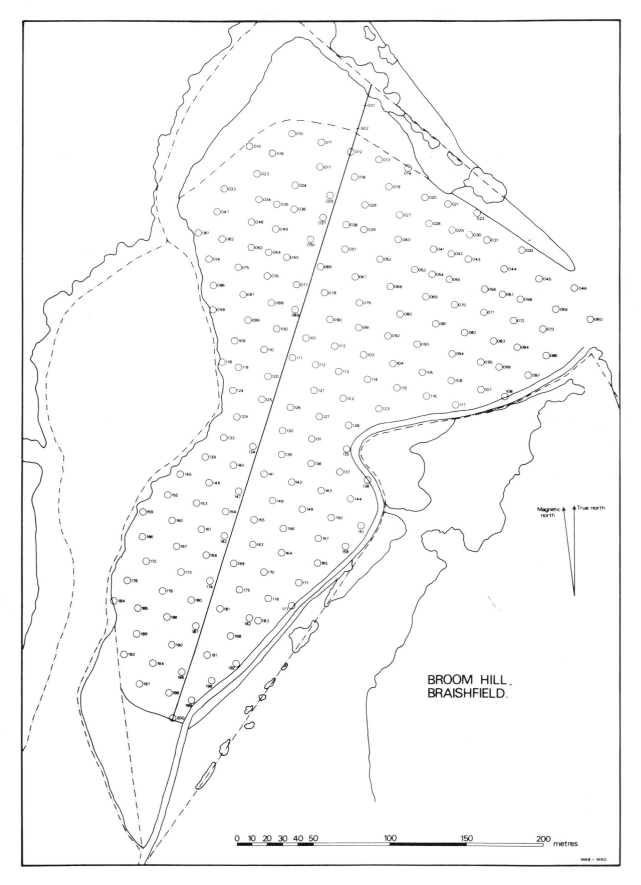

Figure 3.2 Distribution of sampling units across the site area.

of systematically spaced transects to achieve a representative coverage of the site's surface area followed by the selection of individual sampling units. To obtain the required surface coverage a baseline was initially plotted on a 1:1000 map of the site with transects along its length every four metres. Since the distribution of artefacts across the surface was unknown, systematic spacing of transects was decided upon with an arbitrary distance of sixteen metres between transects. To minimise the possibility of the data being skewed by the periodicity of systematic spacing, the first transect was chosen at random from a table of random numbers. This produced a total of twenty-eight transects of varying lengths, sixteen metres apart, along the baseline. All twenty-eight transects were plotted at right angles to the baseline with the centre points of the sampling units located every four metres marked on each. Proportional allocation (Kish 1953; Cochran 1977) was then employed to establish the number of sampling units per transect out of the planned total of 200. Proportional allocation ensures that the number of sampling units selected in each transect will be pro-

portionate to the total number of sampling units from each transect in the population. The number of sampling units in each transect relative to the total population of sampling units is specified by transect weight,

$$w_t = N_t/N$$

where N_t = the number of sampling units in transect t

N = the total number of sampling units.

To obtain the number of sampling units to be selected in each transect, the weight of the transect is multiplied by the total desired size of the sample,

$$n_t = nw_t$$

where n = sample size

n_t = transect weight.

The results of this method for establishing the number of sampling units per transect are summarised in Table 3.2. Distance between sampling units was randomly selected.

Table 3.2 Proportional allocation

transect no. (t)	1	2	3	4	5	6	7	8	9	10	11	12	13	14	15
no. of collection units (N_t)	23	29	27	44	55	70	74	69	64	59	52	45	33	25	23
relative weight (N_t/N)	.022	.03	.026	.042	.052	.07	.07	.065	.06	.06	.05	.043	.031	.024	.022
number of units to be selected (nw_t)	4	5	5	8	10	14	14	13	12	12	10	9	6	5	4

transect no. (t)	16	17	18	19	20	21	22	23	24	25	26	27	28	total no.
no. of collection units (N_t)	30	33	36	38	35	34	31	29	27	23	19	15	12	1052
relative weight (N_t/N)	.03	.031	.034	.034	.033	.032	.03	.03	.025	.022	.02	.014	.011	
number of units to be selected (nw_t)	6	6	7	7	7	6	6	6	5	4	4	3	2	200

Retrospective comments on the Broom Hill design

A number of distinct advantages in both data collection and analysis emerged through the use of the research design. One immediate advantage was the sampling design employed for data collection. The design proved to be an objective and relatively flexible method for setting out the sampling units across the area of the site. The use of systematic spacing, proportional allocation and randomised unit spacing, provided an objective procedure for establishing a "first fit" distribution of sampling units, which was flexible enough to be easily adjusted to fit existing field conditions. At the time of fieldwork, vegetation cover occurring within the area crossed by the first two transects did not allow for any meaningful collection to be undertaken. As a result only twenty-six out of the planned twenty-eight transects could be set out across the site area. Similarly, when it was discovered that only one sampling unit could be collected in transect 28 due to vegetation cover, an additional unit was assigned to transect 11. From the twenty-six transects a total of 191 units were collected out of the initial sample of 200. Only the nine units allocated to the first two transects were not collected. The collected sampling units gave a total surface coverage of 2400.18 m^2 or a 3.28% sample of the ploughed area of the site. Figure 3.2 shows the actual distribution of sampling units across the site. In terms of time, the use of circles as sampling units proved extremely efficient, requiring between seven and ten minutes to set-up and record, with an average collection time of around seventeen minutes.

Another advantage in data collection was the specification of important on-site observational data to be recorded during fieldwork. Data recorded on-site for each sampling unit prior to its collection included slope, direction of ploughing, the presence of any surface vegetation, and the length of time necessary for collection. Each sampling unit was also photographed. Both slope and direction of ploughing had been specified in the research design as being two of the variables relevant to the investigation of surface formation processes. These two variables, together with the presence of any surface vegetation, also provided a description of the surface conditions at the time of collection which was essential for understanding the recovery contexts of the sampling units. The fourth observational variable, collection time, was recorded in the field to provide logistical data for evaluating the relative efficiency of the collection strategy in relation to fieldwork costs.

Perhaps the most important advantage to emerge from the use of the research design was in terms of data analysis where it provided a series of guidelines for an extended analysis of both the controlled and uncontrolled collections from the site. The data requirements of the problems and hypotheses set out within the two problem domains stimulated the development of attribute recording systems for artefact classes aimed at generating data directly relevant to their investigation. Attribute systems were defined on the basis of relatively broad class groups and consisted of a variable number of multistate qualitative and quantitative attributes selected for their potential to describe individual finds in terms of condition, technology, function and style. A total of fourteen multistate attributes were defined for unretouched flakes and blades, eighteen for retouched tools, fourteen for cores, and fourteen for miscellaneous debitage. Twenty-one multistate attributes were defined for pottery. Similar systems were also developed for other artefact classes such as burnt flint and ceramic and limestone roof tiles occurring within the two collections from the site. With the data generated from these attribute systems, it became easier to explore the different data sets individually and in various combinations for meaningful patterning. It was also easier to assess the amount of agreement or concordance (*cf* Carr 1987) between the mathematical distributions of the variables of interest with the assumptions of the statistical and graphical techniques employed in the analysis. On a more general level, the overall structure and organisation of data analysis became more clearly defined and hierarchical in character through the use of the research design. Data or results generated at one level in the investigation of a problem or hypothesis, being used or incorporated into the analysis at succeeding levels.

At the time of writing data analysis has not advanced into its final stages. Results that have been obtained so far indicate that the extant artefact distributions at the site are the product of a series of complex interactions between erosional processes, agricultural ploughing and unsystematic artefact collecting. Bivariate and partial correlations of size and weight with slope and interclass associations with each other have revealed significant patterning produced by the combined effects of erosion and ploughing. It has not been possible so far, however, to analytically separate these two forms of post-depositional patterning. Completed analyses have also revealed that all four of the hypotheses proposed in the research design concerning unsystematic collection bias were correct and had a number of serious implications for the investigation of intrasite structure. The selective bias towards the collection of lithic artefact classes largely removed the majority of temporally diagnostic classes and a considerable proportion of the retouched tools originally present in the plough zone. As a result it has not been possible to distinguish occupation or activity areas for the prehistoric occupations at the site solely on the basis of temporally diagnostic and retouched tool classes recovered during fieldwork. Alternative distributional analyses using technological, functional and stylistic variables are currently being explored for their ability to recognise individual occupation and activity area patterning. The Roman occupation area and its associated activity areas, on the other hand, were clearly recognisable on the basis of mapped distributional data. Associational tests are at present being undertaken to determine if there are any differences in activity area composition that reflect any possible functional differences between them.

Conclusion

In this paper I have argued for the use of problem orientation and explicit research designs in investigating and interpreting surface artefact scatters. My reason for this argument is relatively straightforward and centres around one basic fact, that before we can decide what surface data have to tell us about past behavioural systems, we must determine what kinds of patterning can be detected in the data. Problem orientation and the use of explicit research designs offer a relatively objective way by which methodological approaches and interpretative frameworks for

surface data can be developed, applied, and evaluated for their effectiveness in addressing substantive archaeological problems. This point cannot be stressed too strongly, since many of the current techniques employed for data collection and analysis remain poorly understood in relation to their ability for pattern recognition. Problem orientation and research design in "management" fieldwork, such as evaluations and SMR enhancements, can also provide a way for integrating management and research goals into a single project, thereby increasing resource-use efficiency (*cf* Boismier in press). Despite arguments to the contrary, the only *real* limitation in achieving this situation is an archaeologist's expertise and ability to integrate substantive research questions with management information needs. Finally, and perhaps most importantly, problem orientation and research design allow archaeologists to explore the patterning present in the resource base in new ways which, in turn, may produce new insights into past human behaviour and the character of the resource base. The continued evolution and intellectual health of archaeology as a scientific discipline largely depends on our willingness to explore new and more satisfactory approaches to data collection, analysis and interpretation.

References

Arnold J.B., 1982. Archaeological applications of computer graphics, in Schiffer M.B., editor, *Advances in Archaeological Method and Theory Vol. 5*, 179-216. London. Academic Press.

Asch D.L., 1975. On sample size problems and the uses of non- probabilistic sampling, in Mueller J., editor, *Sampling in Archaeology*, 170-190. Tucson. University of Arizona.

Baker C.M., 1978. The size effect: an explanation of variability in surface artefact assemblage content. *American Antiquity* 43, 288-293.

Binford L.R., 1964. A consideration of archaeological research design. *American Antiquity* 29, 425-441.

Boismier W.A., in press. *The Historic Landscape Project: Archaeological Resources on County Council Owned Farm and Recreation Land*. Planning Department, Hampshire County Council, Occasional Paper No.1. Winchester, Hampshire County Council.

Boismier W.A., nd. Preliminary report of the excavation of Broom Hill, Braishfield, Hampshire. Report to the Department of the Environment, 1982.

Bradley R., 1987. A field method for investigating the spatial structure of lithic scatters, in Brown A. and Edmonds M.R., editors, *Lithic Analysis and Later British Prehistory*. BAR (British Series) 162, 39-47. Oxford.

Brown A.G. and Edmonds M.R., 1987. Introduction, in Brown A. and Edmonds M.R., editors, *Lithic Analysis and Later British Prehistory*. BAR (British Series) 162, 1-8. Oxford.

Carr C., 1987. Removing discordance from quantitative analysis, in Aldenderfer M., editor, *Quantitative Research in Archaeology, Progress and Prospects*, 185-243. London. Sage.

Clark G.A., 1982. Quantifying archaeological research, in Schiffer M.B., editor, *Advances in Archaeological Method and Theory* 5, 217-273. London. Academic Press.

Cochran W.G., 1977. *Sampling Techniques*. Third edition. Chichester, John Wiley.

Dickinson C.C., 1981. *Statistical mapping and the presentation of statistics*. London, Edward Arnold.

Dougenik J.A. and Sheehan D.E., 1977. *SYMAP User's Manual*. Laboratory for Computer Graphics and Spatial Analysis, Harvard University.

Fasham P.J., 1980. Archaeology in wood and field, in Hinchliffe J. and Schadla-Hall R.T., editors, *The Past Under the Plough*, 95- 104. DoE Archaeology Reports. HMSO. London.

Ford S., 1987. *East Berkshire Archaeological Survey*. Department of Highways and Planning, Berkshire County Council Occasional Paper No 1. Reading, Berkshire County Council.

Gaffney C., Gaffney V. and Tingle M., 1985. Settlement, economy or behaviour? Micro-regional land-use models and the interpretation of surface artefact patterns, in Haselgrove C., Millett M. and Smith I., editors, *Archaeology from the Ploughsoil: studies in the collection and interpretation of survey data*, 95-107. Sheffield, University of Sheffield.

Gaffney V. and Tingle M., 1984. The tyranny of the site: method and theory in field survey. *Scottish Archaeological Review* 3, 134-140.

Gaffney V. and Tingle M., 1985. The Maddle Farm (Berks.) Project and micro-regional analysis, in Macready S. and Thompson F.H., editors, *Archaeological Field Survey in Britain and Abroad, 67- 73.* Society of Antiquaries. London.

Goodyear A.C., Raab M.L. and Klinger T.C., 1978. The status of archaeological research design in cultural resource management. *American Antiquity* 43, 150-173.

Hall D., 1985. Survey work in Eastern England, in Macready S. and Thompson F.H., editors, *Archaeological Field Survey in Britain and Abroad,* 25-44. London. Society of Antiquaries.

Haselgrove C., 1985. Inference from ploughsoil artefacts, in Haselgrove C., Millett M. and Smith I., editors, *Archaeology from the Ploughsoil: studies in the collection and interpretation of field survey data,* 7-29. Sheffield, University of Sheffield.

Hill J.N., 1972. The methodological debate in contemporary archaeology: a model, in Clarke D.L., editor, *Models in Archaeology,* 61-107. London, Methuen.

Kish L., 1953. Selection of the sample, in Festinger L. and Katz L., editors, *Research Methods in the Behavioural Sciences,* 175- 239. New York. Rhinehart and Winston.

Lambrick G., 1977. *Archaeology and Agriculture: a survey of modern cultivation equipment and the problems of assessing plough-damage to archaeological sites.* Council for British Archaeology and Oxfordshire Archaeology Unit.

Lambrick G., 1980. Effects of modern cultivation equipment on archaeological sites, in Hinchliffe J. and Schadla-Hall R.T., editors, *The Past Under the Plough,* 18-21. DoE Archaeology Reports. HMSO. London.

Lewarch D.E., 1979. Effects of tillage on artefact patterning: a preliminary assessment, in O'Brien M.J. and Warren R.E., editors, *Cannon Reservoir Human Ecology Project: a regional approach to cultural continuity and change,* 101-149. University of Nebraska, Department of Anthropology, Technical Report No. 79- 14.

Lewarch D.E. and O'Brien M.J., 1981a. The expanding role of surface assemblages in archaeological research, in Schiffer M.B., editor, *Advances in Archaeological Method and Theory* 4, 297-342. London. Academic Press.

Lewarch D.E. and O'Brien M.J., 1981b. Effect of short term tillage on aggregate provenance surface pattern, in O'Brien M.J. and Lewarch D.E., editors, *Plowzone archaeology: contributions to theory and technique,* 7-49. Vanderbilt University Publications in Anthropology No. 27. Nashville, Vanderbilt University.

Mallouf R.J., 1982. An analysis of plow-damaged chert artefacts: the Brookeen Creek Cache (41HI86), Hill County, Texas. *Journal of Field Archaeology* 9, 79-98.

Mueller J.W., 1974. The use of sampling in archaeological survey. *Memoirs of the Society for American Archaeology* No 28.

Mueller J.W., 1975. Archaeological research as cluster sampling, in Mueller J.W., editor, *Sampling in Archaeology.* Tucson, University of Arizona Press.

O'Malley M. and Jacobi R.M., 1978. The excavation of a mesolithic occupation site at Broom Hill, Braishfield, Hampshire: 1971-1973. *Rescue Archaeology in Hampshire 1978,* 16-38.

Percival S.T. and Piggott S., 1934. Neolithic and Early Bronze Age settlement at Broom Hill, Michelmersh, Hants. *The Antiquaries Journal* 14, 246-253.

Redman C.L., 1973. Multistage fieldwork and analytical techniques. *American Antiquity* 38, 61-79.

Reynolds P. and Schadla-Hall R.T., 1980. Measurement of plough damage and the effects of ploughing on archaeological material, in Hinchliffe J. and Schadla-Hall R.T., editors, *The Past Under the Plough,* 114-119. DoE Archaeology Reports. HMSO. London.

Richards J.C., 1985. Scouring the surface: approaches to the ploughzone in the Stonehenge Environs. *Archaeological Review from Cambridge* 4, 27-42.

Rick J.W., 1976. Downslope movement and archaeological intrasite spatial analysis. *American Antiquity* 41, 133-144.

Rogge A.E. and Fuller S.L., 1977. Probabilistic survey sampling: making parameter estimates, in Schiffer M.B. and Gumerman G., editors, *Conservation Archaeology: a guide for cultural resource management studies,* 227-238. London. Academic Press.

Roper D., 1976. Lateral displacement of artefacts due to plowing. *American Antiquity* 41, 372-375.

Schiffer M.B. and Gumerman G.J., editors, 1977. *Conservation Archaeology: a guide for cultural resource management studies.* London. Academic Press.

Small R.J., 1974. *The Study of Landforms.* Cambridge, Cambridge University Press.

Tingle M., 1987. Inferential limits and surface artefact scatters: the case of the Maddle Farm and Vale of White Horse fieldwalking survey, in Brown A. and Edmonds M., editors, *Lithic Analysis and Later British Prehistory,* 87-99. BAR (British Series) 162. Oxford.

Trubowitz N.L., 1978. The persistence of settlement pattern in a cultivated field, in Engelbrecht W. and Grayson D., editors, Essays in memory of Marian E. White. *Franklin Pierce College, Department of Anthropology, Occasional Publications in Northeastern Anthropology* 5, 41-66.

Tukey J., 1977. *Exploratory Data Analysis.* Reading, Massachusetts. Addison-Wesley.

Wood W.R. and Johnson D.L., 1978. A survey of disturbance processes in archaeological site formation, in Schiffer M.B., editor, *Advances in Archaeological Method and Theory* 1, 315-381. London. Academic Press.

Section 2

Landscape Processes: the Effect of Natural and Cultural Disturbance on Artefact Distributions

The papers in this section are perhaps best described as "cautionary tales" of a most disturbing nature. Archaeology has been aware of the influence of post-depositional disturbance for some considerable time, culminating in the appearance of Schiffer's seminal volume *Behavioural Archaeology,* published in 1976. Despite that, the results of surface collection, the artefact distributions upon which so much depends, have rarely given more than a passing mention to post-depositional disturbance. The papers in this section, each representing a very different set of environmental conditions, suggest that to exclude post-depositional influences could lead to misrepresentation of the data and misunderstanding of the results.

To begin with the least disturbing of the three papers, Healy demonstrates how the gradual erosion of the Fenland has led to the emergence of discrete archaeological units, visible by surface collection. It is ironic that through that very process of erosion, disturbing in the extreme, comes a possible explanation as to the whereabouts and target areas for the vast quantities of floorstone excavated from the flint mine complex at Grime's Graves during the later Neolithic period. Through the emergence of "sites" it may be possible in the long term to suggest not only the location but the scale of occupation which was receiving the floorstone. Under normal conditions of surface collection, a general scatter of flint attributable to a specific flint mine complex, might only be interpreted in terms of presence/absence, both chronology and cultural association of the assemblage being largely speculative. In the case where specific locations are open to investigation, the quantification of results may be both more precise, for example a specific place at a specific time, and thus more reliable in terms of supply and demand on a regional scale. The paper therefore demonstrates clearly that the structure or content of surface distributions is as important an attribute as size or density in the analysis and interpretation of surface collections.

But the erosion and manipulation of landscapes will only produce answers under such exceptional circumstances. Both Allen and Gaffney, Bintliff and Slapsak describe examples in which the opposite is the case. Allen's environmental perspective on the processes at work in Downland contexts is both eye-opening and disturbing in the extreme. Both erosion and deposition are constantly at work, to such an extent that only a small percentage of the landscape remains intact. His suggestion that 19% of the chalkland may be buried under colluvium combined with the estimated erosion of 70 cm of chalk from much of the downland is certainly food for thought.

Although Allen's paper outlines the problems most succinctly and suggests that to ignore landscape taphonomy is to exclude a major factor in any interpretation, there is cause for optimism. Clearly we cannot generalise simply by looking at parts of the landscape (the examples of Stonehenge Bottom and the Seven Sisters, Sussex demonstrate that). But "digging holes", implementing a test-pit strategy as part of landscape survey, is one solution. This could provide quantitative support for artefact distributions as well as producing valuable results concerning landscape formation. That the majority of dry valley excavations in the south-east of England have produced virtually all the known evidence for Beaker occupation is significant. That the excavated area never exceeded 0.0007% of the valley surface is disturbing and has major implications for the interpretation of artefact distributions, not just for the chalklands but for any arable landscape.

Field survey on Hvar has also produced significant results for the interpretation of regional distributions, depending not so much on environmental processes as recent agricultural practices, although the former will obviously determine the latter to some extent. It was observed at an early stage of the survey that the various artefact classes within a total collection were being differentially sorted, often up to 50% of artefacts coming not from the field surface but from field walls and stoneheaps. Often the nature of artefact groups and their relationship to each other may be introduced as evidence for diagnostic activity areas where density is unreliable. Just as this would not work on the Downland, it is unrealistic in the case of Hvar as the larger and more visible sherds tend to be removed from the field in greater quantities. The result, that smaller fine ware sherds concentrate in one area and the larger amphora sherds in another will, therefore, produce an unrepresentative and potentially misleading picture of the spatial arrangement within occupation areas.

All the papers in this section are thus examples as to the danger of unconditional interpretation of artefact distributions. The resultant scatter of archaeological debris will, in the great majority of cases, represent the end product of a complex and dynamic system of landscape formation. To understand the distribution, both what it means and how it relates to other components of the social system, we must first acknowledge the extent of landscape formation.

Chapter 4
The Hunting of the Floorstone
F Healy

Introduction

This paper summarises some of the problems which still attend the interpretation of the flint-mining complex of Grime's Graves and examines the potential of contemporary local settlement assemblages and surface collections for elucidating the dispersal and nature of flint mine products. Sites located in Norfolk are followed by their reference numbers in the county Sites and Monuments Record. Chronology is expressed in approximate calendar years BC, derived from the tables of Pearson *et al* (1986).

Grime's Graves

Grime's Graves, Weeting with Broomhill, (Site 5640) lies in south-west Norfolk on the *Terebratulina lata* zone of the Middle Chalk (Figure 4.1), the first locally to contain substantial quantities of flint. The underlying zones, successively exposed to the west of the site, are virtually flint-free (Peake and Hancock 1970, Figure 3, Plate 1). The mined area has been investigated over more than a hundred years, most recently by the Department of the Environment (Mercer 1981) and the British Museum (Sieveking *et al* 1973; Sieveking 1979). This work of the 1970s has shown that the mined and quarried area covers 37 ha within which are between 350 and 500 deep galleried shafts and numerous smaller pits. Both were worked mainly by users of Grooved Ware pottery. Galleried shafts were sunk over a period of between three and four hundred years, from *c* 2600 to *c* 2200 BC, in other words at the approximate rate of one per year. Smaller pits continued to be worked down to *c* 1900 BC (Burleigh *et al* 1979). Output has been calculated as eight tonnes for a shaft with an atypically underdeveloped gallery system (Mercer 1981, 32) or 45 tonnes for a shaft with a more typical extensive gallery system (Sieveking 1979, 35). Both figures are minima, since they apply only to floorstone, the lowest, semi-tabular flint seam to which the shafts were sunk, with no allowance for the flint of the higher seams encountered in the process. Most of the floorstone extracted remains in the knapping floors which carpet the mined area. Mercer (1981, 112), using an assumed efficiency level of 15-20%, estimates the amount of floorstone removed from the galleried shaft, excavated by him in 1971, as between 1.12 and 2.00 tonnes (the equivalent of between 6,150 and 10,250 axes). Applied to the more typical estimated output of 45 tonnes, this would give an annual total of between seven and nine tonnes of floorstone (the equivalent of between 35,000 and 45,000 axes), disregarding the output of smaller pits.

Problems of use and dispersal

The removed output, despite its large estimated size, remains obstinately close to invisible. The form in which most of it was taken from the site is unclear. Products included discoidal knives and axes made on large flakes, the latter generally of distinctive subtriangular outline and plano-convex section (Saville 1981, 51-56). Such axes are infrequent both on the site and beyond it. Other implements made there, such as picks, relate specifically to mining. Others again are the quickly-made flake tools of contemporary settlements. It is difficult to tell how far these represent the manufacture of *ad hoc* implements during (temporary?) occupation, and how far the larger-scale production of such implements, most of which were removed. Levallois-like cores (Saville 1981, 45-48) may reflect the manufacture of chisel and oblique arrowheads, both known from the site, as well as that of discoidal knives. A strikingly low proportion of cores in a later Neolithic knapping floor excavated in 1971 suggests that cores themselves may have been removed (Saville 1981, 69). The debitage from mining-period knapping floors includes material, notably blade cores and blades, which attests the manufacture of end products other than arrowheads, axes, discoidal knives or the normal run of Later Neolithic flake tools (Healy in preparation). Saville concluded that the mining-period industry was a multi-product one, in which axes were relatively unimportant (1981, 67-72). The British Museum's trace element analysis of ground flint axes correspondingly sourced very few to Grime's Graves and many more to the earlier Neolithic Sussex flint mines (Craddock *et al* 1983, 158-160).

The removed output is thus likely to have taken many forms. Flint analysis, by one method or another, is one means by which it may be positively identified. Macroscopic examination of industries and collections from the surrounding area may, however, pose some relevant questions despite being a crude and approximate technique. In Britain macroscopic identification is possible only when artefacts retain considerable areas of cortex, and even then is

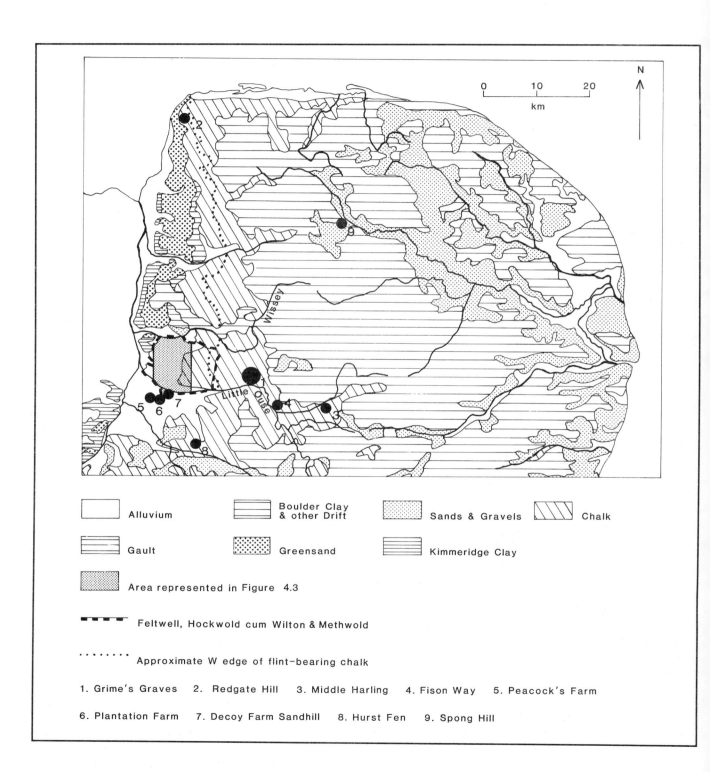

4.1 North-eastern East Anglia, showing simplified geology, location of sites mentioned in the text, and the parishes of Feltwell, Hockwold cum Wilton and Methwold. The western edge of the *Terebratulina lata* zone of the chalk is drawn following Peake and Hancock (1970, Pl. 1), who do not map it south of the Little Ouse.

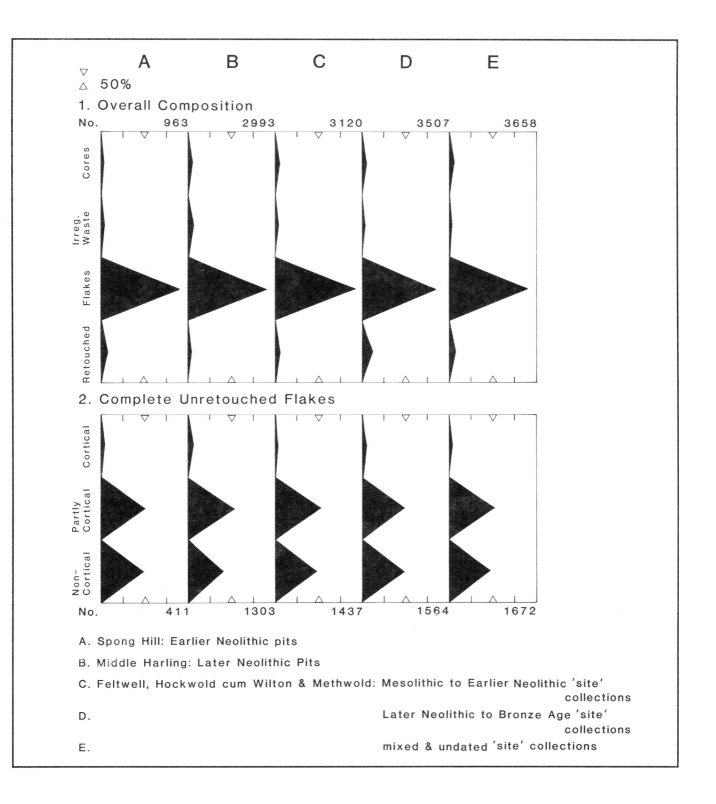

4.2 A comparison of the composition of two lithic assemblages from upland sites located on their flint sources with that of "site" collections made in Feltwell, Hockwold cum Wilton and Methwold in the course of the Fenland Survey.

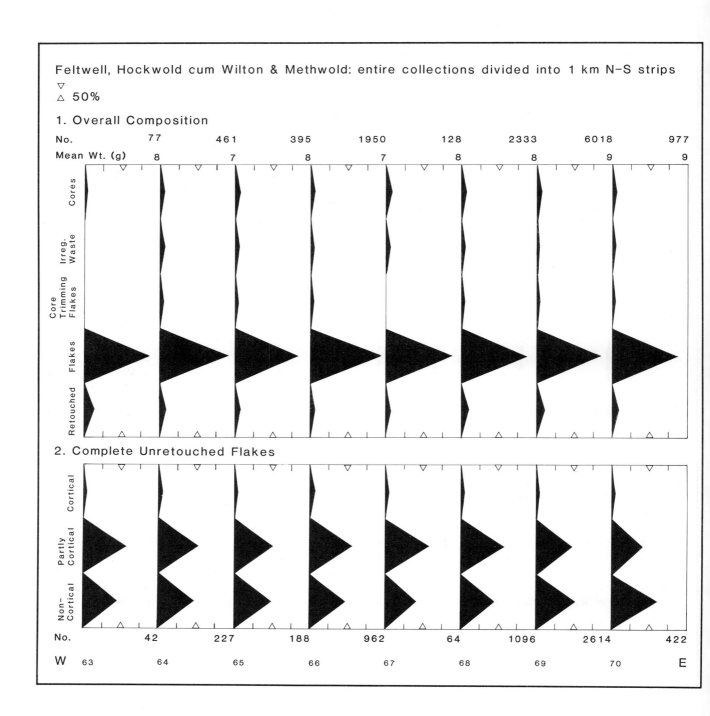

4.3 A comparison of the composition of the entire collections from successive 1 km-wide bands in Feltwell, Hockwold cum Wilton and Methwold, running from the edge of the upland in the east outward into the fen to the west.

more often capable of determining that a piece of flint is NOT from a given source than of suggesting that it is. All Grime's Graves flint is predominantly black and clear with relatively few inclusions. Floorstone is distinguished by its exceptionally thick, creamy cortex, which renders it capable of tentative macroscopic identification away from the site. The flint of the higher seams is indistinguishable from the surface flint of the surrounding Breckland which also includes occasional pieces of floorstone-like material. This abundant surface flint has been derived from the underlying chalk by frost action and weathering, and is superior in size and quality to the till and gravel flints of adjacent areas. Flint-mining at Grime's Graves may perhaps be seen as a specialised aspect of the use of the Breckland as a source area for raw material (Healy 1984, 126-127; Healy forthcoming a).

Macroscopic identification suggests that local settlement assemblages of the mining period contain very little possible floorstone and consist predominantly of flint from the nearest available sources. The industry from pits containing Grooved Ware on Redgate Hill, Hunstanton, 50 km to the north of Grime's Graves (Figure 4.1) is derived primarily of pebbles from the then nearby beach (Site 1396; Healy, Cleal and Kinnes forthcoming). Struck flint from pits containing Grooved Ware and others containing Fengate Ware at Middle Harling, 17 km to the south-east, consists almost entirely of local surface material, with one flake (0.02% of the total) possibly of floorstone (Site 6033; Healy forthcoming a). A largely unstratified and residual collection, including sherds of Grooved Ware and Beaker pottery, from Fison Way, Thetford, only 7 km to the south-east, similarly consists almost entirely of local surface flint, with nine pieces (0.6% of the total) of possible floorstone (Site 5853; Healy forthcoming b).

A primitive process of elimination suggests that efficiency may have been much lower than previously suggested, so that less floorstone than estimated was distributed, and/or that the majority left Grime's Graves in non-cortical form, and would therefore not be susceptible to macroscopic identification. If the latter occurred on any scale, and was uneven in its direction and eventual dispersal, then the movement of cores, blanks, preforms and finished implements might be apparent in enhanced frequencies of non-cortical flakes. A further aspect might be the occurrence of finished implements, perhaps of particular classes, in certain areas or types of context.

The Norfolk Fens

12 km west of Grime's Graves, the sand-covered chalk of the Breckland gives way to a very different landscape, that of the south-eastern fen edge. Here, in a sequence classically defined by Godwin in the 1930s and recently summarised by him (1978, 50-78), a low-lying basin, supporting deciduous forest in the fifth millennium BC, became increasingly wet as the combined result of rising Flandrian sea-levels and tectonic downwarping. Backing-up of the rivers draining into the basin led to peat growth which, in this part of the fen, seems to have spread outward from river channels in the later fourth millennium BC and to have reached a considerable, although unknown, extent by the time of a third millennium BC marine incursion. This was followed in the late third and second millennium BC by renewed peat growth (Hall 1987, 4-5; Waller 1986-87). Subsequent marine episodes resulting in the deposition of silts over northern parts of the basin (Hall 1987, 6-9) did not extend to its landward extremities. In the south-east of the basin, the area under discussion here, the surface of the peat was broken by numerous hillocks, formed generally by fossil late glacial sand dunes, sometimes by dissected chalk of the lower flintless zones. These often carry evidence of Mesolithic activity, while hillocks close to the edge of the fen were repeatedly occupied during the third and second millennia BC. The best-known are Plantation Farm and Peacock's Farm, both in Shippea Hill, Cambridgeshire (Clark 1933; Clark, Godwin and Clifford 1935; Clark and Godwin 1962). South-west Norfolk examples, excavated in the 1960s, are published by Bamford (1982). The density of contemporary occupation, forming a belt running south-west along the fen edge from the river Wissey towards Cambridge, is illustrated by Cleal's distribution maps of middle and late Beaker pottery (1984, Figures 9.6, 9.7).

Fresh hillocks, often with well-preserved occupation debris, are regularly exposed by wastage of the now-drained peat. The area differs from most arable landscapes in that the microtopography ensures that "sites", in the sense of discrete artefact concentrations, are the rule rather than the exception. The area is also distinct for another reason. It is one area in East Anglia to which, at least from the late third millennium BC onwards, flint would have to have been brought, albeit over short distances. Knappable flint is absent from both chalk and sand hillocks. The small, rolled flint pebbles of the Decoy Farm sandhill, Hockwold cum Wilton, do not, for example, seem to have been among the raw materials worked on the site (Site 20054; Healy and Silvester 1985-86, 62). Only low quality flint is present in the boulder clay, sands and gravels of the few larger islands. It is unclear what flint resources would have been available in the basin before peat reached its full extent. They would probably have been confined to river and terrace gravels with occasional patches of till, since the floor of the basin is formed by Jurassic clays (Hall 1987, Figure 2).

The area is thus one in which it may be possible to examine the transport and use of flint from the adjacent Breckland, including flint mined at Grime's Graves, since its dense late third into second millennium BC occupation overlapped with the mining period there.

The Fenland survey

An opportunity to examine this relationship is provided by the Fenland Survey. Since 1981, the Historic Buildings and Monuments Commission has funded and co-ordinated an extensive field survey of the Wash Fenlands, with the aim of recording their environment, stratigraphy, landscape and archaeology. In Norfolk, Bob Silvester, Fenland Field Officer for the county, has recorded many hundreds of concentrations of prehistoric artefacts, most of them previously unknown, on the south-eastern edge of the peat fen. Lithic material collected by him in the three most prolific parishes of Feltwell, Hockwold cum Wilton and Methwold, the location of which is shown in Figure 4.1, forms the subject of the rest of this paper.

Preliminary results

The results presented are provisional, but are unlikely to be substantially modified by the small quantity of material yet to be studied. Only approximately 40% of the total collection to date (1988) of 13,466 pieces from these parishes may be characterised with any confidence. The characterisable fraction of a "site" collection is typically dominated by small, weathered nodules such as occur on the surface of the Breckland. Orange-coloured flint of the kind apparently selected for arrowhead manufacture at Hurst Fen (Clark and Higgs 1960, Figure 9) is present in collections of all periods, but seems to have been most frequently used in the Mesolithic. Possible floorstone, identified by its fresh, thick, unweathered creamy cortex and sound black body, is present in small quantities, and may be represented by further good quality black flint among the non-cortical material.

Floorstone-like material presents particular problems. The same flint seam was mined in recent times to provide raw material for the manufacture of gunflints. The workshop-based aspect of this industry, centred in Brandon, Suffolk, is well-documented, notably by Skertchly (1879). Collections of characteristic debitage make it clear, however, that mined floorstone was transported several kilometres from source and made into gunflints on farms and around villages. While concentrations of such material are unmistakable, they render uncertain the date at which the occasional core or blade fragment of apparent floorstone may have been discarded. Such artefacts have been accepted as having been transported and worked in prehistory only if they are in similar condition (for example in a comparable state of cortication or abrasion) to the bulk of the collection in which they occur, if they have technological features alien to the Brandon industry (such as platform preparation or soft-hammer flaking), or if they are finished implements. Those which meet one or more of these criteria consist mainly of unretouched flakes, but include cores, scrapers and borers.

Figure 4.2 summarises aspects of the composition of the "site" collections from the three parishes, grouped on conventional technological and typological grounds into those which are predominantly Mesolithic to earlier Neolithic, those which are predominantly later Neolithic to Bronze Age, and those which are mixed and/or undatable. The first group, in other words, corresponds to a period when peat was less extensive than it later became, the second to a period of extensive peat cover and also to the mining period at Grime's Graves. They are compared with excavated assemblages from two sites located immediately on the flint sources which their occupants were exploiting, and hence where there was no constraint on raw material availability. The first is Spong Hill, North Elmham, where earlier Neolithic pits were sunk into the glacial outwash gravels which constituted the flint supply (Site 1012; Healy 1988 a). The second is Middle Harling, mentioned above, where the later Neolithic occupants worked the surface flint of the Breckland in which the site lies. The locations of both are shown in Figure 4.1.

There is little difference in overall composition between the four groups, the full reduction sequence being represented equally in upland and fen edge locations. The composition of complete, unretouched flakes presents a similar picture, with cortical and partly cortical flakes as frequent on fen edge hillocks as on the flint-rich upland. This indicates that flint was taken to the hillocks in an unmodified state and worked there, a conclusion confirmed by the presence on them of occasional unworked nodules such as those collected from the Decoy Farm sandhill (Healy and Silvester 1985-86, 62). There is unlikely to have been any substantial transport of prepared (ie largely non-cortical) cores, since their further reduction would have resulted in higher proportions of non-cortical flakes on the fen-edge sites than on upland ones. This does not appear to be the case and a statement to the contrary (Healy 1988 b, 32-3) is now withdrawn.

The later Neolithic to Bronze Age collections are distinguished by two characteristics:

1 A higher frequency of retouched pieces than any of the other groups (Figure 4.2).

2 The highest frequency among the fen edge groups of confidently-identified chalk flint of all kinds, which amounts to approximately a quarter of the later Neolithic to Bronze Age group, but to no more than a tenth of either of the others.

While the first may reflect increased local production of retouched forms, it may equally reflect the introduction of finished implements or the blanks on which they were made. The second is mirrored even at site level. At the Decoy Farm sandhill, which had seen intermittent activity from the Mesolithic to the Bronze Age, gridded collection made it clear that chalk flint was most frequent in an area where later Neolithic and Bronze Age material (including pottery) was predominant (Healy and Silvester 1985-86, 61-62). An increase in the use of chalk flint on the fen edge in this period seems likely to reflect the effects of peat growth (possibly making heterogeneous local sources inaccessible) together with heightened activity in the adjoining Breckland, involving the increasingly systematic exploitation of its flint resources, both superficial and *in situ* (Healy 1984, 126-127).

This does not, however, locate the removed output of Grime's Graves. Most of the chalk flint concerned consists of small, weathered nodules from superficial sources. Possible floorstone accounts for only approximately one percent of the whole later Neolithic to Bronze Age group, a similarly low proportion to those in which it is identified on contemporary upland sites.

It is difficult to reconcile the cost of extracting floorstone to its apparent use for *ad hoc* flake tools such as the scrapers and borers of the fen edge collections, forms which were generally, and apparently satisfactorily, made on surface flint. It is possible to see the excavation of a small, open-cast pit by two to three people in one or two days (Sieveking 1979, 38) as geared to the winning of good quality flint for everyday use. It is less easy to see the excavation of a deep, galleried shaft by twenty people in two (Mercer 1981, 32) to four months (Sieveking 1979, 33-34) in the same terms, bearing in mind that the immediate area abounds in more readily-accessible flint of reasonable quality. The manufacture of the identified *ad hoc* tools and of the flakes on which they were made may have been incidental to that of other products.

The effort expended in winning floorstone, its apparent infrequency in contemporary local contexts, the character of some of the known products, and the multi-product nature of the debitage on the knapping floors would all accord with the manufacture of what have been termed prestige goods. The working of Grime's Graves coincides with the currency of a variety of finely-made flint implements, the extra-functional significance of which is seen in their inclusion in burials and other formal deposits as well as in the quality of their workmanship (Bradley 1984, 46-57). Among these are the more finely-worked examples of discoidal knives and chisel and oblique arrowheads (Bradley 1984, 48-9), both made at Grime's Graves. A raw material won at considerable cost from a restricted source would enhance the significance of elaborately-worked objects. Such artefacts are generally non-cortical, which would make the macroscopic identification of their raw material uncertain. In practical terms, the mass and the high quality of floorstone are ideally suited to the manufacture of any implement which requires a large, sound flake as a blank. The span of the mining period would accommodate the manufacture not only of the prestige goods of the mid third millennium BC, but also the grave goods of the late third and early second millennium, in the form of flint daggers, plano-convex knives and the more elaborate barbed and tanged arrowheads. The multi-product debitage on the site could result from the manufacture of a variety of implements and/or the blanks for them, combined with unspecialised knapping to meet the day-to-day needs of those working there.

The increased frequency of retouched pieces in the later Neolithic to Bronze Age group of fen edge collections (Figure 4.2) could thus result from the import of finished, high quality implements of Grime's Graves flint. The appropriate objects, sometimes made of sound black flint which may be floorstone, are indeed present in the Fenland Survey collections, and abound in the far more selective museum and private collections from the area. Green maps a local concentration of ripple-flaked oblique arrowheads (1980, Figure 42), while his Breckland arrowhead concentration, which comprises the whole of 10 km grid square TL68 (Green 1980, 158) and hence includes the fen edge, has an exceptionally high frequency of "fancy" barbed and tanged arrowheads (Green 1980, 118). Distribution maps compiled more than fifty years ago by Clark (1929) of polished discoidal knives and by Grimes (1931) of flint daggers show strong concentrations along the south-eastern fen edge below the Wissey which have been accentuated rather than blurred by subsequent finds. Plano-convex knives are concentrated in the same zone (Healy 1980, Vol. 1, 305). Both they and elaborate barbed and tanged arrowheads, of both Green Low and Conygar Hill type, regularly occur in local excavated domestic assemblages of the late third and early second millennia BC, as at Plantation Farm, Shippea Hill (Clark 1933, Figure 2).

The hypothetical transport of fine flint artefacts and/or blanks for them from Grime's Graves to the south-eastern fen edge and perhaps further afield might be proved or disproved by flint analysis. If demonstrated, it could be seen as part of the same pattern as the long-haul transport of fine objects into the area, in the form of stone implements, of which there is a major national concentration (Cummins 1978, Figure 1) and, from the late third millennium BC, of bronze and bronzes (Lawson 1984, Figures 6.6, 6.8, 6.9).

The character of fen edge occupation
The lack of a substantial distinction between the composition of industries from upland sites located on their flint sources, fen edge collections dating predominantly from periods of restricted peat cover, and fen edge collections dating from a period of extensive peat cover suggests that flint was freely available there at all times, since it was used no more conservatively or parsimoniously than that of upland industries. This suggests either that, even in the late third to second millennium BC, local supplies were more abundant than they now appear to be, or that there was no constraint on the procurement of upland material. The evidence is examined more closely in Figure 4.3. Here, lithic material from the most productive part of the parishes of Feltwell, Hockwold cum Wilton and Methwold, starting on the extreme edge of the upland in the east and ending in the fen 8 km to the west, is presented in 1 km wide north-south bands defined by the eastings of the national grid. In this case, all the material from each 1 km band is included, regardless of date and of whether it comes from a "site" or from the slight background scatter of the survey area. In addition to the information portrayed in Figure 4.2, the mean weight of the artefacts in each band is recorded, as is the frequency of core trimming flakes.

There is, at least at this crude level, no substantial diminution in overall size (expressed by mean weight) or substantial change in composition from east to west, the complete reduction sequence being present throughout. The absence of core trimming flakes from the 67 - 68 band and of both core trimming flakes and irregular waste from the 63 - 64 band is most readily seen as resulting from the small quantity of material present in both. It may be argued that the 8 km east-west distance represented in Figure 4.3 is too short to register changes in raw material use with distance from source. They amount, after all, to only an hour and a half's walk. But the 8 km, would, at least from the late third millennium BC, have been traversed from hillock to hillock across peat bog, considerably increasing the time and effort involved. The whole is indicative of embedded procurement, in other words of a pattern of activity in which flint was collected with little additional cost in time or labour in the course of frequent traffic between fen edge and upland. This is in turn suggestive of complementary use of both environments by the same communities, a possibility enhanced by the fact that occupation of the fen edge has long seemed less dense north of the river Wissey, where the fen abuts on Kimmeridge Clay, Greensand and Gault, rather than on chalk (Figure 1; Healy 1984, 119). This impression has been confirmed and refined by Bob Silvester's work in the course of the Fenland Survey.

Pryor's interpretation of the later third and the second millennium BC occupation of the western fen edge in terms of seasonal use as summer pasture (1978, 161-163; 1984, 206-208), may well be applicable here. The fauna of sandhills on the south- eastern fen edge seems, as far as it has been studied, to consist overwhelmingly of cattle (Clark 1933, 269; Jackson 1936; Calvocoressi 1967; Bamford 1982, 29-30). A one-to-one economic match between the two sides of the fens is, however, unlikely. They are topographically distinct; extensive contemporary systems of ditched paddocks and droves, like those excavated at Fengate, have not yet been identified on the south-eastern fen edge; and most important, evidence for cultivation, which seems to have been unimportant within the Fengate enclosures (Pryor 1984, 206), is more abundant on the south-eastern fen edge (Healy 1984, 119). A combination of upland cultivation and fenland pasture would provide a context for the frequent transport of flint and other materials between upland and fen edge.

Acknowledgements
I am grateful to the Norfolk Archaeological Unit, and in particular to Bob Silvester for the opportunity of working on material from the Fenland Survey, and to HBMCE for funding the work. The paper was stimulated by suggestions from Alasdair Whittle and Julian Thomas, and improved by comments from Bob Silvester and Julie Gardiner, to all of whom I express my thanks.

References

Bamford H.M., 1982. Beaker domestic sites in the fen edge and East Anglia. *East Anglian Archaeology* 16.

Bradley R., 1984. *The social foundations of prehistoric Britain*. London, Longman.

Burleigh R., Hewson A., Meeks N., Sieveking G. and Longworth I., 1979. British Museum natural radiocarbon measurements X. *Radiocarbon* 21 (1), 41-47.

Calvocoressi D., 1967. Phillips site (Bronze Age) faunal remains, in Kelly T.C., A series of Late Middle Bronze Age sites, Wilde Street, Mildenhall. *Proceedings of the Suffolk Institute of Archaeology* 31(1), 53-55.

Clark G., 1933. Report on an Early Bronze Age site in the south-eastern fens. *Antiquaries Journal* 13, 266-296.

Clark J.G.D., 1929. Discoidal polished flint knives - their typology and distribution. *Proceedings of the Prehistoric Society of East Anglia* 6, 40-54.

Clark J.G.D., Godwin H., Godwin M.E. and Clifford M.E., 1935. Report on recent excavations at Peacock's Farm, Shippea Hill, Cambridgeshire. *Antiquaries Journal* 15, 284-319.

Clark J.G.D. and Godwin H., 1962. The Neolithic in the Cambridgeshire fens. *Antiquity* 36, 10-23.

Clark J.G.D. and Higgs E.S., 1960. Flint industry, in Clark J.G.D. Excavations at the Neolithic site at Hurst Fen, Mildenhall, Suffolk (1954, 1957 and 1958). *Proceedings of the Prehistoric Society* 26, 214-226.

Cleal R., 1984. The Later Neolithic in eastern England, in Bradley R. and Gardiner J., editors, *Neolithic studies. A review of some current research*, 135-160. BAR (British Series) 133. Oxford.

Craddock P.T., Cowell M.R., Leese M.N. and Hughes M.J., 1983. The trace element composition of polished flint axes as an indicator of source. *Archaeometry* 25, 135-163.

Cummins W.A., 1978. Neolithic stone axes: distribution and trade in England and Wales, in Clough T.H.McK. and Cummins W.A., editors, *Stone axe studies*, 5-12. London, Council for British Archaeology Research Report 23.

Godwin H., 1978. *Fenland: its ancient past and uncertain future*. Cambridge University Press.

Green H.S., 1980. *The flint arrowheads of the British Isles*. BAR (British Series) 75. Oxford.

Grimes W.F., 1931. The Early Bronze Age flint dagger in England and Wales. *Proceedings of the Prehistoric Society of East Anglia* 6, 340-355.

Hall D., 1987. Fenland landscapes and settlement between Peterborough and March. Fenland Project 2. *East Anglian Archaeology* 35.

Healy F., 1980. *The Neolithic in Norfolk*. Unpublished Ph. D. thesis. University of London.

Healy F., 1984. Farming and field monuments: the Neolithic in Norfolk, in Barringer C., editor, *Aspects of East Anglian pre-history 20 years after Rainbird Clarke*, 77-140. Norwich, Geo Books.

Healy F., 1988a. The Anglo-Saxon cemetery at Spong Hill, North Elmham. Part VI: occupation during the seventh to second millennia BC. *East Anglian Archaeology* 39.

Healy F., 1988b. East Anglia: lithic resources and use. *Lithics* 8, 32-33.

Healy F., forthcoming a. The prehistoric occupation, in Rogerson A., as yet untitled report on excavations at Middle Harling, Norfolk. *East Anglian Archaeology*.

Healy F., forthcoming b. Lithic material, in Gregory T., as yet untitled report on excavations at Fison Way, Thetford, Norfolk. *East Anglian Archaeology*.

Healy F. and Silvester B., 1985-86. The Decoy Farm sandhill. *Fenland Research* 3, 59-63.

Healy F., Cleal R.M.J. and Kinnes I.A., forthcoming. Excavations on Redgate Hill, Hunstanton, 1970-71. *East Anglian Archaeology*.

Jackson J.W., 1936. Report on the animal remains, in Clark J.G.D., Report on a Late Bronze Age site in Mildenhall Fen, West Suffolk. *Antiquaries Journal* 16, 33-34.

Lawson A.J., 1984. The Bronze Age in East Anglia with particular reference to Norfolk, in Barringer C., editor, *Aspects of East Anglian pre-history 20 years after Rainbird Clarke*, 141-177. Norwich, Geo Books.

Mercer R. J., 1981. *Grime's Graves, Norfolk, excavations 1971-72: volume I*. DoE Archaeological Reports 11. HMSO, London.

Peake N.B. and Hancock J.M., 1970. The Upper Cretaceous of Norfolk, in Larwood G.P. and Funnell B.M., editors, *The geology of Norfolk*, 293-339. Norwich, Geological Society of Norfolk.

Pearson G.W., Pilcher J.R., Baillie M.G.L., Corbett D.M. and Qua F., 1986. High-precision 14C measurement of Irish oaks to show the natural 14C variations from AD 1840-5210 BC. *Radiocarbon* 28 (2B), 911-934.

Pryor F., 1978. *Excavation at Fengate, Peterborough, England: the second report*. Toronto, Royal Ontario Museum Archaeology Monograph 5.

Pryor F., 1984. *Excavation at Fengate, Peterborough, England: the fourth report*. Leicester, Northamptonshire Archaeological Society Monograph 2; Toronto, Royal Ontario Museum Archaeology Monograph 7.

Saville A., 1981. *Grime's Graves, Norfolk, excavations 1971-72: volume II: the flint assemblage*. DoE Archaeological Reports 11. HMSO, London.

Sieveking G. de G., 1979. Grime's Graves and prehistoric European flint mining, in Crawford H., editor, *Subterranean Britain. Aspects of underground archaeology*, 1-43. London, John Baker.

Sieveking G. de G., Longworth I.H., Hughes M.J., Clark A.J. and Millett A., 1973. A new survey of Grime's Graves. *Proceedings of the Prehistoric Society* 39, 182-218.

Skertchly S.B.J., 1879. *On the manufacture of gun-flints, the methods of excavating for flint, the age of Palaeolithic man, and the connexion between Neolithic art and the gun-flint trade*. London, Memoirs of the Geological Society.

Waller M., 1986-7. Palaeoenvironmental report. *Fenland Research* 4, 11-17.

Chapter 5

Analysing the Landscape:
a Geographical Approach to Archaeological Problems

M J Allen

Introduction

Fieldwalking has long been appreciated as a method of artefact recovery. Barclay Wills, writing in 1932, stated that:

> "...flint hunting...is an arduous occupation, and one best done alone. It demands great concentration and is very tiring. You walk along, furrow by furrow, glancing at every stone, and you can only search in comfort when the light is behind you and when the rains have washed the stones".

In 1929 he had written,

> "I have occasionally experienced changes of light which make a subtle difference in the appearance of the stony ground...[when] the sunlight shone with an intensive lurid glare...flinting was then impossible yet a few days afterwards in normal light the spot yielded a good 'bag' each time.".

Field survey thus emerged largely as a method of locating areas of past human activity and enhancing the existing knowledge of known sites (*cf* Fasham *et al* 1980; Foard 1979). More recently, however, the aims of such analyses have been to examine settlement patterning through time over a given landscape, rather than within specific settlement units (eg Flannery 1976). This has given rise to attempts to investigate "archaeological landscapes" and conduct regional surveys (eg Shennan 1985; Holgate 1985; Gaffney *et al* 1985). In addition, the concept of both archaeological sites (Foley 1981; Shennan 1985) and geographical sites (Wagstaff this volume) have been re-defined. Archaeologists have, therefore, started to use field survey data as a tool in its own right rather than simply as a method of discovering suitable sites for excavation (Lewarch and O'Brien 1981; Gaffney et al 1985).

There is, therefore, a new initiative in the analysis of artefact distributions; data have been used in an attempt to examine and identify activity episodes and reconstruct a temporal picture of human patterning in an evolving landscape. Investigations of site formation processes and artefact displacement are, however, necessary for the understanding and interpretation of such distributions. Investigations to date

include the theoretical basis of human action in the landscape (Hayes this volume), the effect of ploughing upon artefact scatters (Clark and Schofield this volume) and artefact recovery rates. It is only when all the human and taphonomic processes involved in the formation of artefact scatters are at least acknowledged, if not fully understood, that any sensible interpretation on a spatial and temporal plane can be attempted. Much energy has been recently expended on these problems resulting in the publication of numerous critiques, analyses and case studies, for example *The past under the plough* (Hinchliffe and Schadla-Hall 1980), *Archaeology from the ploughsoil* (Haselgrove, Millett and Smith 1985) and *The East Hampshire survey* (Shennan 1985). Such studies have examined in detail the specific problems of artefact taphonomy in the ploughsoil (Hinchliffe and Schadla-Hall 1980) and the damage caused to artefacts by cultivation (Reynolds 1978), while further quantitative and methodological approaches have also seen much discussion (Shennan 1985).

The realisation that fieldwalking can be used as an analytical tool with which to assess archaeological patterning on a regional scale thus required, and has received, a reassessment of methodology and the understanding of artefact taphonomy. Despite this, little attention has been paid to the geographical parameters of the region and the taphonomy of the landscape itself. Geographical processes have, and will continue to, mould, alter, erode and obscure the landscape. They must, therefore, have had a profound influence upon the distribution of human activity within the landscape. In addition, and more pertinent in the context of this paper, is that geomorphological processes have biased the present-day distribution of surface artefacts. This is one of the more serious problems that archaeologists working from surface distributions must face.

Therefore, before one can even attempt to interpret artefact distributions from surface collection, it is necessary to understand the nature and past history of the land surface. It is not sufficient just to compare empirical data sets with lithology and soil maps. Many people have attempted to explain the mechanisms of landscape taphonomy and geomorphological processes. Few, however, have looked at its archaeological implications and, more specifically, its implications for the interpretation of surface data. Mills (1985a; 1985b) broadly outlines and discusses the fact that the occurrence of colluvial deposits in the south of France obscure archaeological information, therefore distorting the archaeological record. This has also been adequately demonstrated in southern England by Bell (1983), Smith (1984) and, more specifically, by Allen (1988). In this paper I wish to examine the landscape, not as a hypothetical peneplain, but as a dynamic and complex geomorphological system. The discussion will, however, concentrate upon specific landscapes and processes in order to highlight some of the problems outlined above. The chalklands of southern Britain are examined and can, I hope, be used to draw attention to these, and other, geomorphic problems outside southern England. The importance and significance of erosion and deposition as major processes in the formation of the archaeological record within the downlands is examined with the specific aims of providing:

1 an historical perspective on erosion and the evolving landscape on the macro scale, and
2 theoretical and empirical studies of the disturbance and biased re-distribution of artefacts by erosion.

This will serve, I hope, as a cautionary tale, but will also provide a geographical perspective which will aid archaeological interpretation of the landscape through the analysis of artefact scatters.

The chalklands of southern England

In the following examples, archaeological and erosion data and analyses are drawn from the downlands of southern England for a variety of reasons, not least that they have been the centre of the author's own research for the past 11 years. Much of the area (Figure 5.1) has had a long history of antiquarian and archaeological study, first because monuments are readily visible in this landscape (eg hillforts, barrows etc) and thus provide an initial focus of attention.

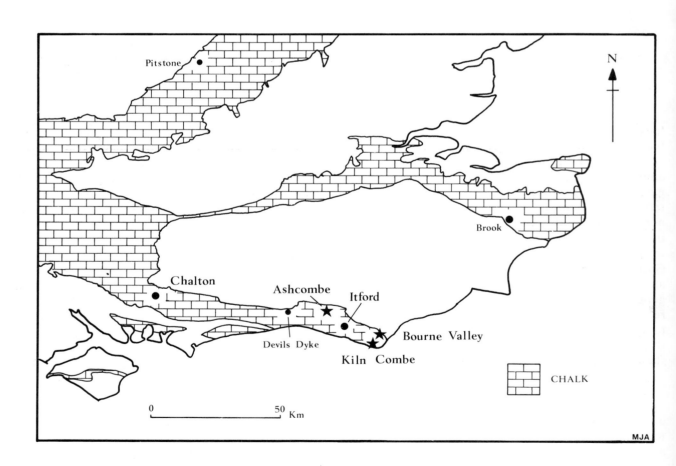

Figure 5.1 The chalk downlands of southern England showing dry valley deposits investigated.

Second, that artefacts were readily recoverable in abundance across the ploughed downscape and finally, but by no means least of these considerations, the general social status of much of the population who inhabited the area, especially in the Victorian period. The area had, and still maintains, a significant bias towards the wealthier and higher social classes who, in Victorian times, could afford to "dabble in archaeology", primarily a pre-occupation of the rich. As a result, many local and county archaeological societies were founded, including Sussex (1842), Wiltshire, formerly Devizes (1853), Kent (1857) and Dorset (1875). The chalklands today remain a centre of archaeological research and should, therefore, be one of our best understood archaeological landscapes, a view which is questioned in the discussions which follow. Recent studies by Boardman (1984a; 1984b; 1986) of landscape processes, specifically erosion, have also been centred on the Sussex Downs, thus making the analysis of erosion mechanics available and enabling consideration of their archaeological implications.

The concept of a continuous archaeological landscape, rather than a series of individual sites, has recently come to the fore (Flannery 1976; Foley 1981a; Butzer 1982) and research designs, fieldwork and excavation strategies are being devoted to the interpretation of complete landscapes. Analysis now tends to concentrate on the collection of off-site as well on-site data combined with environmental evidence, for example at Bullock Down, Sussex (Drewett 1982), the Stonehenge Environs Project (Richards 1990) and investigations by the Trust for Wessex Archaeology in the Dorchester landscape (TWA 1988). This provides an approach which, when well-planned and integrated with other multi-disciplinary analyses, should be welcomed. Unfortunately, however, the landscape has often been viewed as a "plate" from which artefacts have been collected; this has resulted in naivety in the interpretation of land-use and occupation. The following discussion of erosion processes in the downland attempts to show how an appreciation of the natural landscape and an understanding of the (albeit anthropogenically enhanced) processes operating within it, can affect archaeological recovery and, therefore, interpretation and perception of the archaeological landscape. The research of Bell (1983), Smith (1984) and Allen (1988) as well as the author's own unpublished work, allow a better comprehension of how landscape processes interact and relate to the archaeological evidence. The possibility of acquiring "off-site" and "on-site" data has been demonstrated from receptor locations such as dry valleys and lynchets (Allen 1988). When integrated with studies of recent erosion, the processes and mechanics of move-

ment, deposition and burial of surface artefacts can be discussed and their implications considered. From this evidence we may examine the potential for bias in artefact distributions.

Erosion

Chalkland soils today are often thin grey to brown rendzinas of the Andover 1 Series, specifically the Upton and Icknield soils, especially in arable contexts. Deeper soils exist on the tertiary cappings of Clay-with-Flints and these are typically palaeoargillic brown earths of the Carsten Series. This paper is concerned specifically with present day arable areas as it is from these contexts that artefact recovery is possible and from which both past and present erosion regimes have been primarily recorded.

Rates of erosion on the downland have greatly increased as a result of the dramatic change in agricultural practices over the last decade. Field sizes have increased through the removal of hedgerows and lynchets and there is a trend towards double cropping and autumn sowing. Although erosion has existed on the downs for several millennia, the consequence of more intensive and extensive agricultural practices has been a dramatic increase in the rate of erosional episodes and thus net erosion. Soil erosion has become a much published topic within geography, largely because of its agricultural implications. Publications such as *Soil Erosion* (Kirkby and Morgan 1980), *Soil Erosion and Conservation* (Morgan 1979) as well as conference proceedings on soil erosion, for example *SEESOIL* Journal 3 (1986), are just a few examples of an extensive literature. More specifically, however, Boardman has recently recorded and studied modern erosion from arable contexts on the Sussex Downs (1984a; 1984b; 1985). His numerous erosion studies enable the archaeological investigations of colluvium in this area to be put into perspective. Also the implications for artefact distribution and re-distribution can be examined via erosion mechanics.

Erosional and depositional regimes in the landscape, or even within a single valley, will vary over time. Fine grained sediments (ie silts and loams) will be gradually and rhythmically deposited while coarse grained sediments and localised gravel fans are deposited rapidly and infrequently. Their occurrence is dependent upon the specific nature of the surrounding landscape.

Of paramount importance to the erodibility of soils are their characteristics, for example organic content, structure, soil fabric and water content. Soils most at risk are those with a restricted clay content, ie less than 35% (Evans 1980), while the most erodible soil particles are those in the 100 - 300 micron range (Morgan 1979) ie medium-coarse silt as defined by

Allen

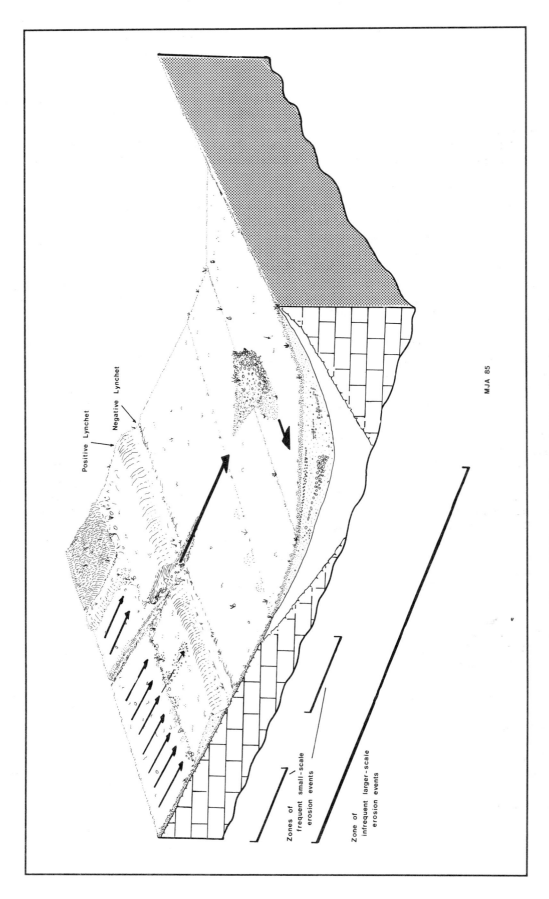

Figure 5.2 Hypothetical reconstruction of erosion regimes

the British Standards Institute. By these criteria Downland soils are generally highly erodible. They have poor soil aggregates and are characteristically silt rich, commonly containing as much as 60% (Hodgson 1967, 131) due to the inclusion of loess. Even on the Tertiary cappings of Clay-with-Flints, where soil aggregates are more stable, the overall silt content is rarely below 40% (Avery *et al* 1959; Hodgson *et al* 1967) and clay content rarely exceeds 30%. Here also, organic matter, which is a contributory factor to soil aggregate stability, is generally low (between 1.7 and 13.2%); soils with less than 2% organic carbon (ie 3.5% organic content) are considered erodible (Harrison Reed 1979, Morgan 1979). Downland soils of the Icknield series type contain between 7% and 11% organic matter under natural vegetation but this is considerably reduced under cultivation, usually to less than 4%. None of the analyses by Moffat and Cope (1984) on chalkland soils showed organic carbon contents greater than 2.3%, while less than 10% of their entire analytical suite produced amounts in excess of 2.0%, with some dropping as low as 0.4%. When organic matter content falls below 2-3%, the basic maintenance of soil structure becomes a problem, especially in silty soils (Bridges and Davidson 1982, 179). The lowering of the organic content as a consequence of arable activity has led to the collapse of many tilled soils (Harrison Reed 1983) thus raising awareness of the significant increase in erosion (Morgan 1979; SEE-SOIL Vol. 3 1986). Many downland soils tend to slake (ie where soil crumbs disintegrate in water into discrete fragments (Pitty 1978)); this results in the formation of a relatively impermeable surface crust reducing infiltration and leading to increased erosion.

There is a growing body of literature indicating that downland soils have been considerably modified by human activity. Evidence supports the hypothesis that thicker, less calcareous soils (ie acidic silty brown earths and calcareous brown earths) existed over much of the rolling downland, with thinner calcareous soils on the slopes and gravel and head deposits in the valley bottoms (Allen 1988; Macphail 1987; Macphail and Scaife 1987; Staines 1988). Brown earth (forest) soil aggregates are certainly more stable than those in thin calcareous soils (ie rendzinas) largely because they are more porous and contain higher contents of organic matter. Brown earths (forest) soils will resist slaking, unlike rendzinas, but are susceptible to erosion by physical impact and transportation by rain drops (Imeson and Jungerius 1976). Such soils were, however, in early prehistory, protected from rainsplash and rain drop impact by the woodland canopy. Hence removal of the woodland was liable to result in soil erosion until a new soil equilibrium was met.

In order to discuss the implications of both erosion and deposition for the analysis of artefact distributions, it is necessary to outline the processes of erosion. For clarity the erosional processes can be divided into two categories. Those resulting from frequent, small scale, erosion episodes which generally involve the removal and deposition of fines (clay to small stones), and those related to larger, infrequent, erosive events which may remove and deposit both larger volumes of material and larger inclusions, for example gravels, stones and boulders (see Figure 5.2).

Low energy frequent events

Low energy erosive events are those which, in general, are frequent and regular occurrences. It is these events that lead to colluvium being deposited and built up by gradual increments over many centuries, probably on a seasonal basis, under different land-use regimes (Imeson and Vis 1984). These are essentially natural processes but are greatly accelerated by anthropogenic effects such as tillage, where bare and broken ground is open to the elements and the activity of the biota.

The erosion of fines (small stones to clay fraction) involves processes of weathering which move material downslope under the force of gravity. These processes include agencies such as rainsplash, hillwash, soil creep, tillage and also soil movement resulting from earthworm action, burrowing insects and mammals as well as soil displacement by larger, hoofed, animals. These are continuous processes resulting in small-scale downslope movement of soil particles and smaller stones of the type recorded since at least 1881, when Darwin wrote in his *Vegetable Mould and Earthworms,* that "...many branching valleys intersect most countries...and that earth is steadily travelling down both turf-covered sides of each valley...here a thick bed of alluvium will accumulate..." (Darwin 1881, 247).

Rainsplash is an important agent, even when overland flow of water occurs. It is the physical kinetic energy of rain drop impact that enables the detachment of soil particles which may then be entrained (Kwaad 1977). When soil is subjected to either *intense* rainfall, where the rate of precipitation is greater than the rate of infiltration, or *prolonged* rainfall, where infiltration capacity is exceeded and the soil becomes saturated, then excess water will lead to overland flow. Once water has been mobilised in this fashion, processes of sheetwash, rilling and gullying may occur depending upon the intensity of overland flow, degree and length of slope etc. The net result, however, is more severe erosion.

Sheetwash

Once overland flow occurs, water will wash off the soil surface in sheets, provided surface morphology is not pre-sculptured into channels. Sheetwash will enable fine material to be transported in suspension once entrained, and coarser particles, including a high proportion of soil aggregates, to be moved downslope by the gravitational force of the flow. Smaller stones (ie chalk pieces up to an average diameter of 6 mm) have also been observed to be moved downslope under these conditions. On the downlands, chalk pieces are frequently moved under these conditions in preference to flint. This is because chalk often occurs in smaller pieces than flint and has a lower specific gravity (2.17 for chalk, 2.65 for flint which is quartz -SiO_2- based). Although sheetwash is a fairly regular occurrence, its erosive effects on grassland are negligible, whilst on open tilled bare earth, material is obviously more readily entrained and moved. Sheetwash will frequently lead to small braided water courses with no pronounced channels. When localised channelling does occur, the down cutting and removal of material results in the creation of networks of small rills. This is rare on grassland (Bennett 1939) but a regular occurrence on arable land.

Rilling

Rills are ephemeral features created by the channelling of overland flow and are often destroyed by the next pluvial event. The formation of rills (or gullies) is dependent upon a number of factors including soil type, slope, velocity and depth of water. Although rilling affects the same part of the slope as overland flow these processes can be distinguished by their relative erosive capabilities. The concentration of flow increases erosive power and hence rilling displays a greater capacity for soil removal and the movement of coarse components. Networks of rills, often only 3 cm deep, have been observed in recent erosion events on the Sussex Downs (Boardman 1984a; 1984b). The deposition of this material often forms fans of soil material above which (ie higher up the slope) well sorted fans of the coarser fragments (eg chalk pieces commonly *c* 6 mm - 14 mm in diameter (see Plate 5.2)) tend to occur.

Higher energy, less frequent events

Generally, high energy events occur with less frequency than their low energy counterparts, and catastrophic events are rare. Boardman has recently postulated a regular cyclical occurrence pattern of 4 - 6 years for extensive modern rilling and gullying events on the Sussex Downs (Boardman pers comm).

Larger rills

Rills are, by definition, ephemeral erosion features.

Nevertheless they can be in excess of 150 m long and 17 cm deep (ie total soil depth on chalk). Larger rills have considerable erosive ability. Boardman, for example, has recorded figures of up to 1.89 tons of soil per hectare removed from arable fields as a result of recent rilling (1984a; 1984b). Deposition occurred as large fans individually constituting *c* 0.26 tons of material (Boardman 1984a). These were often comprised of both fine and coarse components and included a number of large stones up to 20 cm diameter. Occasionally individual flint nodules of 380 cm^3, weighing approximately 1 kg, were recorded (Boardman and Robinson 1985). Differential deposition is commonly noted; the larger stones and flints being deposited at the base of the slope whilst finer flint and chalk material may be transported another 500 m and the silt and clay fraction often over 1 km (Boardman and Robinson 1985).

Gullies

Once larger rills become permanent or semi-permanent features of the landscape they can be classified as gullies. As a consequence of being permanent, water is directly channelled into the gullies, the concentration of flow often stripping out all soil material. They will, therefore, produce exaggerated forms of rill erosion and deposition and have been observed to exceed 200 m in length and be in excess of 0.5 m deep and 1.5 m wide (Boardman pers comm), thus representing a linear swathe of total soil and stone removal across a field. They tend to be straight, taking the steepest and shortest route downslope, and often disregard minor morphological features of the landscape. Deposition at the base of the slope may cover many square metres and include large flints as well as fines.

Although slope is an important factor in all of the erosion regimes described above, Boardman (1984b) has recorded rilling and gullying on slopes as small as 4 degrees while the erosion of fines can occur on slopes as little as 2 degrees (Evans 1978, 69; Butzer 1974). From the processes highlighted above it is evident that erosion must be considered as a major factor in the re-distribution of archaeological material, even on minor slopes. It now remains to consider the implications of erosion to artefact scatters.

Archaeological implications

Having outlined the significant present day erosion processes on the downlands, it is obvious that:

1 artefacts residing in the ploughzone will be affected,
2 sites may be severely denuded/destroyed by erosion, and
3 that sites may also be preserved by deposition.

What follows then is a discussion, on a theoretical rather than empirical level, of the effects of the erosion regimes outlined above upon artefact distributions. From this discussion of present day artefact re-distribution processes, we can examine the consequence of such processes within the landscape as a whole over the past four millennia.

The implications of soil movement

Erosion of fine soil particles by sheetwash and small rills are frequent and regular events and probably will not result in significant downslope movement of artefacts. Nevertheless, the regular removal of the silt, fine sand and very small stone fractions will result in an overall decrease in soil depth on the hill crest and slopes, and a gradual increase in soil depth on valley edge margins at the base of the slope. The effect will be to increase stoniness (ie stones per unit of soil) and thus artificially concentrate artefacts upslope, in areas of soil loss relative to those of non-erosion or soil gain. Areas of deposition will see a relative reduction in artefact density and ultimately, under this regime, total burial. Increase in stoniness and relative artefact density will be reflected in the surface distributions (Figure 5.3).

To emphasise the effect of soil, rather than artefact, movement a hypothetical scenario is considered in which artefact distribution is constant over a landscape, and no downslope component of artefact movement takes place. Take, for example, two 1 m^2 blocks of downland with a soil depth of 15 cm (ie a typical grey rendzina) each of which contains 30 artefacts; one block situated on a slope and suffering erosion, and the other located in the valley bottom, receiving sediment. Initially both areas have artefact densities of 200 per cubic metre. If the top 1 cm is considered as "the surface" then two artefacts per m^2 can be observed. The effects of frequent low energy erosion on this hypothetical landscape will be significant. If uniform erosion of 3 cm of soil material on the slope is envisaged and the uniform deposition of 3 cm in the receptor area occurs, which is within the bounds of both modern and ancient soil erosion (Boardman 1986; Bell 1986), the soil depths will become 12 and 18 cm respectively. The density of artefacts upslope is thus 250 per m^3, whereas downslope it is 167 per m^3. As the number of artefacts on the surface at any one time is dependent upon artefact density and *not* total artefact numbers, it is evident that as soil depth increases, the percentage of the assemblage on the surface will decrease. Therefore, surface artefact densities are 2.50 and 1.67 per m^2 after only 3 cm erosion and deposition respectively (Figure 5.3).

This problem is further compounded when the depth of ploughing and artefacts within the active ploughzone are considered. As soil depth increases, the basal soil profile may become greater than the depth of the plough. All artefacts within this basal zone are below the effects of further tillage and may, therefore, be considered to be outside the system. For instance, if ploughing occurs to a depth of 15 cm, and erosion is considered to have occurred gradually, then the basal 3 cm of the receptor site, which now has a soil depth of 18 cm, will no longer remain within the active ploughzone and artefacts within that basal portion will not be mixed. This represents 17%, or *c* 5 of the 30 artefacts, which do not reside in the active ploughzone. As further erosion occurs the reduction in artefact density will be exaggerated by the reduction in the number of available artefacts in the active ploughzone. Continual erosion will eventually result in vertical dispersal and burial of the assemblage altogether.

Under low energy erosion events, it is likely that artefact density will increase on the hill crest and slopes and decrease at the base of the slope and in the valley bottoms. How often is this scenario, when encountered in the field, generally interpreted as evidence for more intense activity of the chalk ridges and hillslopes? In reality the true archaeological record may be the total antithesis of this.

Artefact displacement

Under slightly more energetic erosion regimes, for example rilling, the movement of artefacts is certainly a possibility. Minor rilling will essentially affect only surface material, though some may be preferentially moved due to difference in bulk densities and specific gravity. Empirical studies, by the author, of natural and artefactual flints demonstrated that their shape was also an important factor.

The specific gravities of prehistoric pottery (mean = 1.93), flint (mean = 2.61) and chalk (mean = 2.17) were calculated and, as might be expected, produced a significant variation. From this it can be inferred that under low energy "fluvial" erosion (rilling), chalk will be preferentially eroded, not only because it displays a low specific gravity, but being very soft (less than 2.5 on the Moh Scale) it is able to weather into small, often well rounded, pieces which tend to roll. Although prehistoric pottery (flint and grog, and flint tempered) produced the lowest specific gravity, its platy shape will not be transported as easily as chalk spheres, while its high surface area may facilitate movement by overland flow. Flint is the heaviest of these materials (specific gravity 2.61) and is, therefore, less likely to be transported under the fluvial conditions postulated. However, experiments by the author showed that in an assemblage of approximately equal proportions of marked natural and struck flint, those which were relatively thin with

82%

46   *Allen*

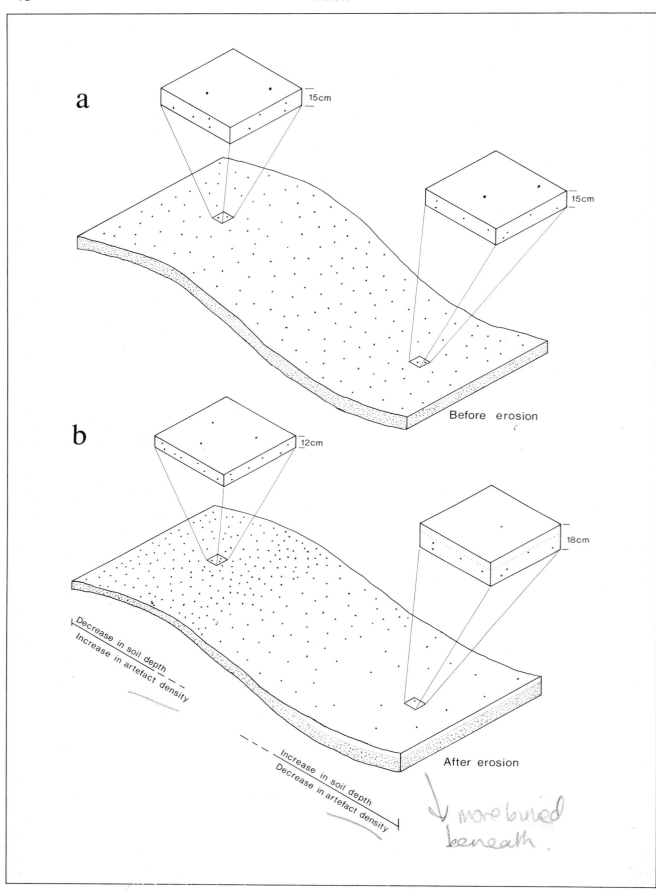

Figure 5.3 Consequences of soil erosion.

flat surfaces were preferentially transported down-slope. 873 flints weighing between 15.2 and 122.4 grams, were spread over a 2 x 45 m strip along an 11 degree slope. A trench was excavated parallel to this strip 10 metres downslope. After two small storm events, 87% of the marked flints recovered in the trap were thin and had flat surfaces, 94% in this class were blade artefacts!

After four years, over 60 flints, over 80% of which were struck flakes and blades, had moved 50 m down-slope and were caught in a second trap. This indicates that downslope movement is possible over large distances. Over time a large proportion of the assemblage may be deposited at the foot of the slope

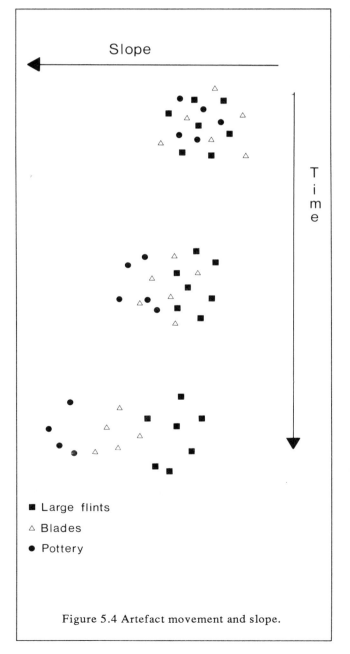

Slope

T
i
m
e

■ Large flints
△ Blades
● Pottery

Figure 5.4 Artefact movement and slope.

and blanketed by finer wash. In real terms, whatever the effects of this erosion are, it must be considered as a potentially serious distortant to artefact scatters.

From the above it is evident that once fluvial energy is significant enough to move small objects, pottery will display the greatest tendency to movement followed by small and more spherical flint artefacts. This implies that discrete artefact distributions have the potential to become "blurred" by the preferential sorting of surface material (see Figure 5.4).

Modern erosion is obviously a factor that must be considered when analysing artefact distributions. Although it may be extreme, due to intensive and extensive agricultural practices, it is evident that colluviation has occurred on the downlands for at least four millennia. This being so, erosion processes operating today have probably done so continually, to a greater or lesser degree, throughout most of prehistory and up until the present. Recent studies of valleys provide an archaeological dimension to these processes but also highlight other severe landscape biases.

Artefact removal
There can be no doubt that severe rilling and gullying can, and does, remove artefacts from the area of human deposition. From recent examples of severe erosion on the Downs it would appear that these processes can also potentially damage well stratified and buried sites. Concentrated channelling processes will indiscriminately remove a small percentage of the ploughsoil, including artefacts. However, as only a thin linear band of soil and artefacts are removed, this will only result in the general reduction of artefact numbers within the gullied or rilled area. Deposition, on the other hand, may result in extreme sorting and redistribution of artefacts. Artefacts are likely to be deposited at the base of the slope while this zone is also the most likely to accumulate finer material. Burial of artefact scatters and redeposited artefacts may, therefore, occur comparatively rapidly. If this is the case, no severe distortion will be noticed from observation of surface artefact scatters upslope, but the lower slopes may be totally obscured. This obviously has major implications when fans of material are not buried and do enter the ploughzone. Large rills can even make deep incisions in valley colluvium and lynchet deposits and hence even buried sites are not totally protected from erosion.

As the processes and examples discussed here are theoretical ones, further examination is required of:

1 modern erosion events and artefact occurrence, and
2 fieldwork data that can be compared with the hypothesis outlined above.

Plate 5.1 Ashcombe Bottom during excavation, July 1984. Photo: Mike Allen.

Plate 5.2 Ashcombe Bottom after erosion event, September 14th 1984. Photo: Mike Allen.

Colluvial studies

Contrary to statements made by both Taylor (1966) and Godwin (1967) that there was no evidence for soil erosion on the chalk downs in the prehistoric and early historic periods, it is abundantly clear that hill-wash is a major component of the downscape as shown by the significant colluvial deposits at Pitstone, Buckinghamshire (Evans 1966), Brook, Kent (Kerney *et al* 1964) and Pegwell Bay, Kent (Kerney 1965; Weir *et al* 1971). More recently, investigations in dry valleys have produced evidence for an almost ubiquitous occurrence of post-glacial colluvium varying from 0.5 m to in excess of 3.5 m in depth. More significantly, Bell (1983) and Allen (1988) have demonstrated that such deposits are directly or indirectly the result of human interference within the environment, rather than a purely natural or climatic phenomenon.

Processes of colluviation have been addressed by geographers and archaeologists alike (Kwaad and Mücher 1977; 1979; Bell 1981b), both of whom have often placed emphasis on the agencies of soil creep,

rainsplash and gravity. Although these are important factors, Allen has argued that erosion may involve higher energy, more rapid processes such as sheet-wash, rilling and gullying (1988). This was demonstrated at Ashcombe Bottom where excavation revealed a Bronze Age gravel fan and a series of chalk lenses resulting from prehistoric rill erosion of arable land. A graphic modern analogy was provided for these prehistoric erosion events at Ashcombe Bottom (Plate 5.1) when, only 10 weeks after excavation had been completed, a severe storm resulted in a large gravel fan and 17 cm of fine sediments being deposited directly over the previously excavated area (Plate 5.2). These modern deposits, on investigation, provided exceptionally good analogies for the Bronze Age contexts excavated, only being separated in time and vertical distance. Burial of archaeological sites can, therefore, be either extremely rapid or very gradual, but in both cases erosion is primarily accelerated by anthropogenic activity, for example tillage.

	a	b	$\frac{a}{b}=$			
	Estimated m² of colluvium in whole cross section	Length of contributing slope in metres	Estimated depth of eroded soil in cm.	Total artifacts excavated	Artifacts per m³ of hand-excavated soil	Date of Erosion
ASHCOMBE BOTTOM Valley TQ 380 106	24	500 m	5 cm	1911	138·1	Beaker ↓ modern
BOURNE VALLEY Lynchet TV 600 994	156	640 m	24 cm	≤ 10,000	256·4	Bronze Age ↓ Saxon
KILN COMBE Valley TV 573 964	90	500 m	18 cm	3109	68·2	Beaker ↓ Medieval
BISHOPSTONE Lynchet TQ 468006	15·4	160 m	10 cm	1985	64	Neolithic ↓ Saxon
ITFORD BOTTOM Valley TQ 441 049	59	1,200 m	12 cm	2103	68·9	Early Bronze Age ↓ Roman
CHALTON Valley B SU 729 160	60	700 m	9 cm	3105	204·3	B.A./I.A. ↓ Modern
CHALTON Valley A SU 721 166	22·6	900 m	25 cm	366	114·3	Neolithic ↓ Modern
HAMBLEDON Spur	≤ 30·6	500 m	6 cm	163	—	? Prehistoric ↓ Modern
HAMBLEDON Coombe	≤ 137·6	680 m	20 cm	167	104·4	? Iron Age ↓ Modern

MJA

Table 5.1 An attempt to quantify a) the extent of erosion represented by surviving colluvium, and b) the numbers of archaeological artefacts in the excavated sections. The final column provides a crude indication of the period over which the erosion occurred. (After Bell 1986).

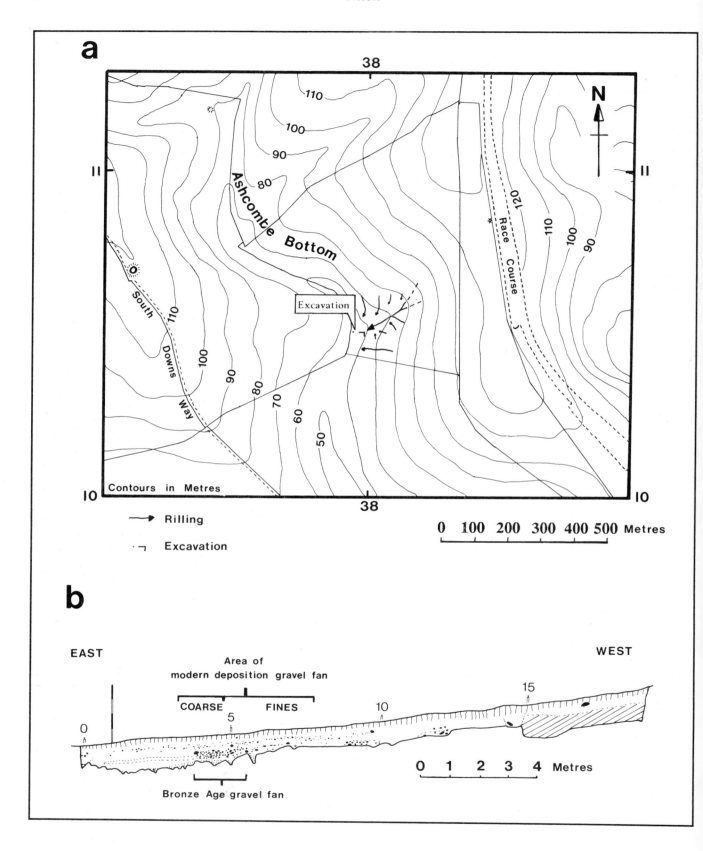

Fig. 5.5 Bourne Valley, Eastbourne

How severe is erosion? (the modified landscape)
The erosion processes described above are only a selection of the processes occurring within the downlands. The landscape is a complex dynamic system of closely integrated processes which change over time in response to external and internal factors. Although we can isolate and monitor precisely those processes occurring today, it is more difficult to indicate rates and frequencies of such processes in the past, not least because the data base from which to draw this information is so small. However, both the nature of colluvium and the artefacts within hillwash provide the basis for the interpretation of ancient erosion events. Only when more intensive and extensive studies of colluvial deposits have been instigated can we really attempt to construct competent models of the true nature of artefact biasing processes in prehistory.

Sediments investigated at a number of sites have contained a vast quantity of identifiable, stratified archaeological artefacts (Figure 5.5; Table 5.1). This indicates not only the occurrence of prehistoric erosion, but also the ancient erosion of prehistoric artefacts. However, Allen (1982), Allen (1988) and Bell (1983) have demonstrated that these deposits are well stratified despite the variation of sedimentological processes involved. The artefact distributions provide a good chronological sequence and display only limited mixing. Although one might have expected biotic activity as well as erosive action to have disrupted and destroyed artefact chronology, it has been shown that these phenomena do not have a serious disruptive effect.

Environmental evidence in the form of Mollusca, soil micromorphology, granulometry and chemistry link the occurrence of the deposits and the artefactual evidence with land clearance and subsequent, large scale, cultivation practices. As these sediments are often appreciable, it is evident that the downlands are largely an anthropogenic landscape composed of essentially "Man-made" soils. As stated above, the scale of sedimentation in dry valleys is highly variable and dependent upon many factors. At Kiln Combe, Sussex, (TV 573 965) nearly 3.0 m of hillwash was revealed in a comparatively major, dip slope, dry valley (Bell 1981a; 1983), whilst at Strawberry Hill, Wiltshire (SU 000 525), a minor scarp slope valley produced 3.3 m of post-glacial hillwash. In contrast the constricted valley at Ashcombe Bottom (TQ 380 106) produced only 1.2 m of colluvium (Allen 1984) and a similar depth was revealed in the extremely broad Bourne Valley, Eastbourne (TV 600 994) (Allen 1983). It would appear that valley morphology seems to bear no relation to the resultant deposits.

Although many dry valleys in southern Britain have been demonstrated to contain colluvium there are exceptions, notably the Seven Sisters, Sussex, and Stonehenge Bottom (Bell and Richards pers comm). Nevertheless, crude estimates based on drift geology, soil maps and fieldwork suggest that *c* 16% of the chalk landscape may be blanketed by colluvium and a further *c* 3% obscured by great depths of alluvium (Scaife and Burrin 1983; 1985). In total it is possible that *c* 19% (ie one-fifth) of the downland landscape previously available for occupation is now obscured and buried by geologically recent deposits. This alone is surprising and often not appreciated by those attempting to reconstruct settlement patterns, but is made more alarming when the archaeological examination of five dry valleys in Sussex produced evidence of four previously unrecorded settlements.

The abundant occurrence of pottery in dry valley deposits does indicate fairly rapid erosion. Certainly at Kiln Combe and Bourne Valley, sherd size can be seen to increase with depth, indicating the rapid burial of material, while residual sherds are significantly weathered and reduced in size. On both of these sites up to 73% of the pottery of any one chronological period occurs within 25 cm of its basalmost example. The remaining 27% occur in the overlying 0.7-1.5 m of colluvium. In each case less than 1% were present on the surface indicating that the ploughsoil on the slopes today contain few sherds of pottery of the type recovered in quantity within the colluvium. Does this indicate that evidence of entire cultural episodes have been transported downslope from valley sides or was the major focus of activity sited on the valley bottoms?

None of these sites are detectable by normal archaeological reconnaissance, least of all as surface artefact scatters. Bell's excavations (Kiln Combe, Itford Bottom and Chalton) were conducted specifically in areas of known archaeology, whereas the excavations at the Bourne Valley, Ashcombe Bottom and Strawberry Hill, undertaken by the author, were conducted due to either the impending destruction of the site or at a location predetermined by the necessity for vehicular access. In none of these valleys did the area of excavation exceed more than 0.0007% of the valley surface! This must, therefore, pose significant questions about our ability to reconstruct archaeological landscapes and identify the location of specific activities within them.

Beaker activity in the downland: a case study
Careful examination of the sediments combined with accurate three-dimensional recording of artefact location allowed distinct, stratified artefact distributions produced in section from a number of valleys (eg Bourne Valley, Figure 5.5) to be integrated with environmental evidence. This provides

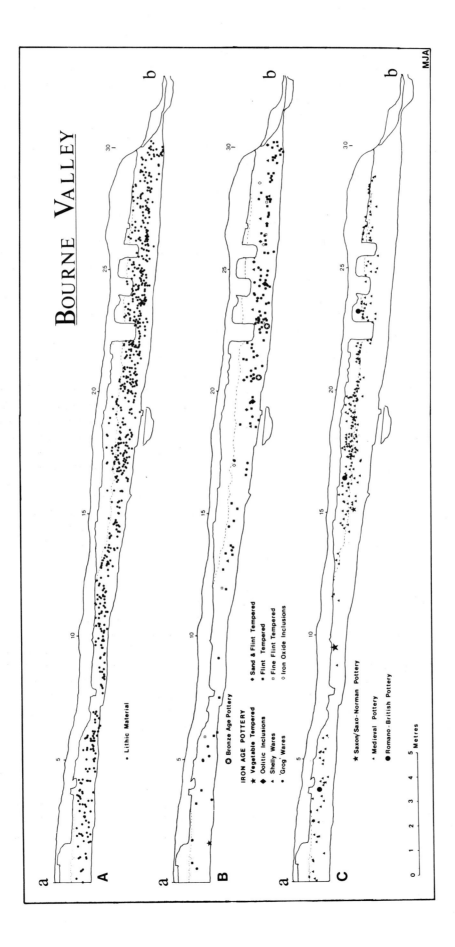

Figure 5.6 Artefact distribution at Bourne Valley.

an ideal situation in which to record off-site landscape studies enabling a wider perspective of landscape evolution to be achieved.

Recent excavations at Strawberry Hill, Wiltshire, Fordington Bottom, Dorset, Newbarn Combe, Isle of Wight and Holy Well Coombe, Kent, have produced evidence alluding to settlement beneath colluvial deposits. In the Bourne Valley, Eastbourne, the density (Figure 5.6) and size of Iron Age sherds was consistent with occupation in the immediate vicinity (Allen 1983). Kiln Combe, excavated by Bell, produced a Beaker occupation phase beneath 2.3 m of colluvium as well as evidence of a 12/14th century medieval farmstead under 0.4 m of hillwash (Bell 1981a, Drewett 1982). Ashcombe Bottom, Sussex, produced a scatter of Beaker pottery associated with a buried soil which have been interpreted as indicative of occupation (Allen 1984). In Wiltshire, recent excavations at Strawberry Hill revealed late Bronze Age activity beneath 2.1 m of hillwash and further, at the base of the valley, two ditches, as yet undated, beneath 3m of deposits.

To exemplify the above, evidence for Beaker activity on the chalk of south-eastern England, especially Sussex, is briefly reviewed. In Sussex alone, there are no less than 28 known Beaker funerary sites on the chalk uplands (Ellison 1978). However, with the exception of North Bersted, situated on the coastal plain (Bedwin and Pitts 1978), only one domestic site was known prior to valley investigation, that of Belle Tout. Here, two sets of upstanding earthworks situated on the cliff edge and, more significantly, located in a dry valley were originally excavated by Toms (1912) and later, in 1968-69 by Bradley (1970). Beaker sherds were located on the old land surface and in the primary fill of the ditch of the larger (now the only extant) earthwork. Bradley's excavations revealed occupation and activity centred on the valley floor and not masked by significant accumulations of hillwash. Investigations of the dry valleys at Kiln Combe and Ashcombe Bottom both produced late Beaker assemblages and have been interpreted as domestic sites. These were well buried and may be described as "chance" discoveries. However, they now constitute no less than 66% of the Beaker sites known from the Sussex chalklands. Looking further afield, the recovery of a single sherd of Beaker pottery in a colluvial sequence at Holy Well Coombe, Kent (Kerney *et al* 1964) has been substantiated by recent large scale excavations revealing extensive Beaker occupation (Bennett pers comm). No other Beaker domestic sites have been published on the chalklands of Surrey, Sussex and Kent, thus it is evident that this class of site during the Beaker period may be exclusively located in valley bottoms and other areas obscured by

sedimentation. The significance and implications of this to field survey is discussed below.

Discussion

This paper has placed emphasis upon "fluvial" erosion on the chalk downs and has largely ignored the downslope movement of artefacts by purely gravitational processes. The latter processes do not seem to be a significant factor on the arable downland. However, Rick (1976) demonstrates this to be a serious component of artefact distributions on steep slopes not subjected to high precipitation. His analysis revealed that some artefact types are more likely to move downslope than others. Although these phenomena do not seem to be a serious problem in the study area considered here, Bell originally suggested (1981a) that large flints on the ground surface could be kicked by grazing animals (cattle and sheep) and roll downslope creating a distinct flint lens on the valley floor. These gravitational processes are biased towards the larger, more spherical objects on the surface; smaller stones and artefacts will be trodden in rather than kicked. Nevertheless this, and the processes described by Rick (1976), may repay further consideration elsewhere.

Denudation of the landscape has not only resulted in the loss of soil, but has also reduced the level of the ground surface on the uplands by severe physical and chemical weathering of the chalk, while erosion has been calculated to have removed as much as 70 cm of chalk (Drewett 1977; 1980) since the fourth millennium BC. It is also clear that severe erosion of the hilltops will displace artefacts from features into the ploughzone. This, and the concentration of artefacts by soil erosion, will facilitate their discovery and retrieval within specific areas. In the long-term, however, severe erosion will obliterate the older and more ephemeral traces of evidence; this may aid the explanation of the paucity of Neolithic and early Bronze Age domestic structures and sites in southern Britain, an hypothesis often favoured because of the abundance of artefacts and monuments in the hilltop zone. However, I would venture to suggest an alternative scenario. Foley suggests that settlements will, for ecological reasons, tend to focus within a particular part of the environment (1981a; 1981b). One can apply this generalisation to any environment and on the South Downs it might be particularly pertinent. If settlement were predominantly valley-based at any time in prehistory, for reasons of communication, sheltered location and suitable habitable terrain, then an entire suite of domestic evidence may remain unrecorded beneath colluvial or alluvial deposits (Allen 1988 and in prep; Scaife and Burrin 1983). Further, this phenomenon is not restricted to southern England, for Butzer (1974, 69) reports that "Bronze Age

conclusion of chapter

valley settlements were buried by as much as 1-2 m of loessic soil wash" in central Europe, while Tolstoy and Fish (1975) have shown second millennium BC artefacts and structures were buried by colluviation in the basin of Mexico. The Mediterranean "Younger Fills", which also bury archaeological evidence, have now been attributed to anthropogenic activity, as exemplified by Wagstaff's seminal paper (1981).

Colluvial deposits will, therefore, create apparent "blanks" in the archaeological record and it is important that a true appreciation of these "blanks" or "black holes", as Groube (1981) describes them, is attempted. Blanks in the archaeological record may reflect a number of factors; lack of fieldwork, nature and quality of fieldwork, destruction of evidence (eg ploughing, industry, development etc) or evidence not available by surface examination (Hammond 1980). Young (1981), for example, demonstrates how the archaeological record in Weardale is biased by open pit coal mining and other environmental factors. Thus, although colluvium may aid in the preservation of relict landscapes, it will also create archaeological "blanks" and must be taken into consideration when examining any site distribution.

Now that artefact scatters are being used to interpret landscape activity, rather than merely to locate "sites" (Lewarch and O'Brien 1981), it is imperative that a comprehensive background knowledge of the landscape is achieved in order to allow the interpretation of artefact distributions. Although one can assume that differential density structure and the form of lithic scatters will reflect the overall distribution of prehistoric activity (Foley 1981b, 183), as Schofield has shown for the middle Avon valley (1987), it is important also to understand the range of geomorphological processes. Understanding the taphonomy of the landscape is important. One must analyse the landscape as well as artefact distributions before venturing into the world of hypotheses and interpretation.

A case for digging holes

Although field survey is precisely that, a survey, involving the recording of surface parameters (ie topographical features and artefact densities), there is a case for sub-surface examination in landscape projects. One of the only ways to establish the degree to which erosion processes have been working in a study area, past or present, is to examine the resultant deposits. Only by this process can potentially datable buried soils be observed in valley locations and thus be integrated into the interpretation of the archaeological landscape. The excavation of small trenches will provide an indication of sedimentation, and, if an adequate section is revealed, this can be recorded and any pottery sherds located whilst clean-

ing or drawing may enable the construction of a crude chronological framework. The Stonehenge Environs Project, directed by Julian Richards, examined extensively the ploughzone artefact distributions on Salisbury Plain around Stonehenge. One major landscape feature within the prescribed area is Stonehenge Bottom and in an attempt to evaluate erosion and the potential of buried land surfaces, extensive augering and limited valley trenching was envisaged. In this specific case, despite superficial evidence to the contrary, no colluvium was recovered and the valley bottom contained a thin brown rendzina (Bell pers comm). This demonstrates that specific assumptions of colluvial occurrence cannot be made and, therefore, that the excavation of soil pits should be seen as a part of any landscape survey project and fieldwalking exercise.

Conclusion
Although the analysis of surface scatters is well suited to large scale studies of human activity in the landscape, it is an inadequate technique for reconstructing complete patterns of past activity and land use, if used in isolation. One important element is the geomorphological perspective on soil erosion. Soil erosion is the best known and documented of all human geomorphological effects (Brown 1970). Erosion, and thus potential burial, is accelerated by devegetation and human activity. Therefore, the greater the activity in the past, the greater the likelihood of bias within that landscape. Any area with evidence of intensive activity may also have areas blanketed by colluvium, while it was specifically these areas in valley bottoms that were probably the centre of prehistoric activity. Therefore, analysis and understanding of the geomorphological processes that influence the archaeological record should form an integral part of field survey and design.

Holgate's view (1985) that field survey of Neolithic landscapes can only be used to put dots on the map is an over pessimistic one. The understanding of biasing and taphonomic processes will allow the full evaluation of a landscape and activities within it. Schofield's (1987) and Shennan's (1985) work provide exciting prospects in field archaeology, yet neither of these have fully appreciated the geographic element of the landscape. It is precisely upon this element that I hope the present paper has shed some light.

Acknowledgements
This paper reached a draft form even before it was offered as a contribution to TAG 1986 and was the result of both comments and encouragement given by the late R.W. Smith to whom I am extremely grateful.

I would like to thank John Schofield for encouraging me to present this paper and for his comments on earlier drafts of the text. I am grateful to Richard Macphail, Arthur ApSimon, Stephen Shennan, Malcolm Wagstaff and Rachael Seager Smith all of whom made valuable comments on earlier drafts of this document, though all opinions and errors remain my own. This was written whilst in receipt of an SERC award.

References

Allen L., 1982. A study of the chronological development of the Bishopstone lynchet by least-squares analysis of the distribution of datable artefacts. *Sussex Archaeological Collections* 120, 207-208.

Allen M.J., 1983. *Sediment analysis and archaeological data as evidence of the palaeoenvironment of early Eastbourne: the Bourne Valley excavation.* Unpublished BSc dissertation, London University, Institute of Archaeology.

Allen M.J., 1984. *Excavations at Ashcombe Bottom: first interim report August 1984.* Lewes: Archaeological Group.

Allen M.J., 1988. Archaeological and environmental aspects of colluviation in south-east England, in Groenman-van Waateringe W. and Robinson M., editors, *Man-Made Soils*, 67-92. BAR (International Series) 410. Oxford.

Avery B.W., Stephen I., Brown G. and Yaalon D.H., 1959. The origin and development of brown earths on clay-with-flints and coombe deposits. *Journal of Soil Science* 10, 177-195.

Bedwin O. and Pitts M.W., 1978. Excavations at an Iron Age settlement at North Bersted, Bognor Regis, West Sussex 1975-77. *Sussex Archaeological Collections* 116, 293-346.

Bell M.G., 1981a. *Valley sediments as evidence of prehistoric land-use in South East England.* Unpublished PhD thesis, London University, Institute of Archaeology.

Bell M.G., 1981b. Valley sediments and environmental change, in Jones M. and Dimbleby G., editors, *The environment of man: the Iron Age to the Anglo-Saxon period*, 75-91. BAR (British Series) 87. Oxford.

Bell M.G., 1983. Valley sediments as evidence of prehistoric land-use on the South Downs. *Proceedings of the Prehistoric Society* 49, 119-150.

Bell M.G., 1986. Archaeological evidence for the date, cause and extent of soil erosion on the chalk. *Journal of the South-East Soil Discussion Group* 3, 72-83.

Bennett H.H., 1939. *Soil Conservation.* London: McGraw-Hill.

Boardman J., 1984a. Erosion on the South Downs. *Soil and Water* 12, 19-21.

Boardman J., 1984b. A morphometric approach to soil erosion on agricultural land near Lewes, East Sussex, in Lukehurst C.T. and Grant R.L., editors, *Issues in Countryside Research*, 1-10. Brighton: Polytechnic, Kingston/Brighton Research Papers.

Boardman J. and Robinson D.A., 1985. Soil erosion, climatic vagary and agricultural change on the Downs around Lewes and Brighton, autumn 1982. *Applied Geography* 5, 243-258.

Bradley R., 1970. The excavation of a Beaker settlement at Belle Tout, East Sussex, England. *Proceedings of the Prehistoric Society* 36, 312-379.

Bridges E.M. and Davidson D.A., 1982. Agricultural uses of soil survey data, in Bridges E.M. and Davidson D.A., editors, *Principles and applications of soil geography*, 171-215. Longman.

Brown E.H., 1970. Man shapes the earth. *Geographical Journal* 136, 74-85.

Butzer K.W., 1974. Accelerated soil erosion: a problem of man-land relationships, in Manners I. and Mikesell M., editors, *Perspectives on Environment*, 57-78. Washington: Association of American Geographers.

Butzer K.W., 1982. *Archaeology as Human Ecology: method and theory for a contextual approach.* Cambridge University Press.

Darwin C., 1881. *The formation of vegetable mould through the action of worms with observations of their habits.* London: John Murray, pub. 1904.

Drewett P.L., 1977. The excavation of a Neolithic causewayed enclosure on Offham Hill, East Sussex, 1976. *Proceedings of the Prehistoric Society* 43, 201-241.

Drewett P.L., 1980. The Sussex plough damage survey, in Hinchliffe J. and Schadla-Hall R.T., editors, *The Past under the Plough*, 69-73. DoE Occasional paper 3. HMSO. London.

Drewett P.L., 1982. *The Archaeology of Bullock Down, Eastbourne, East Sussex: the development of a landscape.* Sussex Archaeological Society Monograph 1.

Ellison A., 1978. The Bronze Age in Sussex, in Drewett P.L., editor, *Archaeology in Sussex to A.D.1500*, 30-37. CBA Research Report 29.

Evans J.G., 1966. Late glacial and post-glacial subaerial deposits at Pitstone, Bucks. *Proceedings of the Geologists' Association* 77, 347-364.

Evans J.G., 1978. *An Introduction to Environmental Archaeology.* London: Paul Elek.

Evans R., 1980. Mechanics of water erosion and their spatial and temporal controls: an empirical viewpoint, in Kirkby M.J. and Morgan R.P.C., editors, *Soil Erosion*, 109-128. Chichester. John Wiley.

Fasham P.J., Schadla-Hall R.T., Shennan S.J. and Bates P.J., 1980. *Fieldwalking for Archaeologists.* Hampshire Field Club and Archaeological Society.

Flannery K.V., 1976. Analysis on a regional level, part 1, in Flannery K.V., editor, *The early Mesoamerican village*, 161-162. London. Academic Press.

Foard G., 1979. Systematic fieldwalking and the investigation of Saxon settlement in Northamptonshire. *World Archaeology* 9, 357-374.

Foley R., 1981a. A model of regional archaeological structure. *Proceedings of the Prehistoric Society* 47, 19-40.

Foley R., 1981b. Off-site archaeology: an alternative approach for the short-sited, in Hodder I., Hammond N. and Issac G., editors, *Pattern of the Past: essays in honour of David Clarke*, 157-183. Cambridge University Press.

Gaffney G., Gaffney V. and Tingle M., 1985. Settlement,

economy or behaviour? Micro-regional land use models and the interpretation of surface artefact patterns, in Haselgrove C., Millett M. and Smith I., editors, *Archaeology from the Ploughsoil : studies in the collection and interpretation of field survey data,* 95-107. Sheffield University Press.

Godwin H., 1967. Strip lynchets and soil erosion. *Antiquity* 41, 66-67.

Groube L., 1981. Black holes in British prehistory: the analysis of settlement distributions, in Hodder I., Hammond N. and Issac G., editors, *Pattern of the Past: essays in honour of David Clarke,* 185-209. Cambridge University Press.

Hammond F.W., 1980. The interpretation of archaeological distribution maps: biases inherent in archaeological fieldwork. *Archaeo-Physika* 7, 193-216.

Harrison Reed A., 1979. Accelerated erosion of arable soils in the United Kingdom by rainfall and run-off. *Outlook on Agriculture* 10, 41-48.

Harrison Reed A., 1983. The erosion risk of compaction. *Soil and Water* 11, 29-33.

Haselgrove C., Millett M., and Smith I., editors, 1985. *Archaeology from the Ploughsoil : studies in the collection and interpretation of field survey data.* Sheffield University Press.

Hinchliffe J. and Schadla-Hall R.T., editors, 1980. *The Past under the Plough.* DoE Occasional paper 3. HMSO. London.

Hodgson J.M., 1976. Soils of the West Sussex coastal plain. *Bulletin of the Soil Survey of Great Britain.* 3.

Hodgson J.M., Catt J.A. and Weir A.H., 1967. The origin and development of clay-with-flints and associated horizons on the South Downs. *Journal of Soil Science* 18, 85-102.

Holgate R., 1985. Identifying Neolithic settlement in Britain: the role of field survey in the interpretation of lithic scatters, in Haselgrove C., Millett M. and Smith I., editors, *Archaeology from the Ploughsoil: studies in the collection and interpretation of field survey data,* 39-37. Sheffield University Press.

Imeson A.C. and Jungerius P.D., 1976. Aggregate stability and colluviation in the Luxembourg Ardennes; an experimental micromorphological study. *Earth Surface Processes* 1, 259-271.

Imeson A.C. and Vis M., 1984. Seasonal variations in soil erodibility under different land-use types in Luxembourg. *Journal of Soil Science* 35, 323-331.

Kerney M.P., 1965. Weichselian deposits in the Isle of Thanet, East Kent. *Proceedings of the Geologists' Association* 76, 269- 274.

Kerney M.P., Brown E.H. and Chandler T.J., 1964. The late glacial and post-glacial history of the chalk escarpment near Brook, Kent. *Philosophical Transactions of the Royal Society* B 248, 135-204.

Kirkby M.J. and Morgan R.P.C., editors, 1980. *Soil Erosion.* London. Wiley

Kwaad F.J.P.M., 1977. Measurements of rainsplash erosion and the formation of colluvium beneath deciduous woodland in the Luxembourg Ardennes. *Earth Surface Processes.* 2, 161-173.

Kwaad F.J.P.M. and Mücher H.J., 1977. The evolution of soils and slope deposits in the Luxembourg Ardennes

near Wiltz. *Geoderma* 17, 1-37.

Kwaad F.J.P.M. and Mücher H.J., 1979. The formation and evolution of colluvium on arable land in northern Luxembourg. *Geoderma* 22, 173-192.

Lewarch D.E. and O'Brien M.J., 1981. The expanding role of surface assemblages in archaeological research, in Schiffer M.B., editor, *Advances in Archaeological Method and Theory* 4, 297-347. Academic Press. New York.

Macphail R.I., 1987. A review of soil science in archaeology in England, in Keeley H.C.M., editor, *Environmental Archaeology: a regional review, vol. II,* 332-379. Historic Buildings and Monuments Commission for England (Occasional Paper 1).

Macphail R.I. and Scaife R.G., 1987. The geographical and environmental background, in Bird J. and Bird D.G., editors, *The Archaeology of Surrey to 1540,* 31-51. Guildford. Surrey Archaeological Society.

Mills N., 1985a. Sample bias, regional analysis and fieldwork in British archaeology, in Haselgrove C., Millett M. and Smith I., editors, *Archaeology from the Ploughsoil: studies in the collection and interpretation of field survey data,* 39-47. Sheffield University Press.

Mills N., 1985b. Geomorphology and settlement studies in archaeology, in Fieller N.R.J., Gilbertson D.D. and Ralph N.G.A., editors, *Palaeoenvironmental Investigations: research design, methods and data analysis,* 175-206. BAR (International Series) 258. Oxford.

Moffat A.J. and Cope D.W., 1984. The Hampshire Chalklands, in Jarvis M.G. and Findlay D.C., editors, *Soils of the Southampton District,* 82-116. Southampton. British Society of Soil Science.

Morgan R.P.C., 1979 *Soil erosion and conservation.* Longman.

Pitty A.F., 1978. *Geography and Soil Properties.* Cambridge University Press.

Reynolds P.J., 1978. Archaeology by experiment: a research tool for tomorrow, in Darvill T.C., Parker Pearson M., Smith R.W. and Thomas R.M., editors, *New Approaches to Our Past: an archaeological forum,* 139-155. Southampton.

Richards J.C., 1990. *The Stonehenge Environs Project.* English Heritage Archaeological Report HBMC London.

Rick J.W., 1976. Downslope movement and archaeological intrasite spatial analysis. *American Antiquity* 41, 133-144.

Scaife R.G. and Burrin P., 1983. Floodplain development and vegetational history of the Sussex High Weald and some archaeological implications. *Sussex Archaeological Collections* 121, 1-10.

Scaife R.G. and Burrin P., 1985. The environmental impact of prehistoric man as recorded in the upper Cuckmere valley at Stream Farm, Chiddingly. *Sussex Archaeological Collections* 123, 27-34.

Schofield A.J., 1987. Putting lithics to the test: non-site analysis and the Neolithic settlement of southern England. *Oxford Journal of Archaeology* 6, 269-286.

Shennan S.J., 1985. *Experiments in the collection and analysis of archaeological survey data: The East Hampshire Survey.* Sheffield University Press.

Smith R.W., 1984. The ecology of neolithic farming systems as exemplified by the Avebury region of Wiltshire. *Proceedings of the Prehistoric Society* 50, 99-120.

Staines S., 1988. The prehistoric soil patterns of the Dorchester environs: a synthesis of soil analyses for excavation along the Dorchester By-Pass, Alington Avenue and Greyhound Yard. Unpublished Report for Trust for Wessex Archaeology.

Taylor C.C., 1966. Strip Lynchets. *Antiquity* 40, 277-284.

Tolstoy P. and Fish S.K., 1975. Surface and subsurface evidence for community size at Coapexco, Mexico. *Journal of Field Archaeology* 2, 97-104.

Toms H.S., 1912. Excavations of the Beltout valley entrenchments. *Sussex Archaeological Collections* 55, 41-55.

Trust for Wessex Archaeology 1988. *Prehistoric Dorchester General Research Day*. Salisbury: TWA.

Wagstaff J.M., 1981. Buried assumptions: some problems of the "Younger Fill" raised by recent data from Greece. *Journal of Archaeological Science* 8, 247-264.

Weir A.H., Catt J.A. and Madgett P.A., 1971. Postglacial soil formation in the loess of Pegwell Bay, Kent (England). *Geoderma* 5, 131-149.

Wills B., 1929. *Downland Treasure*. London:Methuen Ltd.

Wills B., 1932. *Shepherds of Sussex*. Skessington & Son Ltd.

Young R., 1986. Destruction, preservation and recovery: Weardale, a case study, in Manby T.G. and Turnbull P., editors, *Archaeology in the Pennines*. BAR (British Series) 158. Oxford.

Chapter 6

Site Formation Processes and the Hvar Survey Project, Yugoslavia

V L Gaffney, J Bintliff and B Slapsak

Introduction: the archaeology of Hvar

During September 1987, a team of archaeologists from Bradford University collaborated with Ljubljana University in the first season of a projected 10 year survey of the archaeology of the Dalmatian island of Hvar, Yugoslavia. The island possesses a rich and varied archaeological heritage (Figure 6.1) (*cf* Petric 1975). The celebrated material culture associated with excavated Neolithic cave sites on the island has, for example, been extensively researched and published (Novak 1955), whilst the later prehistoric period is represented by the presence of large numbers of tumuli and by hillforts. The island is also noteworthy, however, for the 4th century BC Greek colony of Faros, situated on the site of modern Starigrad, and the 'centuriated' field system associated with that city (Wilkes 1969). The area containing these land divisions, preserved within the modern field layout as a result of their immense drystone construction, has received considerable attention within recent years (Zaninovic 1983; Slapsak and Kirigin 1987; Slapsak and Stancic 1988). Consequently the distribution of numerous Roman villas, the remains of which lie within the fields (Figure 6.2), has already been established.

During the turbulent Migration period, the island was colonised by Slavs, who appear to have initiated the present settlement pattern of the island, whilst during the high- and post-medieval periods the island was possessed in turn by a number of European powers. The sophistication and wealth of the island's inhabitants during this period are testified by the presence of numerous churches and private houses, many of which are associated with the Croatian Renaissance of the 16th century. More recently, the incorporation of the island into the Austro-Hungarian Empire and a significant time-lag in the spread of the Phylloxera epidemic from West to East Europe led to a huge boom in wine output. These events are reflected in the phenomenal spread of terracing and stone clearance cairns over much of the island, including some of the steepest limestone areas of Yugoslavia.

Despite such promise and although Hvar's archaeology is much researched, the evidence is only partially understood. The early prehistoric period on Hvar is an excellent example of this. Despite the international importance of the Neolithic of the area, the virtual confinement of recorded early prehistoric activity to cave sites could not be considered a true reflection of the potential archaeological data. Published material from other areas of Yugoslavia tends to emphasise the existence of open site and off- site activity which appears to be almost totally absent within the recorded archaeological record of Hvar (Batovic and Chapman 1985). Significantly the recovery of off-site lithics within the Starigrad Plain by the 1987 survey team indicates the potential of the island for non site-based work.

Similar problems can be cited for later periods of occupation. Although the 4th century BC Greek colony is attested both historically and archaeologically (Kirigin forthcoming), the evidence of contemporary land-use is poorly represented and little understood. Although much valuable work had been carried out in the area prior to the 1987 survey, the site- and period-specific nature of much of the research reduces the wider utility of the data collected.

Doubtless at least part of the problem of landscape reconstruction on Hvar, as in many other Mediterranean areas, is a result of present land-use (Cherry 1983). Much of the countryside is covered with mediterranean phrygana/steppe vegetation and is characterised by low ground visibility. Massive terrace walls lead to a number of logistical problems during survey, whilst the process of terracing itself results in differential masking and destruction (Gams 1987; Shiel 1988). These problems may now be considered in more detail.

Field methodology used by the Hvar survey project

The first priority of the Anglo-Yugoslav survey of Hvar island has been to establish reliable and quantifiable survey procedures in line with the nature of the terrain. Given the relatively unknown status of the surface archaeology of the island it was decided initially to test the nature of the archaeological data and viability of chosen techniques by surveying a district between Vrboska, on the eastern edge of the Starigrad Plain, and Starigrad (Faros) on the west (Figure 6.3). This zone was surveyed to produce a quantitative distribution of cultural material across the landscape. It was inevitable that the idiosyncratic nature of land

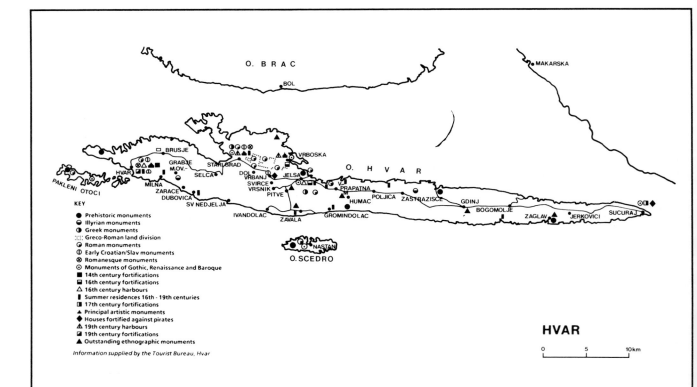

Figure 6.1 Archaeological sites on the island of Hvar, Dalmatia.

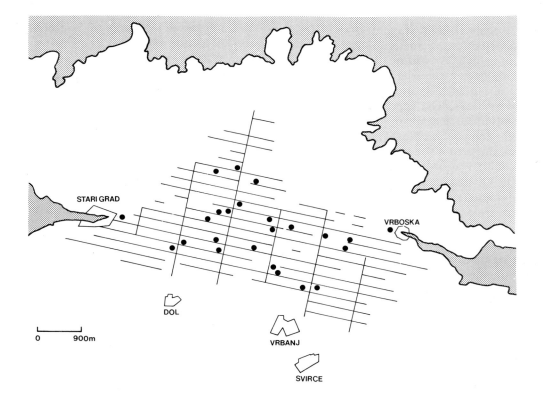

Figure 6.2 Distribution of known archaeological sites on the Starigrad Plain.

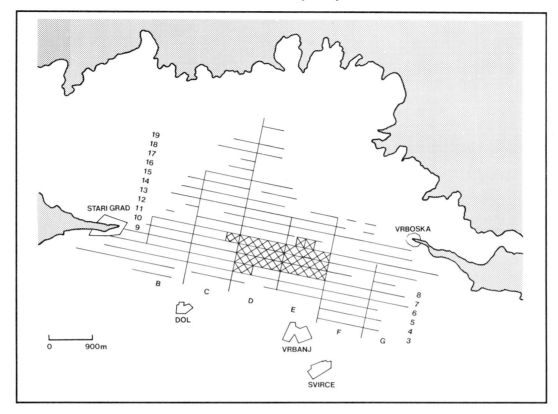

Figure 6.3 Area surveyed during the 1987 field survey season.

divisions on the Starigrad Plain has largely prescribed the nature of the extensive methodology utilised. The fossilisation of the original Greek 'centuriation' within and by a series of massive field clearance cairns and terrace walls, often up to several metres high, has ensured the survival and dominance of a regular grid based on major land divisions of 900 x 180 m and internal subdivisions of 180 x 180 m. This permanent grid is easily identified both from maps and aerial photographs and forms a convenient survey unit (Figures 6.2 - 6.4). Within each grid a series of north-south traverses are being walked at 10m intervals. Each traverse is sub-divided into four recording units of 45 m. Consequently, each 180 x 180 m square contains a total of 72 recording units. We shall term this method *extensive* surface collection.

The field methodology is in many respects a further elaboration of that developed by the Boeotia Survey in Greece (*cf* Bintliff 1985) and the Maddle Farm Project in Britain (Gaffney and Tingle 1989). Within each sub-unit all surface archaeological material is counted using a manually operated counter and all artefacts, except tile, are placed within a bag referenced to the individual 10 x 45 m collection sub-unit. The survey policy is to provide information on all periods of human activity up to, and including, the present. All material is taken back to the survey headquarters for processing and analysis. As ground visibility is an important bias within most Mediterranean based surveys, especially those working outside intensively ploughed areas, data on ground visibility for each 45 m strip are also recorded using a scale of 1 to 10 to denote increasing visibility. All areas are surveyed using this basic technique, thus giving accurate and quantifiable information on both site-location and off-site discard across the Starigrad Plain.

Whilst providing a relatively accurate spatial distribution of material across the landscape, the above techniques do not answer all possible, or indeed relevant, archaeological questions. Therefore, when areas which appear to be associated with habitation or at least concentrated activity are encountered, a more detailed *intensive* survey is carried out. The primary aim of the second survey is to increase the artefact sample from specific locations and to provide further information on the internal structure and nature of the habitation scatter or activity form.

Intensive survey involves two distinct procedures. The first involves the total collection of all surface artefacts within a 10 x 10 m grid. This allows a rapid assessment of the extent and content of the occupation scatter and provides a greater ceramic data base, thus enhancing the likelihood of dating the scatter effectively.

Figure 6.4 Aerial photograph of Greek centuriation on the Starigrad Plain.

The second on-site survey procedure includes a sub-surface survey designed to quantify accurately the absolute density of artefacts within the topsoil. Sub-surface survey has not been widely used in Europe, although the basic principles have been appreciated for some time. Its principle value is to provide information in those areas where visibility restricts the use of traditional survey procedures. In the past it has been used in areas of woodland (Percy 1976) and sand dunes (South and Widmer 1977). Although most often used for intra-site survey (Williams 1986) the technique is now being used within a

wider landscape context (Hayes 1985; Gaffney and Tingle 1989). On Hvar, the technique is particularly attractive as large areas of land are covered by vegetation and consequently suffer from visibility problems.

Sub-surface survey on Hvar has been carried out using a "Tomos" petrol powered posthole drill. This machine, which is fitted with a 20 cm diameter bit, is used to drill small test pits up to 70 cm deep at set intervals on the same grid used for surface collection. The test holes are manually cleared and sorted, all archaeological artefacts being retained. The depth of the test pit is measured allowing a volumetric assessment of the pit's artefact content. This procedure is useful as it allows direct comparison between the sub-surface survey and intensive collection, whilst the volumetric data allow correction to a standard volume for comparison between test pits.

The problem of post-depositional processes

During the 1987 season an area covering 120 hectares was surveyed extensively and four occupation sites examined intensively (three totally, one partially; the total occupation surface studied being 2.82 hectares) using the techniques described above. At a very early stage of the survey, however, it was realised that large quantities of archaeological material were being located, not upon the field surfaces, but upon the clearance cairns and field walls. This appeared to correspond with local agricultural practices, therefore raising serious problems of interpretation. The surface collection strategies adopted for the Hvar survey, in common with virtually all Mediterranean surveys begun within the last 10 years, are variants of techniques developed for use in the semi arid regions of the southern U.S.A. and the temperate regions of north-west Europe. Such techniques are implicitly designed for use within the agricultural regimes and natural weathering conditions prevalent within those regions (predominantly large ploughed arable fields or open desert / Steppe) and are characterised by grid collections which assume a direct link, via the ploughing process or semi arid weathering, between the archaeological entity and the surface distribution. In these specific environments a great deal of work has been carried out to quantify the relationship of surface and sub-surface archaeology, both by experiment (Reynolds 1982; Odell and Cowan 1987; Clark and Schofield this volume; Yorston, Gaffney and Reynolds 1990) and through empirical observation (Bintliff and Snodgrass 1988; Bowden *et al* this volume). It is as a result of such ideal conditions that survey work has been so successful within the southern States and north-west Europe in the past 15 years. There is no reason to assume, however, that such conditions should be expected outside the areas in which grid survey was developed, *or* that any relationship between surface and sub-surface archaeology, based upon assumptions developed in such areas, should hold true. Indeed, initial estimates from the Hvar data suggest that up to 50% of surface artefacts were being recovered from field walls and must be regarded as divorced significantly from their original spatial context.

The processes which lead to such a situation appear to result from the nature of the local geology and topography as well as the agricultural regime practiced within the Starigrad Plain. The modern field system is entirely constrained within the original Greek metrical division of 5 x 1 stadia or 900 x 180 m (Gams 1987). Within this division the land has been continuously sub-divided into a series of very small field units, many of which are terraced with massive drystone walls, a consequence of the sloping topography in the area. These walls are not, however, simply a functional response to land gradient (their scale is far in excess of such a need). Instead they represent the process of stone clearance from the fields. This is common in many limestone environments (Shiel and Chapman 1988) but is present in an extreme form on Hvar as a result of the intensive hand cultivation practised within the Starigrad Plain over the past 2,500 years. Although mechanisation is now used within the Plain, it is still a common sight to see the small tractors used for ploughing being followed by the farmer's family, who will remove any coarse soil elements exposed by the plough. Without doubt the continuing process of clearance is causing a vast modification of the archaeological record. At the time of writing, the cumulative effect of such a modification upon collection strategies and the interpretation of archaeological data was far from clear.

Given the potential scale of post-depositional change in the Hvar landscape, it seemed essential that work was carried out in order to quantify and, indeed, clarify the nature of any potential modification to the survey record. In order to achieve this, information had to be gathered concerning the wall or cairn artefact/field surface artefact ratio and upon the nature of the two assemblages.

An excellent opportunity to achieve this arose when the local authorities at Vrboska gave permission for the construction of a new road over the site of a known Roman villa at Jeze (Gaffney and Slapsak nd). Although the site was not within the district chosen for survey, the threat of road construction demanded that the area should be surveyed to provide information on the extent of the site. It also presented an opportunity to carry out a small scale excavation designed to provide information regarding the artefact content of the topsoil, surrounding stoneheaps and sub-surface features.

The case study: Villa Jeze

The large Roman villa of Jeze lies at the head of a small inlet about 100 metres to the west of the modern village of Vrboska (Figure 6.3). During the 1987 season the site was surveyed both extensively, intensively and using the sub-surface drill strategy described above. A small sondage was also excavated across a terrace wall on the proposed route of the road. This section was later extended to include a

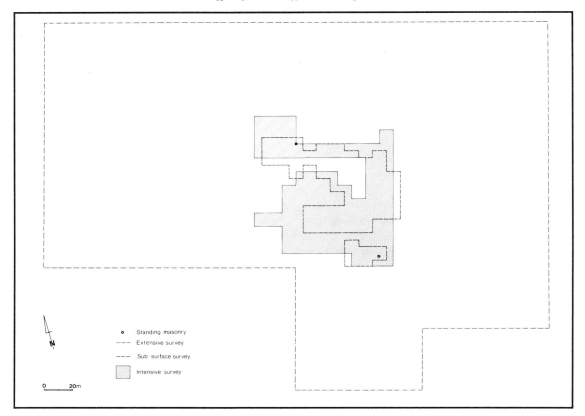

Figure 6.5 Relative positions of survey grids at the Villa Jeze.

5 x 10 m section across the terrace behind the wall and to investigate the wall's relationship with a stone built hut or "trim" which appeared to have been inserted into the terrace wall. The relative positions of the survey grids are shown in Figure 6.5, whilst Figure 6.6 shows the relationship of the extensive grid to field walls, the excavated area and surviving villa walls.

A total of 5.67 hectares was surveyed using the extensive survey technique. This produced a total of 1,531 artefacts, the majority of which were tile and pottery fragments. The distribution of this material suggested that the site lay in the middle of the extensive survey area. Comparison with visibility data (Figure 6.7) indicates that the restrictions of surface visibility prevent a reliable estimate of the probable area of the site. Consequently, visibility data has been used to correct hard data distributions using a simple correction formula devised by the Cambridge and Bradford Boeotia Survey Project (Bintliff 1985). When smoothed, the recorded artefact distribution indicates that the core spread of the site scatter extends over a minimum of 1.8 hectares. The consistent appearance of two separate artefact concentrations in all the plots of the extensive survey data is almost certainly the consequence of areas of very poor ground visibility over the centre of the site.

Analysis of the extensive survey data revealed that

no less than 45% of all material by number, was recovered from stoneheaps. Indeed, the ratio in favour of stoneheaps would probably be even greater if weight were recorded. The contrasting distributions of stoneheap and field surface data are displayed in Figures 6.9 and 6.10. The complimentary relationship between the two groups over the probable core area of the site is quite distinct. This is largely the result of poor ground visibility recorded over this area, although the association of ancient buildings, stone pile accumulation, and stone pile artefact concentrations is a noted feature of the archaeology of the Starigrad Plain. There has been a tendency in the past for the locals to use inconvenient and substantial upstanding masonry as a base for stone clearance piles. Indeed, two terrace walls at the Jeze site are known to contain structural walls, presumably of Roman date (see Figures 6.6, 6.10 and 6.11).

The data provided by extensive survey were used as the basis for the positioning of the intensive survey grid. This was placed over the centre of the surveyed area and covered an area of 0.68 hectares. A total of 4,541 artefacts was recovered from this zone. When corrected for visibility it seems likely that a total of 10,367 artefacts lies over the surface of the site core, giving a mean density of 1.52 artefacts per square metre. Again the majority of the finds were ceramic, mainly tile, dolia or amphorae, although a number of

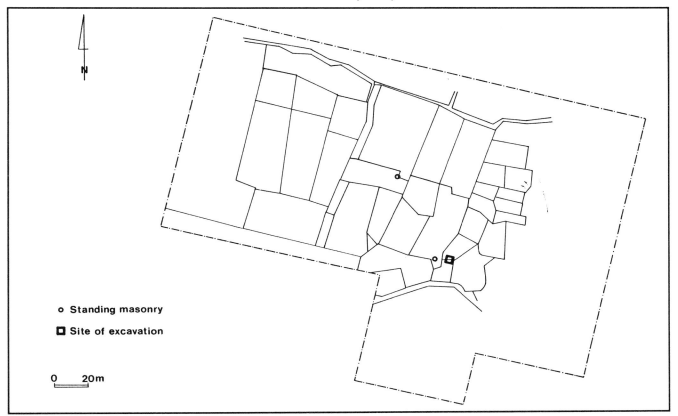

o **Standing masonry**

□ **Site of excavation**

0 __ 20m

Figure 6.6 Field boundaries adjacent to the Villa Jeze excavation.

fragments of painted wall plaster and mosaic pavement, suggesting the presence of a building with some pretensions, were also recovered.

Figure 6.11 indicates the distribution of all artefacts recovered by intensive survey, the distribution tending to confirm the results of extensive collection. The core of the site appears to lie towards the south of the grid with the scatter extending both south and west, while the northern area of the grid shows a marked decline in artefact density. Corrected and smoothed data confirm the picture, but hint at further activity in the northern area of the grid.

When the intensive data are re-analysed in the form of field surface and stone heap collections, a total of 58% of the surface assemblage can be shown to be derived from the stone piles. Once again, the spatial distributions of the two data sets appear to be complementary, largely as a result of the poor ground visibility recorded in the central part of the grid (Figure 6.11 and 6.12). The artefact densities recovered from the stone piles, however, also emphasise the significance of the north western area of the grid, in contrast to the field densities, and despite the good visibility recorded in this area.

The results obtained from the sub-surface drill survey offer an opportunity to assess the reliability of the survey results in an objective way. During this survey a total of 75 boreholes was drilled every five

metres along transects spaced at ten metre intervals, and aligned on the intensive collection grid. A total of 2,445 artefacts was recovered. When considered volumetrically, figures of over 10,000 artefacts per cubic metre of soil were recorded. The majority of objects recovered were ceramic-tile, or pottery, although tesserae, glass, iron slag and mortar were also encountered. The distribution of hard data from the sub-surface survey and the volumetrically corrected distribution are given in Figure 6.13. The discrepancies between these results and those provided by intensive surface survey are considerable. The northern edge of the site, far from being devoid of major archaeological activity is shown to be a principal focus or, at the very least, a continuation of the concentration recorded further south by intensive survey. Distributions of mortar and tesserae (Figure 6.13c) also indicate that the northern area seems to be the position of what may have been a substantial building. The presence of a structural wall within a stoneheap adjacent to the northern sub-surface artefact scatter appears to confirm this.

The opportunity to excavate a small area at Jeze was an ideal chance to examine a portion of the site within the framework of the earlier survey results. The area chosen for excavation lay on the eastern edge of the principal scatter (Figure 6.6), and on the route of the proposed road. Within the trench a ten metre section of a clearance cairn / terrace wall was removed in order to investigate the nature of the archaeological assemblage entering such landscape features. This would also expose the relationship of the terrace wall with a trim (agricultural stone hut) which appeared to have been inserted into the terrace wall (Figure 6.14). Behind the terrace wall a 5 x 10 m area of terrace was excavated. This section was achieved in metre squares through the topsoil and sample sieved in order to provide quantitative information on the horizontal and vertical distribution of archaeological material across the width of the terrace.

The contents of the trench at Jeze, which included a series of Roman graves along the eastern edge of the excavated area, are interesting in their own right. However, the information most relevant to this paper is contained within the comparative analysis of the stoneheap and terrace topsoil artefact assemblage, and the insight the excavated data gave into the nature and effect of agricultural practices on the archaeological survey record.

The destructive nature of terracing can clearly be seen in Figure 6.14. At the rear of the terrace, bedrock lies only a few centimetres below the field surface. Although the soil becomes progressively deeper towards the front of the terrace, immediately behind the terrace wall no stratified deposits survive above a depth of 120 cms. The soil within this zone of destruction is entirely mixed as a result of agricultural activity. Part of the reason for the efficiency of this agricultural destruction can be explained through reference to the nature of viticulture. One method of preparing ground for vines is through the excavation of very deep bedding pits. Several of these trenches were located during excavation and can be seen in the photograph in Figure 6.14. Repeated excavation and relocation of such features over two and a half thousand years have thoroughly homogenised the soil and guaranteed destruction of everything but the deepest archaeological deposits.

The destruction of deposits by agricultural processes is further complicated by the process of intensive field clearance mentioned above. The quantitative scale of this problem can be assessed simply by reference to the ratios of artefacts found on the stoneheaps as opposed to field surfaces during extensive and intensive survey, 48% and 56% respectively. However, the qualitative effect upon surviving assemblages can only be assessed objectively through examination of excavated assemblages. Figure 6.15 attempts this by contrasting a number of different excavated groups and separating out the artefact classes by number, weight and mean artefact weight for each group. Perhaps the most significant points can be seen in the contrast between artefact content

of the topsoil of the Jeze excavation and that found during removal of the "gomila" or stone pile and terrace wall. In contrast to the topsoil, tile dominates the stone pile assemblages both in weight and numbers. Except for specialist forms such as amphorae and dolia, pottery is represented by significantly low numbers. Except for mortar and quern, no other class is represented by more than 1% of the total stoneheap assemblage by number or weight. In contrast, the topsoil assemblage contains very little tile when quantified by numbers of fragments (4%), and even when considered by weight this artefact class only represents 20% of the assemblage. The topsoil is dominated by pottery and unidentifiable ceramic fragments. It must, however, be stressed that a large amount of the oxidised pottery in the topsoil may be amphorae, whilst the unidentifiable ceramic fragments must include large amounts of tile. Unfortunately, the very small size of the sherds involved in the analysis, and the present poor knowledge of amphora fabrics on Hvar prevent a more precise classification at this moment. Their presence indicates that artefact abrasion is a significant problem in the analysis of Hvar survey data, and suggests that the greater susceptibility of pottery vessels to fragmentation is the critical factor.

The two assemblages clearly demonstrate that the process of agricultural clearance of material from field surface to clearance cairns involves the differential sorting of artefact classes. Comparison of the mean artefact weights of material contained within the topsoil and the excavated stone heap at Jeze clearly shows that the principle criterion for sorting is by size. The mean artefact weight is 106 grams in the stone heap, but only 16 grams within the topsoil.

The point is a significant one. Archaeological literature clearly indicates that large objects tend to move to the surface of sites during cultural or agricultural disturbance (Ammerman and Feldman 1978; Baker 1978; Lewarch and O'Brien 1981) and it is these objects which will tend to be removed during agricultural clearance activities within the Hvar agricultural systems.[1] The process of differential sorting may be significant in the analysis of some of the Jeze survey data, especially those results produced through sub-surface survey (Figure 6.13). Here the distribution of artefacts was interpreted to indicate the possible presence of a building in the north western survey area. It is interesting, therefore, that whilst the artefact groups represented within the data set contain relatively large proportions of small building debris, for example mosaic fragments (8%), they contain relatively little ceramic material which could be positively identified as pottery. By contrast, the excavated area at Jeze, which we know does not contain any architectural evidence, contains relatively high

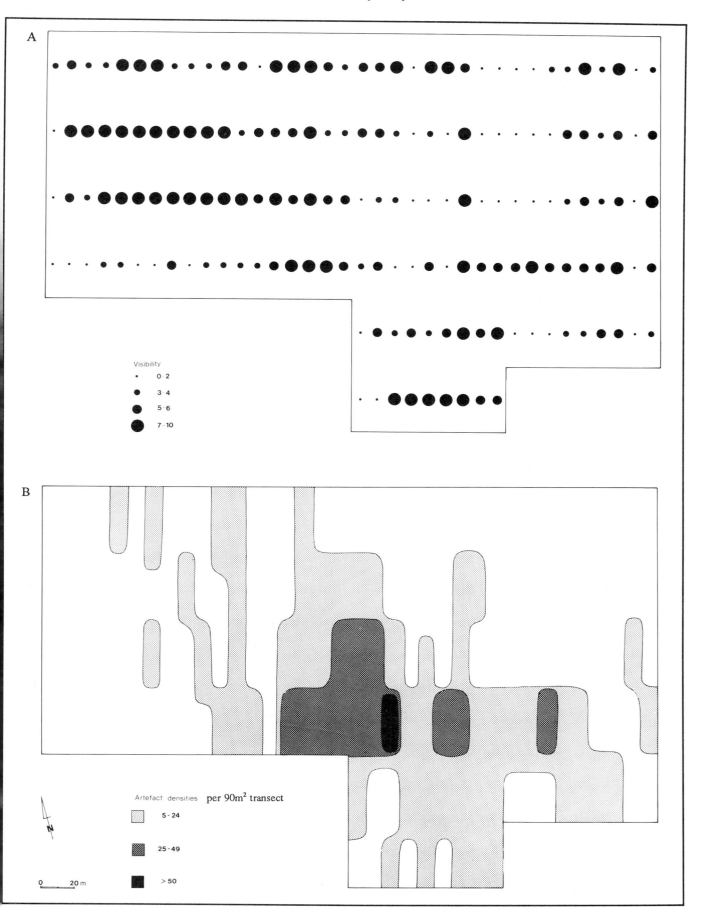

Figure 6.7 Extensive survey results. A) Visibility scores per transect. B) Raw data.

68 *Gaffney, Bintliff and Slapsak*

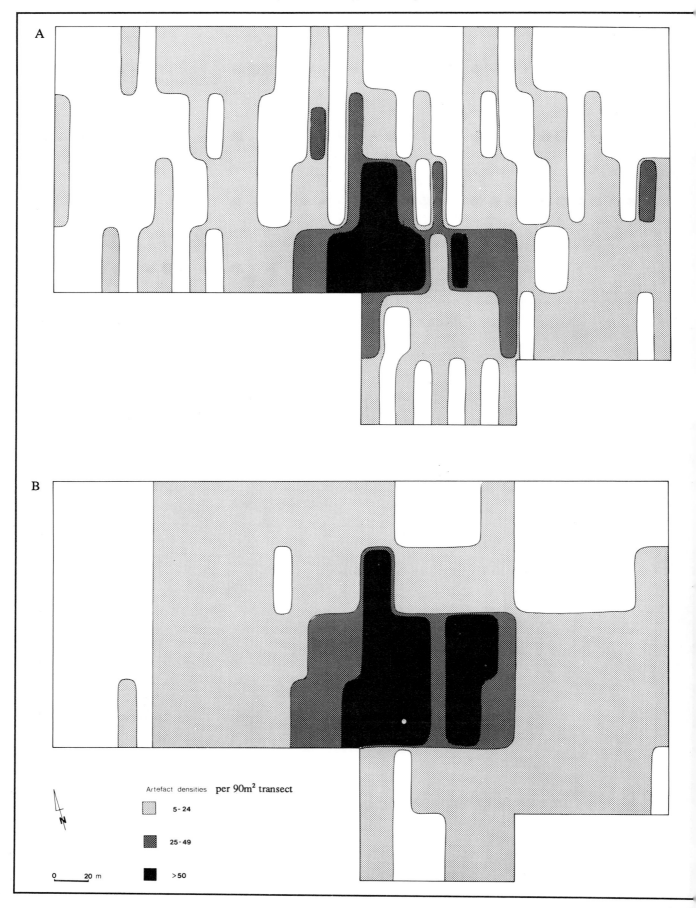

Figure 6.8 Extensive survey results. A) Data corrected for visibility. B) Corrected and smoothed data.

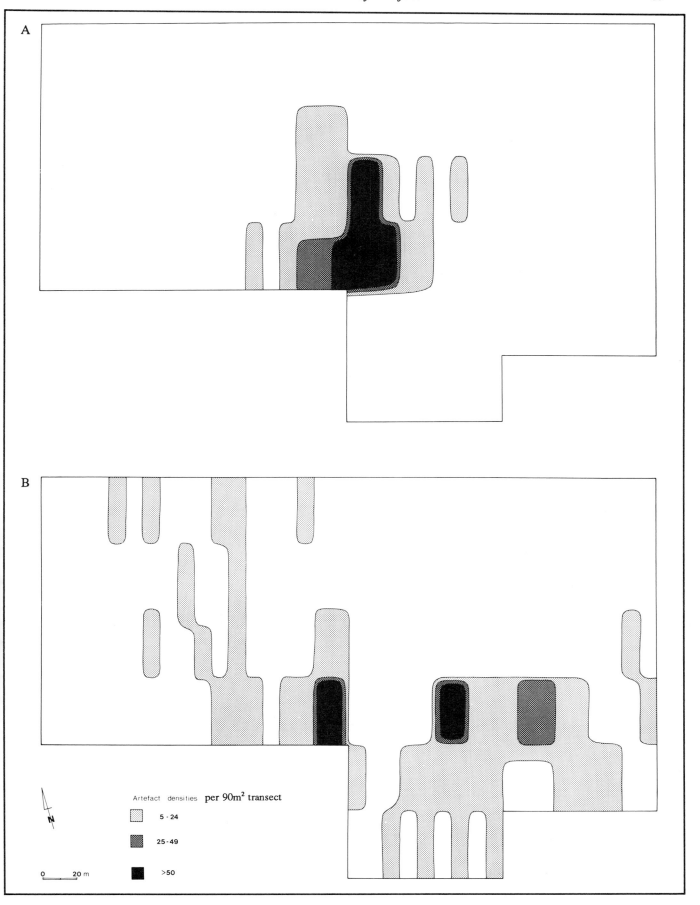

Figure 6.9 Extensive survey results. A) Artefacts collected from field clearance cairns and field boundaries. B) Artefacts collected from the field surface.

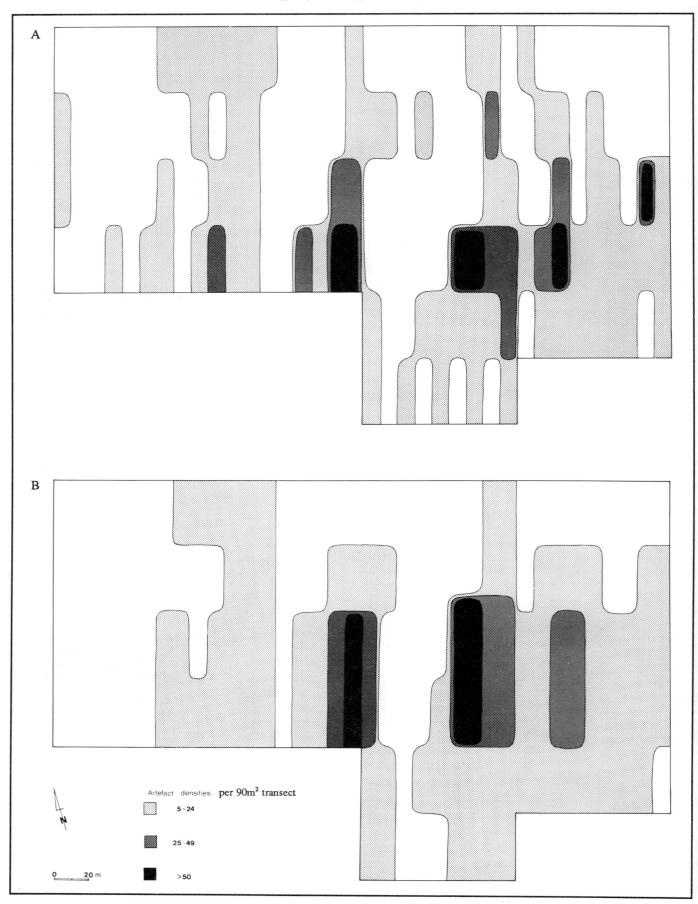

Figure 6.10 Extensive survey results. A) Field surface data corrected for visibility. B) Field surface data corrected and smoothed.

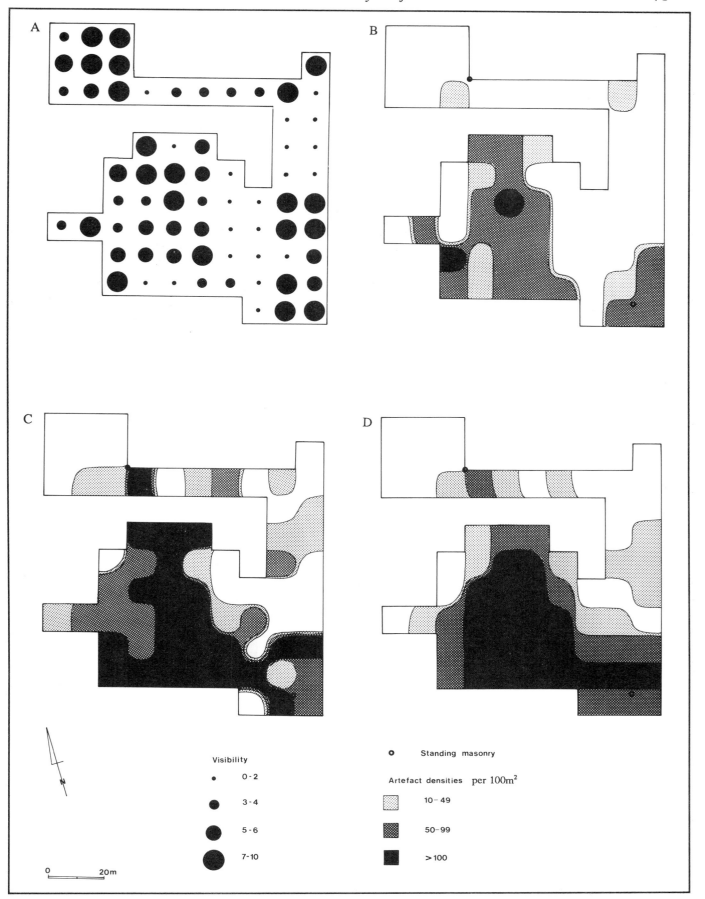

Figure 6.11 Intensive survey results. A) Visibility scores per collection grid square. B) Raw data. C) Data corrected for visibility. D) Corrected and smoothed data.

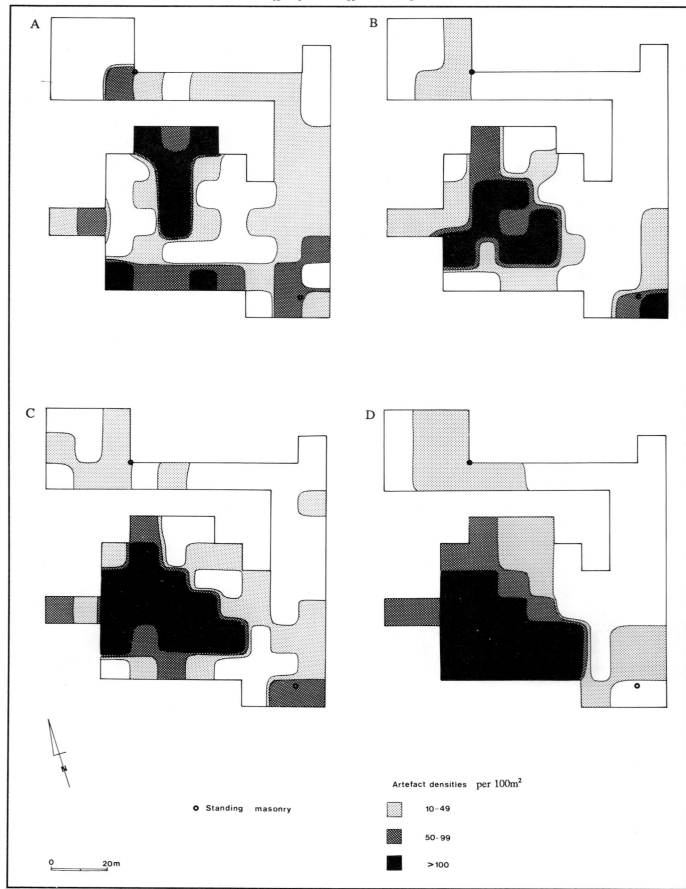

Figure 6.12 Intensive survey results. A) Artefacts collected from field clearance cairns and field boundaries. B) Artefacts collected from the field surface. C) Field surface data corrected for visibility. D) Field surface data corrected and smoothed.

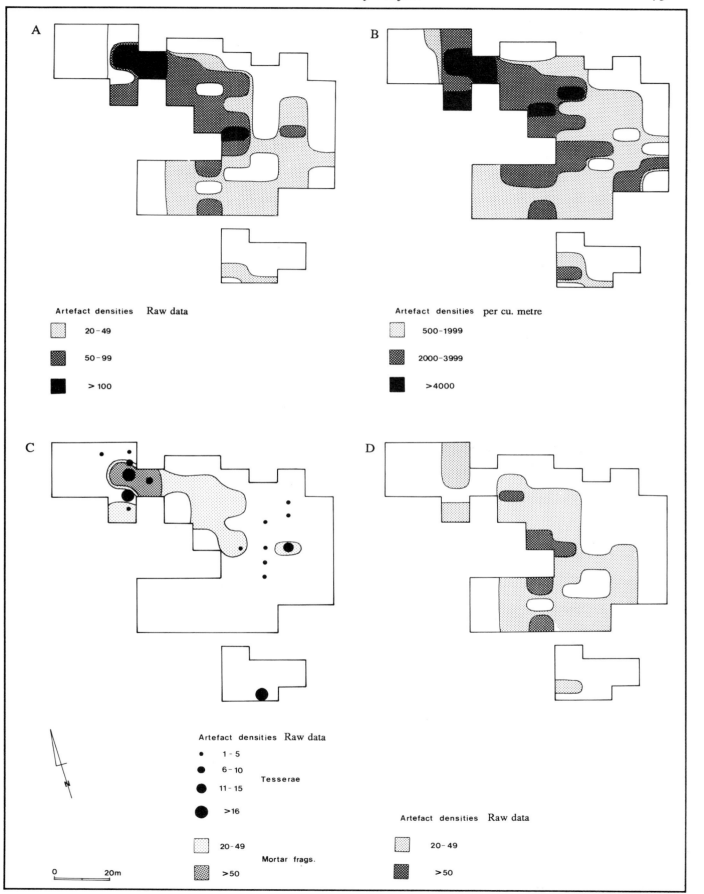

Figure 6.13 Sub-surface survey. A) Raw data. B) Artefact densities per cubic metre. C) Distribution of mortar fragments and tesserae. D) Distribution of all ceramic material.

Figure 6.14 The excavation trench at Jeze showing, A) field terrace wall and clearance cairn (Gomila), B) agricultural hut or "trim" and C) base of vine cultivation trench.

quantities of pottery. Given that post depositional processes seem less likely to affect this artefact group so dramatically, it may be suggested that the contrasting pattern is genuine. It is suggested that the lack of pottery recovered by sub-surface survey may be the result in this case of cleaning within a building, the detritus of such activities probably being deposited beyond the confines of the living area.

The net result is a quantitative and qualitative change in the nature of the assemblage through time. In such a situation some classes of large artefact may be entirely divorced from their original spatial context. Although the Jeze sample is relatively small (the artefact population in Figure 6.15 is 7,081 objects), it is significant that at least one large artefact group, that of quernstone fragments, was only represented in the stoneheap collections. Given that quernstones are

a relatively small part of the overall assemblage, it may be even more ominous to note that over 97% of the tile population by weight now lies within the stoneheap assemblage. Although these proportions will change with the incorporation of stratified deposits into the analysis, the overall picture is unlikely to be modified to any great extent.

It is also significant that the sorting process affects the nature of individual artefact groups internally. At least 30% of the stone heap amphora assemblage is composed of the larger and most diagnostic fragments ie rims, bases and handles. This single group is numerically greater than that representing *all* the sherds which could be positively identified as amphora fragments in the topsoil, despite the fact that the potential number of amphora sherds is far greater within the topsoil if, as we suspect, a large proportion

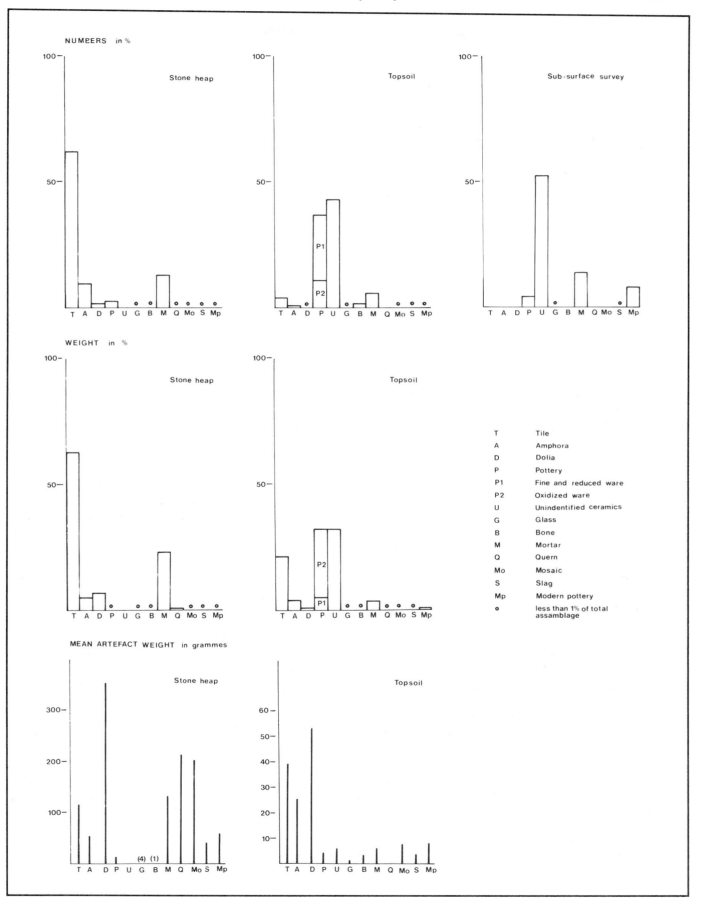

Figure 6.15 Comparison of the excavated assemblages from the stone heap (Gomila) and topsoil contexts at the Villa Jeze.

of sherds classified simply as "oxidised wares" turn out to be amphorae. Consequently, we might expect to find, in time, that the majority of *diagnostic* amphora sherds will have been transferred to the stone heaps. A similar comment could also be passed for the pieces of glass found within the stone heap assemblage. Although the number of fragments found within either assemblage is not great, the pieces within the stoneheap tend to be the larger, diagnostic and "prettier" examples.

Should we then be completely pessimistic about the potential of field survey in environments like that on Hvar? We would suggest not and that what is really needed is an attempt to understand the nature of the assemblage we are dealing with. The extensive surface survey results described above confirm their value as site location tools (Figures 6.7 to 6.10). Detailed analysis of the intensive survey results may, however, demand a more rigorous interpretation. The artefact distributions shown in Figures 6.11 and 6.12 indicate that the grossing of all the information to produce single plots may be too simple. By doing so in Figure 6.11, we have ignored the emphasis that the stoneheap collection would have placed upon the northern part of the site, and the fact that the northern artefact terrace wall concentration relates directly to a structural wall contained within the terrace (Figure 6.12). In order to extract the maximum information from such data it is essential that field surfaces *and* stoneheaps are treated independently, at least in the initial analysis.

Although agricultural practices on Hvar have distorted the nature of the assemblages, some artefact groups, especially those which contain smaller artefacts, may avoid the worst effects and retain some degree of spatial integrity (Baker 1978). The spatial patterning exhibited through the sub-surface survey, interpreted as being related to the presence of a substantial building, may therefore be considered as significant, especially when used in conjunction with the analysis of the sub-surface assemblage shown in Figure 6.15. In this illustration it appears that some small objects implicitly associated with a building, for example mosaic fragments, are represented in relatively high densities (8% of the total) within the sub-surface survey, in contrast to the excavated area, where we can be sure we are outside the principal structure. It may also be significant, therefore, to point out the very low percentages of ceramic material positively identified as pottery within the sub-surface survey in comparison to the excavated area assemblage. If the sample is regarded as adequate, it may be suggested that the pottery data hint at some element of structuring, possibly as a result of cleaning processes which involve the discard of the majority of pottery outside the area of the building.

Evidence from the Jeze excavation suggests, therefore, that it is not sufficient simply to transfer the methodologies developed for the location and analysis of survey data on the wheat growing belts of north-west Europe or the arid lands of America into a Mediterranean context. The agricultural or climatic base for such work, vast machine-worked prairie farms or highly weathered semi-desert landscapes, simply do not exist within the many regions of the Mediterranean. The problems created by intensive terrace agriculture, and outlined above, are alien to the simple application of techniques designed for use elsewhere.

However, such a statement should not be used as an argument against the use of standard surface and sub-surface collection strategies within Mediterranean archaeology. The logical consequence of such an attitude is the demand for a greater concern with local post-depositional patterns and site-formation processes (Schiffer 1976). In order to understand the patterning which is evident within survey data it is essential that archaeologists working within the Mediterranean attempt to come to terms with all the variables at work within the data. Some of this work might seem obscure to the immediate interests of archaeology. A thorough understanding of contemporary agricultural practices and the mechanics of soil movement (Lambrick 1980) might not appear relevant in many cases. In field survey, however, we suggest it would be totally illogical that work should be carried out without any attempt to compensate adequately for such factors. In the case of Jeze it was suggested that the "location logic" behind the distribution of at least 56% of Roman ceramics at the villa site was dictated by post Roman agricultural practices rather than contemporary behaviour.

Such an approach has much to commend itself to survey archaeology and excavation in general. Archaeologists should ensure that they do not unconsciously fall into the trap of "the Pompeii premise" (Binford 1981). The reality of the archaeological record is that it is the most indirect and confused of reflections on past human activity. Any archaeologist who tries to interpret such a record simply as a "fossilised picture" of past human behaviour does so at his/her own peril.

Notes

1 Farmers working in the plain today informed team members that, whilst large objects were removed from the field surface, small objects were allowed to remain as these were felt (rightly) to be beneficial for the soil texture.

Acknowledgements

The authors would like to thank Zoran Stancic for his photogrammetric work at Jeze and Peter Cerce for helping prepare the photographs for publication. However, special thanks are extended to Darja Grossman and the Bradford University Graphics Unit who helped so much in the preparation of this publication through the contribution of their draughting skills. The Centre for the protection of the Cultural Heritage of Hvar also provided much help during the September and November fieldwork seasons.

References

Ammerman A.J. and Feldman M.V., 1978. Replicated collection of site surfaces, *American Antiquity* 43, 743-40.

Baker C.M., 1978. The size effect: an explanation of variability in surface artefact assemblage content. *American Antiquity* 43, 288-93.

Batovic. S and Chapman J.C., 1985. The "Neothermal Dalmatia" project, in Macready S. and Thompson F.H., editors, *Archaeological Field Survey in Britain and Abroad,* 158- 195. Society of Antiquaries Occasional papers 6. London.

Binford L.R., 1981. Behavioral Archaeology and the "Pompeii premise". *Journal of Anthropological Research* 37, 195-208.

Bintliff J., 1985. The Boeotia Survey, in Macready S. and Thompson F.H., editors, *Archaeological Field Survey in Britain and Abroad,* 196-216. Society of Antiquaries Occasional papers 6. London.

Bintliff J. and Snodgrass, A.M. 1988. Off-site pottery distributions: a regional and interregional perspective, *Current Anthropology* 29, 506-513.

Cherry J.F., 1983. Frogs around the pond: perspectives on current archaeological survey projects in the Mediterranean region, in Keller D.R. and Rupp D.W., editors, *Archaeological Survey in the Mediterranean Area,* 375-415. BAR (International Series) 155. Oxford.

Gaffney V. and Slapsak B., nd. Investaj o kontrolnim istrazivanjima na lokalitetu Vrboska-Jeze. Centre for the Protection of the Cultural Heritage of Hvar.

Gaffney V. and Tingle M., 1989. The Maddle Farm Project: an integrated survey of Prehistoric and Roman landscapes on the Berkshire Downs. BAR (British Series) 200. Oxford.

Gams I., 1987. A contribution to the knowledge of the patterns of walls in the mediterranean karst, in *The Proceedings of the International Symposium on Human Influence on Karst,* 76-88. Postojna.

Hayes P.P., 1985. The San Vincenzo Survey, Molise, in Macready S. and Thompson F.H., editors, *Archaeological Field Survey in Britain and Abroad,* 129-135. Society of Antiquaries Occasional papers 6. London.

Kirigin B., Forthcoming. The Greeks in Central Dalmatia, in *The Proceedings of the first Australian Congress for Classical Archaeology.* Oxford University Press.

Lambrick G., 1980. Effects of modern cultivation equipment on archaeological sites, in Hinchliffe J. and Schadla Hall R.T., editors, *The past under the plough,* 18-21. DoE Occasional Papers, No. 3. HMSO, London.

Lewarch D.I. and O'Brien M.J., 1981. The expanding role of surface assemblages in archaeological research, in Schiffer M.B., editor, *Advances in Archaeological Method and Theory.* 4, 297-342. Academic Press. New York.

Novak G., 1955. *Prehistorijski Hvar.* Zagreb.

Odell P. and Cowan F., 1987. Estimating tillage effects on artefact distributions. *American Antiquity* 52, 456-484.

Percy G., 1976. Use of a mechanical auger as a substitute for exploratory excavation at the Torreya (8Li8) site, Liberty County, Florida. *Florida Archaeologist* 29, 24-52.

Petric N., 1975. Arheoloska istrazivinja otoka Hvara. *Hvarski Zbornik* 3, 243-268.

Reynolds P.R., 1982. The ploughzone, in *Festschrift zum 100 jahrigen Jubiläum der Abteilung Vorgeschichte der Naturhistorischen Gesellschaft Nürnberg,* 315-340. Nürnberg.

Shiel R.S. and Chapman. J. 1988 The extent of change in the agricultural landscape of Dalmatia, in Chapman J. C., Bintliff J., Gaffney V.L. and Slapsak B., editors, *Recent Developments in Yugoslav Archaeology,* 31-44, BAR (International Series)431, Oxford.

Schiffer M.B., 1976. *Behavioural Archaeology.* Academic Press, London.

Slapsak B. and Kirigin B., 1987. Starigradsko polje na otoku Hvaru. *Arheoloski Pregled,* 207-8. Ljubljana.

Slapsak B. and Stancic Z., 1988. A modular analysis of the centuriated field system of Faros, in Chapman J.C., Bintliff J., Gaffney V.L. and Slapsak B., editors, *Recent Developments in Yugoslav Archaeology,* 191-199, BAR (International Series) 431, Oxford.

South S. and Widmer R., 1977. A subsurface sampling strategy for archaeological reconnaissance, in South S, editor, *Research Strategies in Historical Archaeology,* 119-150. Academic Press. London.

Wilkes J.J., 1969. *Dalmatia.* Routledge and Kegan Paul, London.

Williams M.W., 1986. Sub-surface patterning at Puerto Real: a 16th century town on Haiti's north coast, *Journal of Field Archaeology* 13, 283-296.

Yorston R., Gaffney V.L. and Reynolds P.R., 1990. Simulation of Artefact movement due to cultivation, *Journal of Archaeological Science* 17, 67-83.

Zaninovic M., 1983. Greek Land Divisions at Pharos. *Archaeologica Iugoslavica,* 20-21.

Section 3
Integrating the Surface Collection

Surface collection has often been isolated both as a field technique and subsequently as a data set in interpretation. Distributions are described in terms of population density and settlement location without concern for the relationship between "real-life" communities and their material remains. To remedy this situation we need to understand, both in quantitative and qualitative terms, what it is the surface collection represents. In this section it is argued that by integrating the results of surface collection with those of controlled experiments, excavation and even the use of theoretical land-use models, a fuller understanding of the nature of surface distributions may result.

The three themes described above are explored by the contributions to this section. In the opening paper Hayes offers a number of theoretical models for land-use around agricultural settlements, describing the nature of the agricultural regime and the archaeological signatures likely to appear. Although they take no account of post-depositional disturbance and changing land-use through time, the models are indications of what we might expect to find under certain conditions. They suggest that pottery distributions will not simply reflect the distribution of habitation areas. Instead they bear witness to the nature, extent and intensity of land-use in the areas around settlements.

Clark and Schofield's paper suggests that the role of controlled experiments should be more widespread, if only to determine the range of variation in terms of surface representation and displacement which may occur within a survey area. They further suggest that such experiments may profitably be integrated with the results of excavation to produce

specific values by which assemblages may be represented in a fragmentary state. That only a handful of surface artefacts may represent settlements on the scale of Black Patch and that similar quantities are recovered from the majority of fields on the Hampshire chalklands highlights the scale of the problem faced.

Bowden *et al* continue discussion on a similar theme, again highlighting the difficulty of establishing a general surface/sub-surface relationship either in terms of quantity or nature of the assemblage. Surface distributions may reflect the location of underlying features. They are just as likely, however, to appear as a mirror image as was the case at Maddle Farm and Weathercock Hill. One interpretation suggested by Bowden *et al*, adding to those suggested in Section 2, may reflect a policy of organised or formal refuse disposal involving the removal of artefacts from the area of habitation. This may appear either in terms of artefact density or in the nature and association of specific artefact groups.

Both at Weathercock Hill and Maddle Farm final interpretation could not have been possible without returning both to surface collection and the more traditional sub-surface archaeology while both case studies build on the suggestions made in Chapter 6, that surface data cannot be viewed simply as the archaeological signatures left behind by specific types of activity. Thus by viewing surface collection in the context of excavation, even on a limited scale, both the nature of that relationship and a clearer picture of the dynamics of human behaviour responsible for creating it, may be ascertained.

Chapter 7
Models for the Distribution of Pottery around Former Agricultural Settlements

P P Hayes

Introduction

In regional scale archaeological surveys the "site" is often used as the principal unit for recording and analysing material collected in the field. It does not necessarily imply the site of a former building while its precise meaning may vary between surveys. "Site" is sometimes defined objectively, as a minimum number of artefacts in a limited area (eg Hall 1985,30), or subjectively, as a discrete concentration of artefacts showing up against a low background level of isolated sherds (eg Mills 1985,83). Both approaches recognise that "sites" are usually surrounded by a low-density scatter of artefacts. This non-or off-site material has attracted increasing attention in recent years. Foley (1981), for example, has discussed the archaeological potential and limitations of analysing distributions of off-site artefacts and has presented a study of past human behaviour based on an analysis of their density within a region. Quantifying variation in the level of background scatter does seem to offer important opportunities to develop new methods for behavioural studies. This paper, however, explores a simpler possibility: the use of presence/absence patterns.

The approach adopted in this paper is deductive. The aim is to investigate theoretically how the agricultural activity of a settlement should be reflected in the distribution of pottery fragments around it. After making some behavioural assumptions, simple models are generated for a number of farming systems. The models predict characteristic distribution patterns and their relationship to classes of soils. The models also have some socio-economic implications.

The paper is intended as a thought experiment. Although the models are not based on arbitrary assumptions, no attempt will be made to prove their validity. This is because the purpose of the paper is not to present perfect models but to suggest that field survey evidence can usefully be approached in this way, working from theory towards observation. It is not a purely theoretical exercise, however. It has practical implications for future survey designs: if we can imagine what we might usefully find we can work out how to look for it. The models presented here are believed to be valid but, if it transpires that they are not, perhaps because they are based on incorrect assumptions or contain faulty reasoning, the remedy is to substitute correct assumptions or reasoning and so generate better models. Objection may be taken to the simplicity of the models. They are, however, meant to be simple. They are ideals intended to aid the structuring and understanding of observations. Their value can only be assessed by their utility, by the clash of reality against the ideal.

The main reason for confining the discussion to theory is the need for brevity and clarity. On the other hand, it is easier to understand the models and assess their likely usefulness if some examples are given. Illustrations from the real world will, therefore, be suggested where they are known to the author. Unfortunately there seem to be few relevant case studies, possibly because in the absence of models of this sort there is no reason why anyone should present their survey data in an appropriate form. One of the implications of the models for survey methods is that we need to record and publish densities of site and off-site material at a scale and in a manner which can be used to look for patterns of this kind.

Generating the models

The models are concerned with patterns of deposition. They ignore post-depositional processes, such as soil erosion, colluviation, alluviation and the differential survival of different kinds of pottery. That is not to suggest that post-depositional processes are unimportant or can be totally ignored (Allen this volume). It is self-evident that no interpretation or analysis of real survey data can afford to ignore the question of bias caused by differential recovery of material due to different rates of post-depositional loss in different parts of the survey area. Neither can one ignore the possibility of differences resulting from varying levels of skill or application among the fieldworkers. Nor can one ignore the problems of variations in the visibility of artefacts connected with sherd fabric, soil colour and weathering, or the angle and brightness of the light at the time of survey. But these are all irrelevant to the question of the validity of the models and the general approach. Post-depositional and survey bias are separate issues, worthy of attention but relating to application rather than theory. However, the recoverability of reliable patterns is such an important practical problem (because the models rely on patterns created by sherd scatters and "blank" areas) that it will be discussed again whenever it is particularly relevant to a specific model.

It is a precondition for all the models that pottery was in use and reached the settlements in sufficient quantities to produce detectable distribution patterns. If sherd densities are generally rather low it may be still possible to produce a reliable sample by increasing the survey intensity. This would unfortunately mean reducing the survey area (given the same resources of people and time) so sooner or later the survey area will be too small to reveal those patterns which are larger in scale. At the very least, pottery should be sufficiently common for the models to be useful when dealing with the Roman and medieval periods in those areas of Europe and North Africa which formed part of the Roman Empire.

Four broad classes of behaviour are assumed to account for the deposition of the majority of sherds. This assumption can, of course, be varied to produce new models but it is essential to make the assumption(s) explicit. The four activities are:

Rubbish disposal

Until the development of communal refuse collection for disposal in large rubbish dumps, most domestic refuse, including broken pottery, seems to have been discarded close to where it was made or used, resulting in high concentrations of artefacts and bones in the immediate vicinity of permanent or long-term occupation. This behaviour probably accounts for the majority of local concentrations of sherds and domestic or industrial debris recognised by field archaeologists as "sites".

Manuring

The value of adding humus to arable land by incorporating animal and vegetable ("green") manure or compost has been known since at least the first century AD (White 1970,125-137) and may well date back to the early development of farming. Sparse scatters of abraded sherds commonly found on fields in Britain have long been interpreted as the product of manure spreading (Bowen 1961,6). The models assume that this took place, resulting in a lower density but more extensive scatter of sherds around the "sites". For various reasons areas of permanent pasture are likely to have received little or no transported manure (and therefore few pieces of broken pottery). Pasture is manured directly, by the animals as they graze. Midden and manure-stack material is usually in short supply and heavy to transport. Its use will, therefore, tend to be limited to the more intensive arable land, as close as practicable to its source.

Burials

Some sherds found by surveys may have come from whole pots deliberately buried in the past, for example for funerary purposes or to conceal a hoard of coins. These have been ignored in the models. The number of sherds will usually be too small to affect the general patterns or, in the case of major cemeteries, their origin will be apparent because of the distinctive pottery types or associated grave goods. Nevertheless, the possibility of funerary sherds should always be borne in mind, while it might be possible to devise models for their distribution in relation to settlements and arable and pastoral land.

Miscellaneous breakages

Pottery lost or broken in transit (falling off the back of a cart) or when used at a temporary activity area (the hay-maker's midday drink) might be expected to add a few sherds to the landscape but these too have been ignored as they will rarely be common enough to affect the patterns on the scale of these models. The importance of miscellaneous sherds will tend to increase as the intensity of survey increases or (possibly) as the general abundance of sherds decreases. As an example of the low levels of ceramic debris found on pasture, the author surveyed over 30 sq km (3000 ha) of former fen in south Lincolnshire (Figure 16 in Hayes 1985,50) known from historical sources to have been used quite intensively as common grazing and for a variety of wetland activities for several centuries in the medieval period. Only two medieval sherds were found. In complete contrast, off-site sherds were plentiful on the medieval arable land next to the fen.

Two of the four activities discussed above (rubbish disposal and manuring) have been selected as the most significant and have been used to generate the models. It is not really possible to prove the validity of these behavioural assumptions but they are not arbitrary, being based on field observation, knowledge of farming systems, and reason. It might be possible to find alternatives but the real test is utility or fitness for purpose: if these or any substituted assumptions produce models which achieve their purpose then they are valid. Their purpose is to enable us to use the patterning of off-site pottery scatters to suggest past farming systems and to make testable predictions (eg as to soils) which can then be used to try to disprove the suggestion. An important study which also interprets distributions of sherds in terms of rubbish disposal and farming practice, supported by fieldwork results, has been published by Crowther (1983).

The title of this paper limits the models to rural areas in the past, although the models in Group 2 (below) do involve urban areas while Group 3 may apply to large villages or small towns. Rubbish disposal in the twentieth century is much more regulated, even in rural areas. No model has been included for the modern development of municipal collection and disposal in large dumps. But town and country cannot be kept entirely separate. Interaction between them will certainly have taken place when a town's need to dispose of large quantities of household sewage and animal droppings coincided with the need for manure in an intensively cropped zone of land around the town. This is an element in von Thunen's classic model of land-use (Chisholm 1968,27) where the zone of land immediately surrounding the town is devoted to horticulture and dairying, producing food for the town's inhabitants. In such circumstances a mutually beneficial trade in manure is likely to develop, resulting in the transport (in the manure) of large numbers of sherds from the town and their distribution immediately around it (see Wilkinson (1982) for an archaeological example and a more detailed discussion). Such a relationship between a small town and the surrounding countryside should produce sherd scatters similar to the models in Groups 2 or 3 (below), depending on whether the agricultural land was farmed from the urban area or from farms scattered around it.

The models
The models are not "identikit pictures". It is not sufficient to match an observed distribution with a theoretical pattern. Each model predicts some of the physical and social attributes which should be associated with the real-world pattern. These must be checked. One limitation of the models is that they present a static view: a single "snapshot" of a working system. If the system changes, the archaeology may become confused, though this need not produce an insoluble problem. For instance, if the time taken to change the agricultural system is sufficiently long, there may be changes in ceramic technology or style, making it possible to devise a phased model. A simple example is given in Group 3.

In the illustrations (Figures 7.1 to 7.3) the system of land-use is shown on the left and the predicted sherd distribution on the right.

Group 1: Models for simple mixed farming

Model 1(A): individual infield-individual outfield
This should be the easiest of the systems to establish and to run. It ought, therefore, to be characteristic of early farming communities or pioneer settlements, where the influence of social and settlement hierarchies is low or absent. Each settlement unit is small and situated on good quality arable land. Since each unit contains both arable and pastoral elements it can

operate independently. Piecemeal expansion of settlements is thus possible and there is no need for a complex social organisation. Taking the group as a whole this system offers low-risk agriculture because the unintensive land-use reduces the risk of ecological disaster and the independence of the units means that the failure of one need not affect the others.

This most simple of systems has several disadvantages. Individual units are vulnerable to attack by enemies, to the ravages of pests, to bad harvests and to problems within the family group, such as the death of a key individual. On a regional scale, productivity is less than it might be. If the region contains a high proportion of arable land some will have to be included in the less productive outfields because each farm needs its own piece of pastoral land. On the other hand, if the region has a high proportion of land which is potentially good pasture but is unsuitable for arable farming (eg highlands or areas with wet clay soils), much of it cannot be settled because each settlement must have its own piece of arable land. Models 1(B) and 1(C) attempt to overcome this defect.

The salient features of the predicted pottery distribution produced by model 1(A) are that there should be small concentrations of sherds and other domestic debris ("sites") situated on easily tilled soil. Each site is surrounded by a diffuse scatter of sherds (still on light soil). The sherds in the diffuse, low-density, scatters should be more abraded (and possibly smaller) than those on the "sites". The scatters are separated by empty land capable of being used as pasture.

The distribution of "sites" across the region may be irregular. Some of the pastoral areas might be next to woodland or other non-agricultural land, allowing hunter-gatherer activities to form part of the total economy. This would result in large areas which now appear archaeologically empty. In Britain the arable soil is likely to be light and well-drained (eg sandy): soil which is probably not regarded as first class arable land by modern farmers.

As this is essentially a subsistence-orientated system, pottery is expected to be predominantly home-produced and probably scarce. If so, the scarcity of pottery will limit the practical usefulness of the model. Another possible difficulty is post-depositional environmental change. Spurious patterns resembling model 1(A) could be created by erosion, or burial by hillwash (colluviation), or by alluviation, for example if water-borne sediments partially cover a landscape of hummocks and hollows common on some glacio-fluvial sands (Hodge *et al* 1984,232). Such distortions are, however, detectable and they only underline the need for a geomorphological survey to accompany each conventional archaeological field survey.

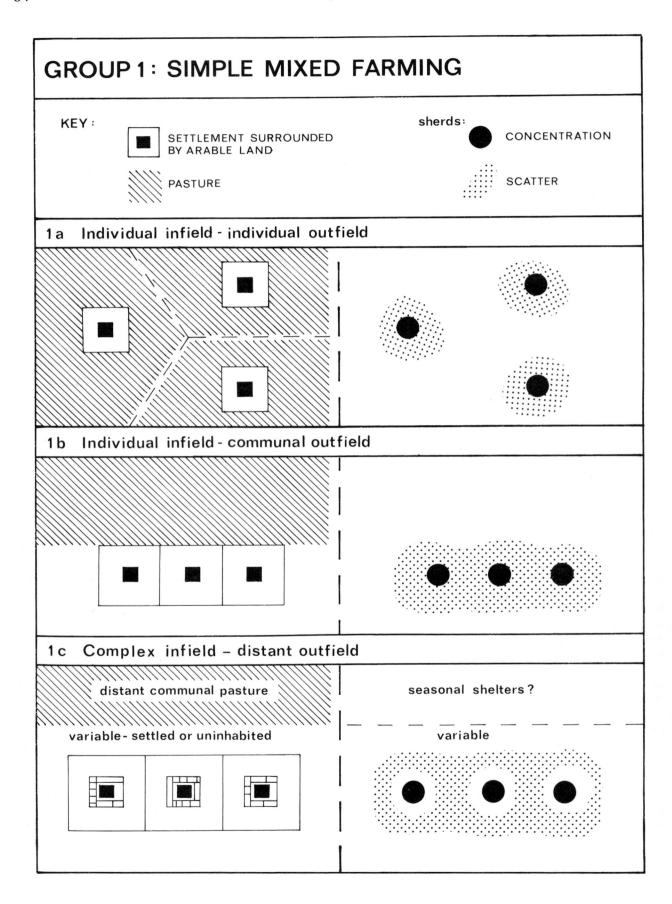

Figure 7.1 Models for Group 1: simple mixed farming.

Model 1(B): individual infield-communal outfield
This is still in essence a simple way in which to combine arable and pastoral activities. It differs from 1(A) in that the settlements are brought together on a sufficiently large piece of arable land and the adjacent pastoral land is used communally. Pasture can be used in common much more easily than arable land. Thus the individual units retain some of their independence and do not form a properly nucleated village. Total productivity should be higher than in 1(A) because fuller use can be made of the available soils. It is easier to avoid having to use potential arable land as pasture. Also, larger areas of pasture can be brought into the agricultural system because it is easier to find adjacent zones of potential arable and pastoral soil than to find individual arable holdings conveniently surrounded by pasture. In 1(A) large areas of non-arable land must be left unsettled, used only for hunting or gathering, even if they would make good pasture.

By bringing the settlements closer together their individual vulnerability is reduced and social contact and interaction are made easier; but there is a price to pay. A social mechanism is needed to agree the zonation and resolve conflicts arising out of increased proximity and the shared pastoral resource. Some of the agricultural production will have to be used for social purposes rather than for subsistence. However, the amount of production which has to be diverted into the social system should be low so this model remains within the capacities of a pioneer group or a non-market economy.

The predicted pottery distribution is of concentrations of sherds and settlement debris, more closely spaced than in 1(A), set in a more or less continuous low level scatter along a band of well- drained, sandy or loamy soil, with an adjacent blank area on land suitable for pasture. The increased productivity, social interaction and complexity might result in greater ceramic variability, perhaps with some non-local pottery, but this aspect of the model lacks a proper theoretical basis.

In England this model seems most likely to be useful for middle Bronze Age to middle Iron Age agricultural settlements on bands of loamy soil such as river gravel terraces. Practical application might still be hindered by a general scarcity of pottery but this ought to be a less universal problem than for model 1(A).

There is again the possibility of partial loss of the original sherd pattern due to subsequent erosion or deposition. Also, in this model it is harder to be sure of correctly identifying and delimiting the pasture land. As the pasture is communal it may have few or no internal divisions (to distinguish it from woodland) and the next strip of arable soil might be quite distant. It might be possible to use pollen analysis to estimate the extent of woodland and pasture but more locally specific indicators, such as mollusc shells, beetle and plant fragments, are unlikely to be recovered from dated contexts away from the settlements.

Model 1(C): complex infield-distant outfield
This more complicated arrangement makes it possible to increase pastoral production by using the mobility of animals and the seasonality of their needs. The animals are brought closer to the settlement when they need protection and time-intensive care, for example when producing young, or when supplementary feeding with stored fodder is employed to carry larger numbers through the leanest season. At other times the animals can be sent far away to feed. There is thus no need to limit the pastures to a distance around the settlement which represents a compromise between extensive and intensive needs. The link between the arable and pastoral elements in the system is broken. They no longer need to be physically close together, and the pastoral element itself is seen as having separable components. This represents a considerable conceptual advance, enabling the group to utilise distant, seasonally unusable, land and perhaps helping to alter their perception of territorial and group potential.

For the purposes of the models the key feature is that some of the land immediately around the settlement is used for livestock management instead of growing crops. Ideally this area should contain evidence of partitioning into small paddocks or stalls. These may superficially resemble horticultural plots but there will be at least one important difference. The confined animals produce so much manure that it has to be collected and removed. The obvious destination is the arable land, on which domestic refuse will also be deposited. There will, therefore, be few sherds left in the area used intensively for animal husbandry and an increased number on the arable land.

The greater organisational complexity of this model requires the diversion of more effort (or energy) into the socio-economic system. This might be achieved directly, by each individual devoting some time, or indirectly, by using part of their food production to support a few people who deal with the organisational needs. "Support" in this sense is used widely and includes not only the provision of food, clothing and shelter, but also of objects, structures and social events needed to reinforce group cohesiveness and acceptance of constraints. Another cost is the loss of arable production through use of arable land close to the settlement for pastoral purposes, or

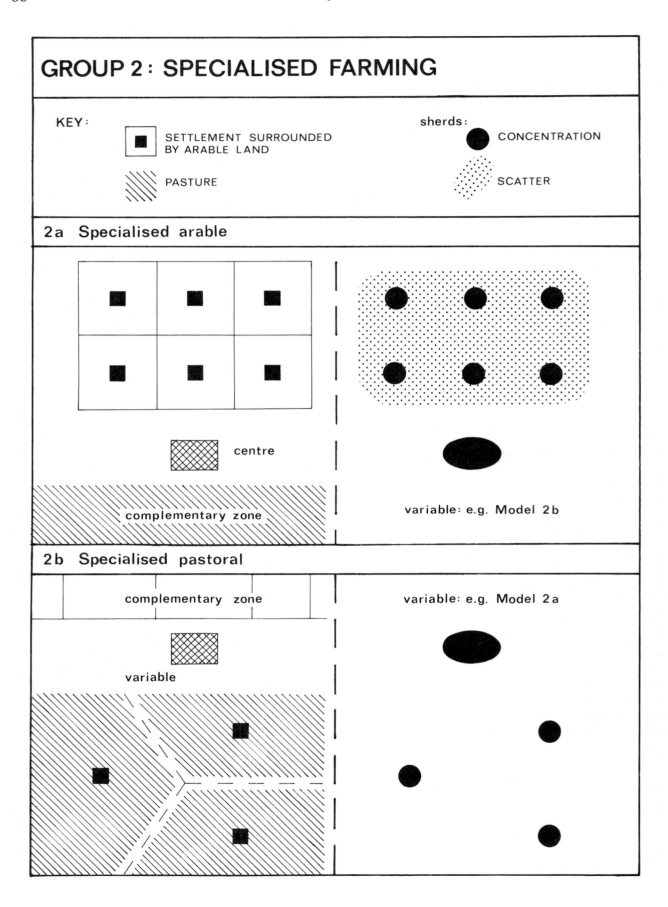

Figure 7.2 Models for Group 2: specialised farming.

the loss of time if the settlement is moved further from the arable land. These costs have to be offset by increased pastoral production through more efficient feeding and stock-care, and by the ability to increase the grazing area by using distant pastures. Arable production may actually be a little higher as a result of more intensive manuring of the infields.

Adoption of system 1(C), not necessarily to the exclusion of 1(A) or 1(B), should increase the total food production in regions with otherwise under-used grazing potential. It could be used to satisfy the need for increased production due to population growth, or in response to greater scope for capital acquisition by individuals arising out of socio-economic changes. It allows greater flexibility in the siting of settlements and this makes it possible to settle in or produce food from previously under-utilised areas. Greater locational freedom would also confer advantages in times of conflict, allowing the settlements to be moved to defensive locations. If defence were important it would be simple to adapt the arrangement of 1(C) by bringing the settlements even closer together, surrounding them with a defensive wall or stockade, and perhaps placing the whole compound on top of a hill.

The predicted pottery distribution is a scatter of sherds over land suitable (in the relevant period) for arable agriculture with characteristic empty areas ("haloes") around the concentrations of domestic debris. The patterning should be clearer than in previous models. The higher productivity of the system and the requirement of a more complex social structure make it more likely that sufficient quantities of durable pottery will have been acquired. More intensive manuring of the infields should also make them more visible and ideally there should be signs of small, non-domestic, enclosures within the central "halo". Pottery should be varied and include some fine, perhaps imported wares (although this may depend more on access). The density of settlement or its wealth should be higher than would be predicted from the productive capacity of the land around the settlement. The pastoral zone should contain seasonal shelters, though it might be archaeologically difficult to detect and relate them to the main settlements. Similar problems apply to the identification of the pastoral zone itself as this may be a considerable distance away and transhumance or semi-nomadic movements might be involved.

This is one of the more interesting models as several variations are possible, each of which may provide insights into the agricultural and social realities which produced them. In a European context the socio-economic requirements suggest that the model might be most useful from the middle of the Bronze Age at least into Roman times, but not to the total exclusion of other models.

The sherd-scatter density map of Tell Sweyhat's catchment (Wilkinson 1982,330) appears to show an almost perfect example, although this could be fortuitous. The Tell, in the mid-Euphrates valley, Syria, is in a suitable location, close to the feasible limits of dry farming, surrounded on three sides by the hills of the Jezireh plateau. The main occupation dates were in the Bronze Age (late 3rd millennium BC) and the Hellenistic period (*c* 300 BC). There is virtually no scatter of sherds within 500 m around the tell. Then there is a pennanular scatter up to a distance of about 2 km, followed by a decline to virtually none. Areas close to the tell totally lacking in sherds were explained, on the basis of two soil pits, as the product of masking by post-depositional sedimentation. This must be a factor, but even if it is accepted as the only explanation, the area immediately around the tell still has a low density (under 40 sherds per 100 sq m) compared to the outer, pennanular, area which has over 40 (in parts over 60) sherds per sq m. Wilkinson interpreted the high density scatter as the product of the manuring of cultivated land. Model 1(C) would predict that the half kilometre around the tell was used for intensive animal husbandry (assuming the animals were excluded from the tell itself). In suitable conditions this might be testable by analysing phosphate levels, mollusc shells or the remains of beetles obtained from the soil. The model would also predict seasonal use of the Jezireh plateau, though identifiable and datable structures or other evidence might be difficult to find.

The option of bringing the animal compounds within the settlement area should not be forgotten, particularly if the need for defence was the main reason for adopting a system of this type. The fortified mesa settlement at Magrusa 1, in the Wadi Zem Zem, Tripolitania (Jones *et al* 1980,13) is a possible example.

Group 2: Models for specialised farming

So far the models have been concerned with mixed farming. In essence, simple mixed farming (Group 1) creates an artificial and simplified ecosystem which is unstable and needs human direction and control if it is to survive. The benefit to the farmer is a significantly increased yield from selected organisms. Specialised farming carries simplification a stage further. Instability becomes structural: each farm is in a sense incomplete and only survives because the larger system enables surplus production to be exchanged. From the viewpoint of the individual farm very little of its production is retained. This differs from farms falling within Group 1 which retain most of their production. Group 2 farming systems, therefore, need and reinforce complex social and exchange systems.

88 *Hayes*

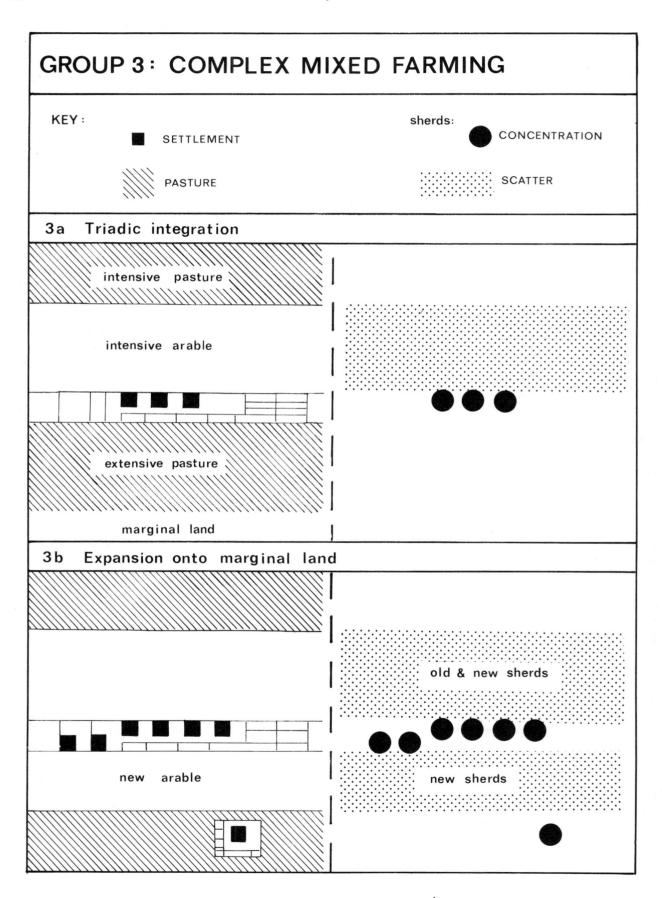

Figure 7.3 Models for Group 3: complex mixed farming.

Specialisation sacrifices risk-spreading within the individual farm in order to achieve greater production. Intensification of cultivation and the move towards monoculture bring increased vulnerability to ecological disaster. The vulnerability of the farms is further increased by their dependence on external demand for their produce. Adoption of this riskier type of farming might, therefore, be a mark of confidence in the political and economic stability, including the confidence which springs from control. On the other hand specialisation could arise out of economic necessity or political compulsion.

Group 2 models are likely to be associated with complex societies, especially states. A tendency to "boom and bust" is to be expected, at least in early examples. Farms may be established quite suddenly in areas previously not used for agriculture. Later the system may collapse, equally suddenly, either for no apparent reason, or accompanied by an environmental disaster which could be regarded as either the cause or the consequence of the collapse.

Both models presented here include an urban centre but it might be possible for mobile pastoralists and sedentary farmers to deal directly. Animals could be brought from a pastoral region to a specialised arable region immediately after harvest. In feeding over winter they would manure the arable fields. The two farming groups could exchange produce before the pastoralists returned to their region for the summer. Such an arrangement would use the social system to replace the economic (eliminating the need for an administrative or marketing centre) and would enable two pre-state societies to have mutually dependent specialised farming systems.

Model 2(A): specialised arable
Arable produce is often bulky and is usually best exchanged within a few months of harvest. Unless there is considerable demand and a cheap means of bulk transport arable production is likely to take place near a centre for the exchange, consumption or processing of the crop. This dependence on higher-level demand and exchange would make it necessary, in a real-life example, to take into account locational models such as those put forward by Smith (1975).

The predicted pottery distribution is a regular arrangement of "sites" (local concentrations) set within a continuous low-intensity scatter on good arable land within range of a consumption or exchange centre. Ideally the centre should also have access to the products of a complementary, primarily pastoral, zone. As this is a system dependent on exchange, pottery on the arable zone should be abundant and varied, including non-local wares.

In Europe, apart from post-medieval examples, the model seems most likely to be applicable in the Roman period and in areas where a good expanse of wheat-growing land exists near a town: see 2(B) below. There may be complications very close to the town, caused by the intensive horticultural/dairying zone discussed earlier. Also, in the Roman period, villa-estates are often found near to towns. Their systems have not been examined; they may adopt a less risky, more conservative and self-sufficient system, and their presence may distort the pattern.

Model 2(B): specialised pastoral
This model is not intended to cover specialisation in dairy products since that is an activity which, like large-scale horticulture, ("market gardening") is likely to be closely associated with an urban centre. Until the development of fast and refrigerated transport, perishable dairy products would normally be exchanged, processed or consumed quickly and close to their place of production. The specialised production of meat is quite different. It is not necessary for the pastoral area to be close to the consumption centre because animals can walk long distances to market; nor is there quite the same need to consume the products quickly.

Specialist pastoral systems are very flexible and few generalisations can safely be made about them. Production of animals for their meat can be described as a less efficient use of land than growing plants for human consumption because only about 10% of the energy in plants consumed by herbivores is passed on to carnivores (Phillipson 1966,48). Despite this theoretical inefficiency, pastoralism survives for a variety of reasons. Maximum production of calories is not necessarily an important requirement of land use, except perhaps for non-importing communities with a very high population density. Dietary needs and preferences, economic factors (including competing producers and the value of by-products), climate and other environmental constraints, and the gross and relative energy inputs which are required, are just some of the considerations which might override simple ecological efficiency. For similar reasons it is not safe to make the generalisation that, because of their relative ecological inefficiency, pastoral systems should support lower populations than would be the case if the area in question were used for arable agriculture.

It follows that to understand a particular system it is important to know its social, economic, environmental and historical context. With that proviso, it is possible to suggest a few circumstances which ought generally to favour the adoption of specialised pastoralism. The most obvious are environmental. Land unsuitable for arable agriculture (given the available technology) may be usable as extensive grazing. Examples may be found in arid zones, lowland wetlands, upland moors and alpine pastures. Non-environmental factors are also relevant. For example, specialised pastoralism might be favoured by moderately complex societies faced with political instability, because animals constitute a more concentrated and mobile form of wealth than arable crops. It is more difficult to steal a complete herd or flock than to devastate the cornfields of an isolated farmstead.

The characteristic pattern of sherd distributions associated with model 2(B) is of discrete local concentrations ("sites") varying from isolated examples through loose clusters to small complexes, with virtually no general or "background" scatter between them. Since the specialised system is exchange-orientated one would usually expect a centre (for consumption or exchange) and a complementary (arable) zone, but these may be some distance away. These characteristics, particularly the negative feature (the absence of non-site material) necessitate care in using the model. A lack of sherds may be due to factors such as post- depositional loss (perhaps due to erosion or alluviation) or poor conditions for the survival or visibility of sherds, or because in the past the land was forested. A suitable range of evidence needs to be evaluated to rule out these possibilities. On the positive side, there may be signs of enclosures suitable for animal husbandry while the soil characteristics and climate may rule out arable farming. Other possible lines of evidence include analysis of soil phosphate levels and patterns, sub-fossil indicators of past vegetation (eg beetles, pollen or seeds) and faunal and artefactual evidence from the sites. As in model 2(A), the proportion of non-local pottery should be high, except possibly on the poorest sites.

The Fens of eastern England in the Roman period seem to offer an excellent archaeological example of a specialised pastoral system. The maps accompanying the text of Phillips (1970) illustrate the large complexes of enclosures and droves, with relatively few concentrations of sherds, characteristic of Romano-British settlements on the alluvial parts of the Fenland. There is virtually no off-site scatter (Hayes 1987,21) and non- local pottery is common. Although the area has now been artificially drained and converted into arable land it seems probable that in Roman times it was a vast and ancient saltmarsh (Hayes 1988,323). It would have been totally unsuitable for growing crops on any large scale, but offered an enormous, naturally treeless, expanse of high quality pasture to anyone prepared to accept the risks involved in attempting to exploit it.

In a recently published study of the region around Levroux, central France, Mills contrasts the virtual absence of off-site medieval pottery in that region with the results of his earlier survey in the Limagne (Auvergne), where off-site medieval pottery was common. He attributes this to the different agricultural systems of the two communities. The Levroux area concentrated on rearing sheep and goats whereas the Limagne was prime arable land (Mills 1988,92). In both cases the settlement pattern consisted of dispersed farms and local centres (towns) so they appear to be examples of models 2(A) and 2(B). It is interesting that the medieval farming system around Levroux shows great stability (few farms were abandoned). This indicates that by medieval times, at least in central France, the inherent weakness of the market-orientated specialist system, its tendency to "boom and bust", had been overcome.

Group 3: Models for complex mixed farming

Model 3(A): triadic integration

The systems in Group 2 may be more productive than those in Group 1 but they will only be fully efficient if each farming zone is particularly and uniformly suitable for its specialised use. Such zones do exist, for example in mountainous regions or on extensive plains. But Group 2 systems are less well suited to undulating land-surfaces in temperate climates, which will have a varied pattern of optimum land use. Another limitation of Group 2 systems is that they are in principle inherently more at risk from disasters, either internal (associated with monoculture) or external (due to reliance on the consumption or exchange centre) than Group 1. Group 3 systems overcome these limitations and so increase both production and stability. This is achieved by including both arable and pastoral land within a single territory, adding a third element (intensive pastoral), and farming the whole of the territory as a unit. The classic example is the English medieval village, say in the Midlands, which has communal open fields (arable), hay meadows (intensive pastoral) and ordinary pasture (especially on uplands or wetlands unsuitable for arable or meadow).

If the territory contains a suitable mixture of sub-environments, each may be used for its optimum purpose. Also, the intensive pastoral component enables the maximum sustainable size of herd or flock to be increased. This is achieved by producing and storing supplementary fodder such as hay for use in late winter and early spring. The quantity of fodder available during the leanest season tends to be the principal factor limiting the herd or flock size. The additional diversity within the farming system has the advantage of helping to overcome its instability and the risk of total disaster.

An integrated and complex system of this sort is capable of being very productive and can attain a high degree of self-sufficiency, but there is a cost. As with the systems in Group 2, integration and direction of the system have to be achieved socially. Some of the agricultural surplus has to be "wasted" by being used to develop and support social, political and economic structures, though in Group 3 the surplus does remain (at least in principle) within the territory. A more serious problem is that this kind of system is vulnerable to intervention or take-over by outsiders. Seizure of the higher levels of the social or economic structures should bring control of the agricultural system and its surplus. In real-life examples it will probably be necessary to supplement the farming model with (at least) a model of the exchange system, because it seems unlikely that the territory will be totally autonomous and self-sufficient. The possibility of a non-hierarchical web of virtually independent territories should not be overlooked.

In the field this sort of system should be easy to identify. The large settlements, located to take advantage of a variety of ecological zones, should produce an abundant scatter of sherds on the land most suitable for arable farming (using contemporary technology) and both the intensive and extensive pastoral zones should be identifiable by a combination of absence of sherds and the nature of their soils. Medieval examples may also produce documentary evidence for land-use.

Model 3(B): expansion onto marginal land
This model has been included to make the point that it should be possible to devise models of systems which change through time. 3(B) is a simple example in which a system like 3(A) has been modified in order to increase production, perhaps in response to an increase in population. This has been achieved by turning some of the pasture into arable and creating new pasture on marginal land which was previously unused. The effect is to create a new, less dense, off-site scatter of sherds and (if the distance to the new pasture warranted it) a new, subsidiary "site" (local concentration of domestic sherds and debris). The factors affecting the location of rural settlements discussed by Chisholm (1968) are relevant to this model, and indeed to all the previous models.

Some forms of intensification might not be identifiable in this way. Hall (1982,19) discusses how production may sometimes have been increased by changing from a classic two-field system (medieval English Midlands) to a three-field system. If that did not involve taking in new ground it does not appear to be detectable.

The earlier models used only presence/absence patterns. Presence/absence may also be sufficient for model 3(B), provided the ceramic typology makes it possible to ascribe reasonable numbers of sherds to the pre- and post-expansion periods. If not, ie if the same pottery occurs on both the old and the new arable land, then it will be necessary to obtain reliable samples from the two areas and to calculate numbers of sherds per unit area. The old arable should have higher densities of the older wares.

In practice several problems might be encountered. The predicted higher total density of sherds on the older arable might not be observable. If the expansion of the arable land coincided with greatly increased pottery usage (eg through increased population or cheaper pottery) the large quantities of newer pottery might mask the small number of older sherds, even to the extent that the error margin on the sampling could exceed the density of the older sherds. Differential survival might also cause problems, particularly if the old and new arable are on different kinds of soil, which is quite likely. However, these problems should not be insurmountable. They are mentioned only to bring out the importance of using the models critically and of using multiple lines of evidence whenever possible.

Discussion
Three groups of farming systems have been presented, together with models which predict their characteristic patterns of sherd distribution and various other attributes, environmental and social. These other attributes are essential elements of the models, which are intended as examples of the application of a deductive approach to the interpretation of artefact scatters.

The models within each group have the following in common:

Group 1: integration of two elements (arable and pastoral).
Group 2: specialisation on one element; integration achieved through an external centre.
Group 3: integration of three elements (arable, pastoral and intensive).

It is interesting that these models, developed theoretically, appear to have an evolutionary aspect when translated into possible archaeological examples, even if they do not amount to a simple evolutionary sequence. In western European terms, Group 1 is characteristically prehistoric (Neolithic to Iron Age) although some Roman and post-Roman examples are also likely. Roman villas might fall into this group: if so they could be regarded as more conservative and less entrepreneurial than some "native" farms, such as those in the Fens. Group 2 could apply at various times from the Roman period onwards, but only if environmental and social conditions were suitable for specialisation. The obvious example of Group 3 is the medieval village but it is possible that earlier examples occur.

The chronological aspect should not, however, be over stressed. Time is not, in any direct sense, an important determining factor. Similarly, the models are not intended to provide an easy way of attaching pre-printed interpretative labels to survey data. Instead, they suggest ways of moving from the field evidence to an understanding of the human activity from which it is in part derived. Past behaviour, especially the repetitions of the farming year, should be recoverable by imaginative use of the sherds scattered around former agricultural settlements. Even if only a generalised and imperfect understanding is obtained, its usefulness may extend beyond mere rec-onstruction of farming systems and contribute to our understanding of past social and political activity.

Acknowledgements

I would like to thank Nigel Mills for inviting me to contribute the paper to his session at the TAG conference in Cambridge in 1984 on which this article is based, and for subsequent long and useful discussions. Thanks are also due to John Schofield and Tony Wilkinson for their helpful comments and information and Jonathan Hayes for preparing the figures.

References

Bowen H.C., 1961. *Ancient Fields*. London. British Association for the Advancement of Science.

Chisholm M., 1968. *Rural settlement and land use*. London. Hutchinson.

Crowther D., 1983. Old land surfaces and modern ploughsoil: implications of recent work at Maxey, Cambridgeshire. *Scottish Archaeological Review* 2, 31-44.

Foley R., 1981. *Off-site archaeology and human adaptation in eastern Africa: an analysis of regional artefact density in the Amboseli, southern Kenya*. BAR (International Series) 97. Oxford.

Hall D., 1982. *Medieval fields*. Princes Risborough, Aylesbury. Shire Books.

Hall D., 1985. Survey work in eastern England, in Macready S. and Thompson F.H., editors, *Archaeological Field Survey in Britain and Abroad*, 25-35. London. Society of Antiquaries.

Hayes P.P., 1985. Fenland Project field survey 1984-5, Lincolnshire: the western Fens (1). *Fenland Research* 2, 49-54.

Hayes P.P., 1987. Developments in the analysis and presentation of survey results: Roman pottery in the south Lincolnshire Fens. *Fenland Research* 4, 20-27.

Hayes P.P., 1988. Roman to Saxon in the south Lincolnshire Fens. *Antiquity* 62, 321-326 and Figures 1-3, 317-319.

Hodge C.A.H., Burton R.G.O., Corbett W.M., Evans R. and Seale R.S., 1984. *Soils and their use in eastern England*. Harpenden. Soil Survey of England and Wales.

Jones B., Barker G. and Hayes P.P., 1980. Libyan valleys survey. *Libyan Studies* 11, 11-36.

Mills N., 1985. Iron Age settlement and society in Europe: contributions from field surveys in central France, in Macready S. and Thompson F.H., editors, *Archaeological Field Survey in Britain and Abroad*, 74-100. London. Society of Antiquaries.

Mills N., 1988. L'apport de la prospection au sol, in Buchsenschutz O., Coulon G., Gratier M., Hesse A., Holmgren J., Mills N., Orssaud D., Querrian A., Rialland Y., Soyer C. and Tabbagh A., *L'evolution du Canton de Levroux d'après les prospections et les Sondages Archéologique*. Levroux: Association pour la Defense et l'Etude du Canton de Levroux.

Phillips C.W., editor, 1970. *The Fenland in Roman times*. London. Royal Geographical Society.

Phillipson J., 1966. *Ecological Energetics*. London. Edward Arnold.

Smith C.A., 1975. Examining stratification systems through peasant marketing arrangements: an application of some models from economic geography. *Man* 10, 95-122.

White K.D., 1970. *Roman Farming*. London. Thames and Hudson.

Wilkinson T.J., 1982. The detection of ancient manured zones by means of extensive sherd-sampling techniques. *Journal of Field Archaeology* 9, 323-333.

Chapter 8

By Experiment and Calibration: an Integrated Approach to Archaeology of the Ploughsoil

R H Clark and A J Schofield

The question of what surface scatters represent has come under increased scrutiny in recent years. As the scale and number of regional surveys has increased, so too has the demand for a simple answer, an equation by which the surface scatter can be interpreted in the "real-life" terms of settlement patterns and population density. In reality, that simple equation appears both complex and elusive. One response has been the excavation of artefact scatters, and although this may provide a simple equation of surface-subsurface proportions, it is an equation which is both static and unique to a specific context. If we are to establish the nature of that equation at a more general level, then some idea of the dynamic processes are necessary.

It is now accepted that a number of processes go to make up the archaeological record. The effect of spatial organisation has been discussed at some length, Binford (1978) and Behm (1983) for example pointing out that discard patterns will not always correspond with the activity areas which generated them. As Binford has suggested, "spatial patterning of discard material does not necessarily mirror the distribution of activities, since dispersal patterns arising from "tossing" or "dumping" may produce distributions that are inversely related to the patterns of use activity" (1978,356). Natural processes have also been discussed, suggesting factors such as colluviation, erosion and deposition as affecting the appearance of the archaeological record (Schiffer 1976; Allen this volume). However, it is really a third category, agricultural disturbance with which this paper is concerned. Attention will be focused on the relationship between patterns in the ploughsoil and the nature and content of sub-surface assemblages. It is argued that sites or specific locations cannot be distinguished from background noise, especially in areas where activity - whether industrial or domestic - continued in a largely unbroken sequence throughout the later prehistoric period. Although variations in density will be marked under certain conditions (eg Tingle 1987,93; Ford 1987,110), to suggest that high density represents the location of a specific site implies first, that everything in the site is chronologically distinct from everything outside it,

and second that the background noise is in some way different in terms of the type of behaviour represented. This need not be the case, as papers in this volume suggest.

This paper combines evidence from a ploughzone experiment west of Salisbury, Wiltshire with excavated lithic assemblages from southern England. Although this degree of calibration and cross-reference is considered useful for understanding surface distributions at a regional scale, its main value is as a cautionary tale. Sites, in the sense of excavated settlements, will produce an enormous range of density variation suggesting that one or two flint artefacts may represent settlement activity to the same extent as 200 flint artefacts from an area of similar size. Thus variations in surface density are considered more representative of *scale* than of the *type* of activity, a more reliable measure being the composition of flint collections.

Background

Lateral movement

The question of how far material moves in the ploughsoil is one which has been approached largely by the implementation of controlled experiments. These have varied both in scale and in terms of their climatic, pedological and topographic setting. On level ground, for example, it has been suggested that after two or three decades of ploughing, artefacts may be displaced by anything between 20 cm and 10 m (Roper 1976). Gingell and Schadla-Hall suggest that although material is lifted by the plough, it is not widely spread (1980,111), while Ammerman's experiments in southern Italy suggest that after two years and possibly six or more ploughing episodes, the mean distance that an individual tile may move will vary between 1.18 m and 1.74 m. Mean values taken at a later date show a more or less consistent pattern of increase with time. Although displacement could not be called pronounced, a few tiles had moved as much as 5 m, with many tiles no longer within 2 m of their starting position (1985,38).

Downslope movement may also influence the degree of lateral displacement. Rick, for example,

working in Peru suggested a positive correlation between slope angle and lithic distributions, noting that
the smaller material tended to travel further (1976).
Ammerman also identified this trend but to a lesser
extent (1985) with few tiles moving as much as 5 m
after as many as nine ploughing episodes (ibid,39).

Another approach has been to evaluate the various
agricultural processes responsible for lateral displacement. Gill (1967), for example, notes that
although ploughing is only the first stage in the tillage process, it is the stage at which most soil
movement occurs. Other cultivation processes subsequent to ploughing serve to break down large clods
of earth, level the surface and destroy weeds but
never cause as much soil movement (a point contra-
dicted by the experiment described below). The
results, therefore, tend to suggest that lateral displacement in the ploughsoil is a cumulative process.
That displacement is often limited may be the result
of a "rocking motion" as suggested by Foard
(1978,362) and Nicholson (1980,24) while regional
variations may well be the result both of the intensity
and type of agriculture and the nature of the soil. In
an arid environment with light soils, artefact movement may be less than in a temperate climate where
heavier soils predominate. The extent to which material will aggregate under the plough and other
cultivation equipment (the "drag factor") will obviously be more significant in the latter causing
greater displacement.

Experiments only appear to be useful, therefore,
where they relate to a *specific* region defined on the
basis of environment, climate and the nature and
intensity of agricultural activity; adopting the results
of experiments from southern Italy or from across the
Atlantic to attempt the interpretation of surface distributions from Hampshire would be inappropriate.
Although much of the machinery and agricultural
systems may be similar between regions, the unique
combination of soil structure, microtopography and
the history and intensity of arable farming is unlikely
to be so uniform.

Assuming then that by studying the relative proportions and spatial limits of artefact groups within
surface scatters, and further that lateral movement
will influence the distribution to a varying but limited
extent, it should be possible to identify activity areas
(sites or patches) by surface collection *if* they appear
as distinct from their surrounding scatters (the background noise). One example where this has been the
case and where distinct activity areas have been
identified is at the Phillips Spring Site in Missouri,
discussed by Downer (1977). By use of distribution
maps and factor analysis, and by maintaining distinct
artefact categories, clear distribution patterns were
apparent in an area under intermittent cultivation for

at least a century. Downer noted, for example, a
correlation between unworked stone, primary and
secondary flakes and shatter, all of which cluster
together towards the south-west of the site (1977,
Fig.1). Contrasting with that is the distribution of
utilised flakes which form a general scatter
throughout the area (ibid, Fig.2), a pattern which
suggests comparison with Behm's secondary refuse
deposit (1983). In addition Trubowitz (1978) has suggested that cultivation does not remove the general
relationships of intra-site settlement pattern. Analysis of the Claud 1 Site in the Geresse valley, New
York, for example, showed that despite ploughing,
the pattern of artefact distribution on the surface
remained constant over three years and that the
general pattern was not destroyed.

It would appear, therefore, that in certain situations - depending on agricultural intensity, the
climatic and soil regimes, the extent of sub-soil patterning and the frequency of artefacts - aspects of
intra-site patterning may be visible on the surface.
We may consider this possibility in the context of
lowland Britain, bearing in mind that the area has a
history of intensive agricultural activity combined
with a long and largely uninterrupted occupational
sequence.

The surface/sub-surface equation
The relationship between material on the surface and
the quantity and types of material in the ploughsoil is
critical to our appreciation and understanding of surface scatters. We may suggest that where over 90%
of material from a disturbed subsoil feature appears
in the ploughsoil (Gingell and Schadla Hall
1980,111) there are grounds for optimism. With such
a large proportion "floating around" in the soil, patterns on the surface may be expected to emerge,
whether they represent habitation *per se*, or other
specialised activity areas, for example, quarries. Pattern replication is only possible, however, where a
reasonable frequency of lithic material appears on the
surface and where the settlement or activity area is a
discrete unit (ie separate from any earlier or later
occupation and distinct from the surrounding scatter). A number of examples illustrate this. Smith's
work in the Ewerne Valley, Dorset (1985,344) did
identify patterns of struck and burnt flint. These appeared mutually exclusive with concentrations of
cores occurring in discrete zones within a general
surface distribution. One pronounced cluster was investigated and was found to mark the position of a
stream edge burnt mound. This was followed by a
more systematic experiment involving three levels of
analysis: systematic surface collection, rapid and intensive excavation. Two observations could be made:
First, that for every 330 artefacts within the plough-

soil, only one would be collected by total surface collection (a recovery rate of 0.30%), and second, that by line walking at 15 m intervals, only 0.07% would be collected from the surface. With such a small quantity, not only activity areas but the scatter itself would, in many cases, be barely visible.

A further example of pattern replication is provided by Parker Pearson's work at Churston, Devon. In this case activity areas of early and late Neolithic and early and late Bronze Age date could be recognised within the general surface distribution, while it was further suggested that around 2% of the assemblage was visible on the surface (1981). Although in contrast to the figure presented by Smith (1985), the results at Churston compare well with those from the Lambourn barrow group (representation of 2.79%), those from work in Devon and indeed with the figure of 2.0% from the excavation of a Roman pottery scatter (Tingle 1987,89).

In summary, therefore, we may suggest that the potential for identifying specific activity areas will depend both on the nature and intensity of agricultural activity and on the occupational history for a given region. Where both are high (as is the case in lowland areas of southern England), potential for recovery of discrete locations will be low and vice versa. In such areas an alternative approach to the interpretation of surface distributions should be sought. It is in this area that the role of calibration between ploughzone experiments, geared to specific agricultural and topographic zones, and known assemblage characteristics from excavated sites can be exploited. Once we have established what a specific type of activity should look like on the surface - in terms of density and assemblage composition - we can return to our surface collections and consider first, whether it is worth looking for sites at all, and second, what a viable and practical alternative might be. These questions may now be considered.

A ploughzone experiment

The results presented represent three seasons work on a ploughzone experiment started in the autumn of 1985 and located at Park Farm, Teffont-Magna, 15 km to the west of Salisbury (NGR SU 0020 3115). It was our opinion that, although results have come from similar experiments in the last decade (eg Ammerman 1985, Lewarch and O'Brien 1981), these results were limited to specific regional contexts defined here by factors of geology, topography, and soil type as well as by the type and intensity of agricultural activity.

As we have already seen in the context of downland Britain, Gingell and Schadla-Hall (1980) have

Table 8.1. Grouping and characteristics of experimental assemblage

area in trench	artefact group	size range (cm)	spacing	quantity
1	large flint nodules	12–20	clustered	25
2	large river pebbles	10–20	clustered	80
3	small river pebbles	2–10	clustered	250
4	large flint flakes	10–20	clustered	65
5	small flint flakes	2–10	clustered	300
6	large flint nodules	12–20	scattered	10
7	large river pebbles	10–20	scattered	30
8	small river pebbles	2–10	scattered	70
9	small flint flakes	2–10	scattered	200
TOTAL				1030

suggested that 90% of the sub-surface assemblage should be represented in the ploughsoil at any one time, while Smith (1985), Tingle (1987,89) and Parker-Pearson (1981) have argued that between 0.30%, 2.00% and 2.79% of the ploughzone assemblage will be present on the surface. There is, therefore, a need for further experiments, both to ascertain the validity of these calculations and as a means to a more accurate interpretative framework for surface data in general.

Our aim was to establish a research design based on the results of those experiments referred to above, and to use them as models or hypotheses which could then be examined in relation to a specific area. The results could then be applied to the surface data accumulating in the area of central-southern England, with the possibility of methodological implications in a wider regional context.

The field chosen for the experiment lies on a stonefree, sandy grey loam, thereby preventing any confusion between the experimental material and coarse components already in the soil. The field lies on a gradual north-east/south-west slope, and has been under intensive cultivation for wheat and barley for over a decade. In September 1985, a total of 1030 flint flakes and pebbles were deposited in a trench measuring 5.0 m by 0.5 m. The trench was subdivided into nine zones into which the various classes of material were placed (Table 8.1). Each class thus occupied a spit 50 cm square with the exception of class 9, the scattered flint, which occupied an extended area of 1.0 m x 50 cm. The assemblage was buried consistently to a depth of 0.2 m to correspond with the depth of ploughing. However, to avoid any inaccuracy in this area, full records of plough depth and direction are being kept by the farmer. In each of the three seasons, ploughing and subsequent cultivation ran perpendicular to, and hence across, the excavated trench thus providing ideal conditions for the investigation of lateral dispersion amongst the experimental assemblage.

The agricultural equipment used consisted of a Deutz DX1 10 four wheel-drive tractor weighing 4.75 tons, and a Downswell four-furrow reversible mouldboard plough, with 14 inch (0.35 m) furrows. Further cultivation included the use of an S-spring-tine cultivator, designed to break the soil furrows up prior to the drilling of the seed corn. For the first year, cultivation followed in the same direction across the 5m trench, by means of the technique known as "one-way ploughing". By this method, a reversible plough makes it possible to turn all the furrows in one direction, thereby moving all soil the same way (Lambrick 1977,4).

The experimental data were recorded by means of metre-square drawing frames, with the precise location of each item recorded on plans at a scale of 1:20. Material was not collected but left on the surface; this was to enable the monitoring of data visibility throughout the year, thereby including weathering, soil movement and surface conditions as variables. This would maintain the entire assemblage (ie a constant population) within the ploughsoil at any one time.

After three seasons, the results of six individual episodes are available. The details of each are as follows (The numbers will be used throughout the remainder of the text):

i   1985: After the first plough/cultivation episode. Weather conditions during the autumn of 1985 necessitated rapid application of the seed corn after ploughing. It was therefore impossible to treat the two processes individually. There was not sufficient time to record the distribution prior to cultivation.

ii   1986: After harvesting and before ploughing. Under stubble conditions the surface was inspected, but only very few flakes were visible.

iii 1986: After ploughing. It was possible to record the distribution between the two episodes, thanks largely to the cooperation of the farmer.

iv   1986: After cultivation.

v   1987: After ploughing.

vi   1988: After cultivation. The wet winter delayed cultivation until the spring.

From these results a number of points can be made. In terms of horizontal displacement, there was enough movement of flint to suggest that displacement was limited, while the percentage of items visible on the surface suggests that figures quoted elsewhere may underestimate surface visibility. Work in future years may confirm this. The results are divided into three sections, two descriptive and one interpretative, all of which have implications for the way surface distributions may be understood. Results after both ploughing and cultivation are presented in graphic form in Figures 8.1 to 8.3 while results of each collection episode are presented in Table 8.2.

Lateral displacement

Of the 32 pieces of flint recorded on the surface in the first year, the maximum displacement value was 2.41 m compared with a mean value of 1.04 m for flakes and 0.84 m for pebbles (Figure 8.1 and Table 8.2). It is also interesting that, although sideways movement is minimal, it does nevertheless occur, material in this case being consistently shifted to the left of the plough. Obviously this will not be repeated from year to year as the direction of movement is affected by such factors as plough direction and in-

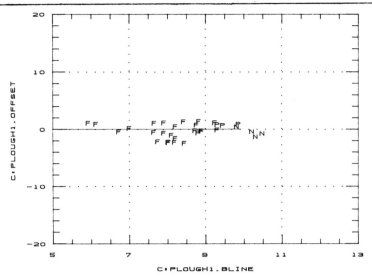

Figure 8.1 General visibility plot after episode 1. The original position of the trench is indicated by a solid line; the x axis presents the scale of lateral displacement (m) and the y axis longitudinal displacement (m). F indicates the location of flint flakes, P the location of pebbles and N the location of nodules. North is to the right of the diagram.

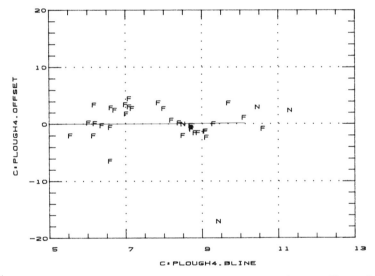

Figure 8.2 General visibility plot after episode 3. For notes on interpretation see Figure 8.1.

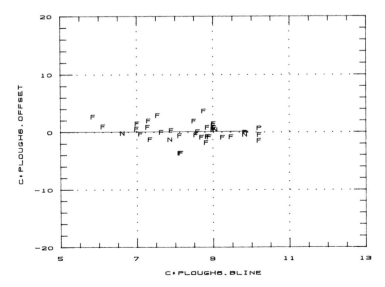

Figure 8.3 General visibility plot after episode 6. For notes on interpretation see Figure 8.1.

Table 8.2. Summary of results (sd = standard deviation)

	surface representation		displacement			
	n	%	mean	sd	min	max
Episode 1						
nodules	4	11.43	0.87	0.31	0.33	1.15
pebbles	3	0.70	0.84	0.09	0.72	0.95
flakes	25	4.42	1.04	0.68	0.06	2.41
TOTAL	32	3.11				
Episode 3						
nodules	3	8.57	0.51	0.13	0.32	0.60
pebbles	41	9.53	0.37	0.20	0.06	0.86
flakes	33	5.84	0.69	1.23	0.01	6.32
TOTAL	77	7.48				
Episode 4						
nodules	3	8.57	1.83	1.31	0.01	3.04
pebbles	0	-	-	-	-	-
flakes	33	5.84	1.90	1.48	0.02	6.40
TOTAL	36	3.50				
Episode 5						
nodules	5	14.29	0.84	0.42	0.31	1.51
pebbles	2	0.47	0.16	-	0.10	0.22
flakes	25	4.42	1.03	0.79	0.01	2.90
TOTAL	32	3.11				
Episode 6						
nodules	4	11.43	0.55	0.41	0.14	1.22
pebbles	2	0.47	0.39	-	0.01	0.76
flakes	31	5.49	1.23	1.03	0.02	3.72
TOTAL	37	3.59				

tensity. It was, however, the case that the original grouping of artefacts remained visible at a general scale at this early stage of the experiment, even though the discrete divisions were lost. This is most clearly illustrated by the four flint nodules to the north of the trench, and in the overall distribution of clustered flint (Figure 8.1).

In the second year of the experiment and after both ploughing and cultivation, both the maximum distance, the mean and standard deviation for flakes had all increased to around twice that of the first season (Figure 8.2 and Table 8.2). The maximum distance moved had increased to 6.40 m, the mean distance was now 1.90 m and the standard deviation 1.48 m. In addition, the general zones apparent after the first season were less clearly defined, affected largely by plough direction which, for the second year, was opposite to that of the first. The large flint nodules were again apparent in the second year of the experiment. After both ploughing and cultivation three nodules were visible, the main difference being displacement. After ploughing the maximum displacement value was 0.60 m and the mean 0.51 m. After cultivation, however, the maximum value was 3.04 m and the mean 1.83 m.

Disturbance after only ploughing also produced a very different picture for the other artefact groups. Maximum displacement for all three groups of artefact was only 0.94 m (excluding two outliers, both flakes, which travelled over 4.0 m from the trench). This provided mean values of 0.41 m and 0.37 m for flakes and pebbles respectively (again excluding the two outliers) and low standard deviations.

After the third season, general trends could be seen to be emerging (Figure 8.3 and Table 8.2). After ploughing, for example, displacement is limited but greater than that of the previous year. The maximum distance was 2.90 m and the mean value, 0.84 m, 0.16 m and 1.03 m for nodules (n=5), pebbles (n=2) and flakes (n=25) respectively. After cultivation these values did increase, at least for pebbles and flakes, although to a lesser extent than in the previous year. Flakes (n=31), for example, display a maximum displacement of 3.72 m and a mean value of 1.23 m while pebbles (n=2) display a maximum distance of 0.76 m and a mean value of 0.39m. What is surprising, however, is the significant variation between pebble frequency after ploughing in the second and third years, a point which will be discussed in the following section.

A further point, which may simply be a reflection of overall density, is the tendency for clustered material to travel further than that in the scattered category (this tendency was only visible from the first years results; after that the grouping became blurred). The maximum displacement value for scat-

tered flint, for example, was 1.71 m, as opposed to 3.96 m in the clustered category, while the mean displacement values were 0.73 and 1.62 m respectively. This may suggest that where material is densely packed within the ploughsoil, not only will it appear on the surface in greater quantity, but it may also tend towards greater lateral displacement. This may be particularly relevant in the case of the larger "industrial" assemblages described in the final section.

Surface representation

The results of the various observation episodes are shown in Table 8.2. A number of points arise from these in terms of the percentage of material occurring on the surface. On the one hand there was a notable variation between scattered and clustered flint from the first year's results, ie 3.00% and 6.85% respectively (Figure 8.1), confirming the point made above about "packing" and density of material in the ploughsoil (see also Allen this volume). Second, there were the overall recovery rates of 4.42% for flint flakes (n=25) and 0.70% (n=3) for pebbles after ploughing and cultivation in the first year. It was only from the second years results, however, that the most significant patterns began to emerge. After ploughing

Figure 8.4 Predicted behaviour of artefact classes in response to ploughing. a) flakes, b) pebbles. Direction of plough: right to left.

7.48% (n=77) of the total assemblage was visible on the surface. Of the various artefact groups, 8.57% of nodules were visible, 9.53% of pebbles and 5.84% of flakes, none of which had moved very far from the location of the trench. After cultivation, however, a very different picture was presented. Only 3.50% (n=36) of the total assemblage was visible, despite the percentage of nodules and flakes remaining constant at 8.57% and 5.84% respectively. The high visibility of pebbles after ploughing was, however, reversed, none appearing after cultivation.

Perhaps the most significant factor, particularly in terms of interpreting the results of surface collection, concerns the enormous discrepancy between the movement of pebbles - which, it may be argued replicate the behaviour of cores - and that of flint flakes. In the first year, for example, only 3 of the 430 pebbles were visible on the surface. They displayed a maximum displacement value of 0.95m and a mean of 0.84m. This, combined with the number recovered, is significantly less than that displayed by flint flakes and is perhaps explained by the standardised form of pebbles in relation to the more irregular shape generally displayed by flint flakes. Rounded pebbles would react to the action of the plough in such a way that they would turn on their own axis within the soil (Figure 8.4b), much as a ball would in water. Flakes on the other hand do not have the same regular shape and would be affected in different ways according to how they were struck, their position and orientation within the soil, weight and tendency to breakage (Figure 8.4a).

The third year again produced a variable set of results, although less so than the second year. After ploughing 3.11% of the assemblage was visible (compared with 7.48% the year before), a difference largely accounted for by the proportion of pebbles, only 0.47% (n=2) contrasting with 9.53% the previous year. Of that total, 14.29% (n=5) of nodules were recorded and 4.42% (n=25) of flint flakes. After cultivation the total figure was increased to 3.59%, nodules reduced to 11.43% (n=4), pebbles remained constant and flakes increased to 5.49% (n=31).

In summary, therefore, two main points emerge. First, that there appears some consistency in the proportion of individual artefact groups occurring after the ploughing and cultivation episodes. After episode one, representation was 2.72% in total. This included three nodules, 0.70% of pebbles and 4.42% of flakes. After episode four, total representation was 3.50%, including 8.57% of nodules, no pebbles and 5.84% of flakes. After episode six, the total had increased to 3.59%, including 11.43% of nodules, 0.47% of pebbles and 5.49% of flakes. Although individual figures vary, the proportions for the three artefact groups appear remarkably constant. This leads into a second

point. After some initial fluctuation, the total percentage represented on the surface appears to have settled to around 3.50%. The most reliable figures are probably those after ploughing and cultivation which amount to 2.72%, 3.50% and 3.59% respectively. Future years will determine whether this is the case or whether further fluctuation is likely. If so it may be possible to determine what factors are largely responsible.

The cause of displacement

The cause of displacement and the reason for a bias towards irregular shaped and perhaps larger artefact classes is commonly put down to the action of the plough. Indeed, the term "plough-damage" is one widely used in the discussion of surface artefact collections and the formation processes responsible for them. It was, however, an aim of the experiment to examine to what extent this really was the case. Certainly Tingle (1987) has observed that far greater quantities of material are brought to the surface by the plough than by other types of agricultural equipment. Table 8.2 demonstrates both in terms of displacement and representation, the extent to which results may vary between ploughing (referring here to use of the mouldboard plough) as a single isolated episode, and ploughing and sowing whereby the use of an S-spring-tine cultivator is a subsequent process. The results are clearly different in two ways: First, that overall a higher proportion of material is visible on the surface, 7.48% and 3.11% where ploughing occurred as an isolated process. This difference is largely accounted for by the greater frequency of pebbles visible on the surface after episode 3 in comparison with that of episode 2. After both ploughing and cultivation, however, the figures were 3.11%, 3.50% and 3.59%. A suggestion might be that after ploughing in episode 3 much of the material was still "packed" into the ploughsoil and hence greater frequencies were brought to the surface in groups. By episode five that density had decreased and, as a consequence, artefacts existed within the ploughsoil more as individuals. A lower proportion would, therefore, be disturbed.

The second distinction concerns displacement. Where ploughing has taken place without secondary cultivation, the mean distance travelled by flint is 0.41 m with a standard deviation of 0.26 m and a maximum of 0.94 m for episode 3, and, for episode 5, 1.03 m with a standard deviation of 0.79 m and a maximum of 2.90 m. For pebbles the mean distance is 0.37 m and 0.16 m, the standard deviation is 0.20 m and the maximum 0.86 m and 0.22 m respectively (as n=2 for episode 5, no standard deviation was recorded). Where cultivation has occurred, the movement of flint is represented by mean values of 1.04

Table 8.3 Assemblage characteristics for domestic sites, excavated in southern England.
Maximum recovery estimates are based on figures suggested by the experiment (3.5% for flakes and tools, 0.5% for cores); minimum recovery estimates are based on the figure of 0.30% (after Smith 1985).

Site	present			no. on surface						total visible with 15m line-interval (20%)						% of total		
	waste	tools	cores	waste min	waste max	tools min	tools max	cores min	cores max	waste min	waste max	tools min	tools max	cores min	cores max	waste	tools	cores
Wakefords Copse (Bradley and Lewis 1974)	416	13	22	1	15	0	0	0	0	0	3	0	0	0	0	92.2	2.9	49
Wawcott 1 (Froom 1976)	4084	74	72	12	143	0	3	0	0	2	29	0	1	0	0	96.5	1.8	17
Thatcham (Wymer 1962)	16029	257	283	48	561	1	9	1	1	10	112	0	2	0	0	96.7	1.6	17
Downton (Neo.) (Rahtz 1962)	1478	120	98	4	52	0	4	0	0	1	10	0	1	0	0	87.1	7.1	58
Hemp Knoll (Robertson Mackay 1980)	2045	52	83	6	72	0	2	0	0	1	14	0	0	0	0	93.8	2.4	38
Black Patch (Drewett 1982a)	11918	116	149	36	417	0	4	0	1	7	83	0	1	0	0	97.8	1.0	12
Hurst Fen (Clark *et al* 1960)	14500	800	570	44	508	2	28	2	3	9	102	0	6	0	1	91.4	5.0	36
Downton (Meso.) (Higgs 1959)	36529	579	416	110	1279	2	20	1	2	22	256	0	4	0	0	97.3	1.5	11
Farnham (Clark & Rankine 1959)	36095	1121	1137	108	1263	3	39	3	6	22	253	1	8	1	1	94.1	2.9	30
Oakhanger (Rankine *et al* 1952)	76400	2965	705	229	2674	9	104	2	4	46	535	2	21	0	1	95.4	3.7	09
mean (n=10)																94.2	3.0	28
standard deviation																3.1	1.8	16

Table 8.4. Assemblage characteristics for industrial sites. Recovery rates predicted as for Table 8.3.

Site	area	flakes total	flakes per ha.	no. on surface min.	no. on surface max.	total visibility per ha. by 15m line walking min.	max	Reference
Sta Nychia	810.0 ha	50,398,661	62,220	187	2,178	37	436	Torrence 1986
Demenegaki	737.5 ha	31,750,564	43,051	129	1,507	26	301	Torrence 1986
RIV 1814 Hill	3.9 ha	38,000	9,743	29	341	6	68	Singer 1984
Grime's Graves	16.5 m sq	80	38,000	144	1,680	29	336	Healy 1985
Grime's Graves	16.5 m sq	185	112,000	336	3,920	67	784	Healy 1985
Grime's Graves	1.0 m sq	160	1,600,000	4,800	56,000	960	11,200	Healy 1985

m, 1.90 m and 1.23 m, standard deviations of 0.68 m, 1.48 m and 1.03 m and maximum values of 2.41 m, 6.40 m and 3.72 m. These are substantially different from those figures apparent after ploughing and suggest that displacement is largely the result of cultivation.

It is, therefore, the plough which causes most material to appear on the surface, by inverting the furrow and exposing an area of ploughsoil previously buried. The plough is not primarily responsible, however, for first, sorting the material into shape classes, and second, displacing material laterally across the surface. In relation to the logistics of surface collection it is argued, in line with previous authors (eg Shennan 1985), that the ideal conditions are between ploughing and sowing at a time when the ploughsoil has been sufficiently weathered to cause maximum visibility. It is also interesting to note that under stubble conditions, in even light and after substantial weathering, only one flake and two pebbles were visible by surface inspection.

"Calibration": the excavated assemblage

The term calibration is used to describe proportional weighting of an excavated assemblage on the basis of results described in the above experiment. The section is an attempt to demonstrate how these results may assist in the identification of activity areas through surface collection. It should be stressed that the calculations take no account of differences in size or shape classes and that the excavated assemblages are derived simply from published excavation reports and are not totals derived from cubic areas. Examples were chosen at random from southern England and, in a few cases, from overseas, the only requirement being that each should represent a settlement or occupation area (see Table 8.3) or areas of industrial activity (Table 8.4). The former vary both in scale and in date with the smallest assemblage - 416 artefacts - from the Mesolithic site of Wakeford's Copse, Hampshire (Bradley and Lewis 1974) and the largest - 76,400 artefacts - from The Warren, Oakhanger, Hampshire (Rankine 1952). It should be stressed however that the assemblage from Oakhanger is exceptional, the next largest being 36,000 artefacts from both Farnham and the Mesolithic assemblage from Downton. For the sake of argument, cores will be examined in relation to those figures displayed by pebbles in the experiment (0.5% representation), while flakes will be used to represent the proportion of the assemblage made up of waste material and tool types (3.5% representation). These figures were calculated from the mean value after ploughing and cultivation over the first three seasons and afford comparison with figures of between 5 and 6% suggested by Ammerman (1985), Lewarch (1979) and

Odell and Cowan (1987). It should be stressed however that the maximum figure is based solely on the results of the experiment described above and that a minimum figure of 0.30% (after Smith 1985) should also be considered; other estimates suggesting varying results may be equally valid. It is also assumed that the total assemblage would be in the ploughsoil. If we were to adopt Gingell and Schadla Hall's (1980) estimate that only 90% will be present in the soil at any one time, then the proportions presented in Tables 8.3 and 8.4 should be further reduced by 10%. The results may now be considered in terms of the two "site-types", domestic and industrial.

Domestic

What the results suggest in terms of the surface-subsurface equation is that for a settlement or occupation area the size of Wakeford's Copse, a maximum of 15 flakes, no cores and no tools may be expected to appear on the surface over an area up to twice the size of the original site, depending on the extent of lateral displacement. If we adopt Smith's 0.30% recovery rate, then it would be unlikely for a single artefact to be recovered by line- walking at 15m intervals, while the results of the experiment suggest a possibility that three flakes may be collected. For a more substantial site like Thatcham the figures are rather more encouraging. Taking the same minimum and maximum collection values, anywhere between 48 and 561 flakes, one and nine "tools" and one core may appear on the surface. By line walking, however, these are reduced substantially between ten and 112 flakes, nought and two "tools" and no cores. What this suggests above all else is that a site on the scale of, for example Hurst Fen, Black Patch or Thatcham, may no longer maintain the status of site - at least not on the basis of density alone - once integrated within the ploughsoil. This will depend on the scale of adjacent artefact distributions and the intensity and history of arable farming in the area. That is not to say, however, that a distinction between types of activity cannot be made from the results of surface collection. Indeed if we concentrated more on the *combination* of density and content of surface scatters rather than trying to establish their status merely by density, our interpretation of the settlement system - which is after all a primary aim of ploughzone archaeology - may appear a little more straightforward.

In terms of assemblage composition, a number of points seem to emerge (Table 8.3). First, that the proportion of tools (excluding modified flakes) appears relatively low. At Black Patch for example, only 1.0% of the total assemblage consisted of tools, while at Thatcham and Wawcott a similarly low figure of 1.6% and 1.8% was suggested. The highest scores appear at the Neolithic sites of Downton and

Hurst Fen where between 5.0% and 7.1% of the assemblage were tools. Cores are also relatively infrequent, although this may vary in relation to the distance between settlement and quarry. At Black Patch, for example, only 1.2% of the assemblage consisted of cores while at Downton that figure was 5.8%. Waste will also vary, although in general a figure of less than 90% is unusual.

In summary, therefore, despite a chronological range from Mesolithic to Bronze Age, variations in size and flint density of the individual sites and locational differences, the proportion of artefacts display similarity. Indeed the standard deviations for the three groups (waste, cores, tools) are low, at 3.1%, 1.8% and 1.6% respectively. It remains to be seen whether these variables can be seen as distinct from those displayed by industrial locations.

Industrial
Again all observations concerning observed and expected density figures are based upon those suggested by the experiment and their relationship with known assemblages, either from excavation or survey. Quarry and extraction sites may produce vast quantities of characteristic waste material and as such are likely to appear as discrete clusters of archaeological debris. A range of examples are quoted although variations in the recording of debitage may cause some inaccuracy in the density figures (Table 8.4). Torrence (1986,204), for example, quotes the production rates from the obsidian quarries at Sta Nychia and Demenegaki on the island of Melos. From these examples the density of waste material per hectare is calculated at between 62,220 and 43,051 respectively, while a further example suggests a figure of 9,744 (Singer 1984,40). Adopting the minimum and maximum figures quoted above, this would produce a total of between 35 and 3,527 pieces per hectare of which between seven and 709 would be recoverable by line-walking at 15m intervals. From the figures presented for Grime's Graves, it is suggested that up to 1,600,000 items of debitage may occur within the ploughsoil in a single hectare unit (After figures of 160 artefacts within a single metre square adjacent to the pit excavated by Greenwell in the 19th century (Healy 1985)). This would produce a surface minimum of between 4,800 and 56,000 and a total visible through line-walking of between 960 and 11,200 per hectare.

In terms of assemblage composition, two factors are likely to appear predominant in the location of lithic quarries. One will be the low proportion of retouched artefacts and tools. With 1.7% of the assemblage at Wawcott and Thatcham and 1.2% at Black Patch appearing the minimum number to occur on settlements in the region, a figure of less than

1.0% may be considered representative of quarry sites. This is simply a rough estimate by which the two types of activity might be distinguished; where regional survey is concerned a more realistic measure may be a distinction based on standard deviations above and below the mean. The second factor is the high proportion of primary waste in relation to that occurring in a settlement area. The total waste frequency will appear greater than 90.0% for settlement areas and greater than 98.0% for quarries, with the number of cores - which we might expect to be higher than for settlement areas, particularly where the settlement area is close to the quarry - underrepresented. In addition to these aspects of composition, density may appear considerably higher than for settlement areas - assuming as we must a standard length of occupation. At Sta Nychia (Torrence 1986) for example, one of only few quarries where appropriate figures were available for comparison, a range of between 45 and 709 artefacts would be collected by line walking at 15m intervals. At Thatcham, one of the larger settlements, that figure is smaller, between 12 and 183 artefacts. Only one mis-fit was encountered, the site of Oakhanger where flint density, when collected within a single hectare square, would be similar to that from Sta Nychia.

It is, therefore, possible to distinguish domestic and industrial by density, although there is the possibility of overlap between big or long-term settlements and small or short-term quarries. A more reliable distinction could be made on the basis of composition or the contents of a flint scatter. A combination of the two is considered the most appropriate solution.

From these examples and from the results of the experiment a number of points can be made:

1 Disturbance under intensive agriculture will make the delimitation of sites as discrete units virtually impossible, at least in southern England. From the figures regarding domestic locations, application to the results of surface collection in the Avon (Schofield 1987) and Meon valley surveys (Schofield this volume) would produce sites on the scale of Thatcham or Black Patch in the majority of fields investigated.

2 That the need for sites is lost when such a clear distinction can be drawn between two specific types of activity. Where such a wide variety of influences may determine lithic density, and where overlap occurs between industrial and domestic activity, the nature of the collection is considered a more appropriate measure of the type of behaviour represented.

3 It is argued that although an equation such as that

presented in this paper can be considered relevant to most lowland areas of southern England, individual equations are required for other areas.

Conclusions: the role of calibration

Millett (1985,31) has suggested that, "by measuring the amount of material culture appearing in specific dated contexts on excavations, we may begin to establish what a surface distribution of similar material means". There are two problems with applying this to lithic distributions: First, that flint is difficult to date. Although a number of attempts have been made to isolate chronological trends in the lithic data available, (eg Ford 1987), technological variables cannot be ignored, for example relating to the frequency of blades. On the rare occasion when a diagnostic artefact is recovered, there is the problem of establishing whether or not it is associated with the general scatter within which it was found. That artefacts were found together does *not* mean that they were necessarily used together. The second problem is that southern England - and particularly the river valleys - are one continuous flint scatter. Although areas of high and low density do emerge, to refer to the high density areas as "sites" may be unrealistic. As we have suggested in this paper, settlements on the surface may be represented by anything under 183 flints in an area probably twice the size of the excavated area at That- cham. This figure was encountered in many of the fields walked in the Meon valley as well as a large

proportion in the Avon valley, west Hampshire (Schofield 1987). Surely we are not going to settle for referring to every field as a "site"?

In this paper we argue that to understand what surface scatters mean in a given region, this degree of calibration combined with the results of an experiment - which are undoubtedly dependent on pedology and microtopography - is a vital part of the survey. We do not suggest that the results of this experiment tell us exactly what we can expect within the plough- soil as a whole; it may simply act as a guide which, in conjunction with results from similar experiments conducted elsewhere, should provide a range of per- centages upon which we may depend as a reliable measure of ploughsoil content. By calibrating results of the experiment with the total assemblages from domestic and industrial contexts, observed results from surface collection may be compared with ex- pected results for specific types of activity.

Acknowledgements

We should like to thank the farm owner, Mr E.C.Clark, for his help and co-operation in conduct- ing the ploughzone experiment. Also to be thanked are Martin Millett, Mike Allen, Bill Boismier and Stephen Shennan for commenting on earlier drafts of the paper and Chris Webster for assistance with the STATGRAPHICS programme. They are not however responsible for the views expressed in the text.

References

Ammerman A.J., 1985. Ploughzone experiments in Cala- bria, Italy. *Journal of Field Archaeology* 12, 33-40.

Behm J.A., 1983. Flake concentrations: distinguishing be- tween flintworking activity areas and secondary de- posits. *Lithic Technology* 12, 9-15.

Binford L.R., 1978. Dimensional analysis of behaviour and site structure from an Eskimo hunting stand. *American Antiquity* 43, 330-361.

Bradley R.J. and Lewis E., 1974. A Mesolithic site at Wakefords' Copse, Havant. *Rescue Archaeology in Hampshire* 2, 5-18.

Clark J.G.D., Higgs E. and Longworth I.H., 1960. Excava- tions at the Neolithic site at Hurst Fen, Mildenhall, Suffolk, 1954, 1957 and 1958. *Proceedings of the Pre- historic Society* 26, 202-245.

Clark J.G.D. and Rankine W.F., 1939. Excavations at Farn- ham, Surrey, 1937-1938, the Horsham culture and the question of mesolithic dwellings. *Proceedings of the Prehistoric Society* 5, 61-108.

Downer A.S., 1977. Activity areas, surface collection and factor analysis at the Phillips Spring site, 23H1 216, Missouri. *Plains Anthropologist* 22, 299-311.

Drewett P.L., 1982. Later Bronze Age downland economy and excavations at Black Patch, east Sussex. *Proceed- ings of the Prehistoric Society* 48, 321-400.

Foard G., 1978. Systematic fieldwalking and the investiga- tion of Saxon settlement in Northamptonshire. *World Archaeology* 9, 357- 374.

Ford S., 1987. Chronological and functional aspects of flint assemblages, in Brown A.G. and Edmonds M.R., edi- tors, *Lithic analysis and later British Prehistory: some problems and approaches,* 67-86. BAR (British Series) 162. Oxford.

Froom F.R., 1972. Some Mesolithic sites in south-west Berkshire. *Berkshire Archaeological Journal* 66, 11- 22.

Gill W.R., 1967. Soil dynamics in tillage and traction. *Agricultural Handbook* 316. Agricultural Research Service, US Department of Agriculture.

Gingell C. and Schadla Hall R.T., 1980. Excavations at Bishops Cannings Down, 1976, in Hinchliffe J. and Schadla Hall R.T., editors, *The past under the plough* 109-113. DoE Occasional Publications No.3. HMSO. London.

Healy F., 1985. Recent work at Grime' s Graves, Weeting with Broomhill. *Norfolk Archaeology* 39, 175-181.

Higgs E., 1959. Excavations at a mesolithic site at Down- ton, near Salisbury, Wiltshire. *Proceedings of the Pre- historic Society* 25, 209-232.

Lewarch D.E., 1979. Effects of tillage on artefact patter- ning: a preliminary assessment, in O'Brien M.J. and Warren R.E., editors, *Cannon Reservoir Human Eco- logy Project: a regional approach to cultural conti- nuity and change,* 101-149. Technical Report 79-14. Division of Archaeological Research, University of Nebraska, Lincoln.

Lewarch D.E. and O'Brien M.J., 1981. The expanding role of surface assemblages in archaeological research, in Schiffer M.B., editor, *Advances in Archaeological Method and Theory* 4, 297-342. Academic Press. London.

Millett M., 1985. Field survey calibration: a contribution, in Haselgrove C., Millett M. and Smith I., editors, *Archaeology from the ploughsoil: studies in the collection and interpretation of field survey data* 31-38. Sheffield University Press.

Nicholson R.J., 1980. Modern ploughing techniques, in Hinchliffe J. and Schadla Hall R.T., editors, *The past under the plough* 22-25. DoE Occasional Publications No. 3. HMSO. London.

Odell G.H. and Cowan F., 1987. Estimating tillage effects on artefact distributions. *American Antiquity* 52, 456-484.

Parker Pearson M., 1981. A Mesolithic and Bronze Age site at Churston, south Devon. *Proceedings of the Devon Archaeology Society* 39, 17-26.

Rahtz P.A., 1962. Neolithic and Beaker sites at Downton. *Wiltshire Archaeological Magazine* 58, 116-141.

Rankine W.F., 1952. A mesolithic chipping floor at the Warren, Oakhanger, Selborne, Hants. *Proceedings of the Prehistoric Society* 18, 21-35.

Rick J.W., 1976. Downslope movement and archaeological intra-site spatial analysis. *American Antiquity* 41, 133-144.

Robertson Mackay M.E., 1980. A 'head and hooves' burial beneath a round barrow, with other Neolithic and Bronze Age sites on Hemp Knoll near Avebury, Wiltshire. *Proceedings of the Prehistoric Society* 46, 123-176.

Roper D., 1976. Lateral displacement of artefacts due to plowing. *American Antiquity* 41, 372-375.

Schiffer M.B., 1976. *Behavioural Archaeology.* Academic Press, New York.

Schofield A.J., 1987. Putting lithics to the test: non-site analysis and the Neolithic settlement of southern England. *Oxford Journal of Archaeology* 6, 269-286.

Singer C.A., 1984. The 63-kilometre fit, in Ericson J.E. and Purdy B.A., editors, *Prehistoric quarries and lithic production,* 35-48. Cambridge University Press.

Smith R.W., 1985. *Prehistoric human ecology in the Wessex chalklands with special reference to evidence from valleys.* Unpublished PhD thesis. University of Southampton.

Tingle M., 1987. Inferential limits and surface scatters: the case of the Maddle Farm and vale of the White Horse fieldwalking survey, in Brown A.G. and Edmonds M.R., editors, *Lithic analysis and later British prehistory: some problems and approaches,* 87-100. BAR (British Series) 162, Oxford.

Torrence R., 1986. *Production and exchange of stone tools: prehistoric obsidian in the Aegean.* Cambridge University Press.

Trubowitz N.L., 1978. The persistence of settlement pattern in a cultivated field, in Engelbrecht W. and Grayson D., editors, *Essays in Northeastern Anthropology in Memory of Marion E. White.* Occasional. publications in NE Anthropology 5, 41-66.

Wymer J.J., 1962. Excavations at the Maglemosian site of Thatcham, Berkshire, England. *Proceedings of the Prehistoric Society* 28, 329-361.

Chapter 9

Skimming the Surface or Scraping the Barrel: a Few Observations on the Nature of Surface and Sub-surface Archaeology

M C B Bowden, S Ford, V L Gaffney and M Tingle

Introduction

The continuing academic interest in archaeological field survey is a rather puzzling phenomenon. Cynically, one is tempted to suggest that the relatively poor data base often associated with surface collection has ensured its popularity as a perfect arena for the "cut and thrust" of academic debate. However, if this was the case in the past, it certainly is not today. Field methodologies have improved considerably over the last decade and the quality of recovered data has risen in consequence. Yet, in spite of these promising developments, there still appears to be some difficulty in incorporating survey results within the general body of archaeological theory.

This lack of appreciation for the relationship between surface survey and archaeology as a whole, seems to be reflected in the continued isolation of the subject at a number of British Theoretical Archaeology Group (TAG) conferences. It seems inappropriate that a permanent conference whose purpose is the debate of theoretical issues should single out an individual *field technique* for intensive and prolonged discussion. Yet there have been no less than four TAG sessions dedicated to surface survey between 1982 and 1986. Surely this is a sign of academic confusion rather than of a desire for healthy debate?

One can illustrate this problem with reference to the concept of the "site". Few archaeological topics have generated as much discussion within recent years as the problem of site status and definition amongst survey archaeologists. The value of much of this discussion is questionable. Ethnographic work has clearly indicated the need to approach the study of human behaviour at larger scales (Foley 1981) and enough data has now been published to emphasise that the primacy of the site in many forms of archaeological investigation simply does not make sense. From the moment a behaviouralist analytical position is adopted by archaeologists such arguments become largely redundant.

Parallel to the problem of the role of sites, has been that of their precise nature. The persistent question as to what sites *are* in the survey-specific sense is undoubtedly a reaction to earlier naive interpretations of survey data. Many early works attempted to force survey data into preconceived perceptions of sedentary habitation sites, often in areas or periods in which such concepts were inapplicable (Gaffney and Tingle 1984). It is strange that such a position should be adopted when we consider that no such situation exists within excavation archaeology. During excavation we expect to encounter situations in which evidence for human activity may be found with or without habitation structures. The archaeologist who claimed that all people did on excavated sites was "live" (whatever that means) would be regarded with justifiable suspicion. Yet, implicitly, this is what many survey archaeologists were attempting to prove until the early 1980s. The predictable confusion resulting from such an interpretative stance was an inability to incorporate the majority of survey results within the body of general archaeological data.

The site, therefore, is simply an archaeological construct, a convenient unit of investigation whose size and shape varies with contemporary knowledge or research aims.

If field survey is an unnaturally isolated branch of archaeology, how can the situation be remedied? In the notes for contributors, distributed by the TAG field survey session organisers in 1986, it was suggested that part of the "problem" of field survey lay in the fragmentary nature of survey data. This is a disturbing suggestion as it implies that the results provided by surface data are somehow less reliable than those provided through other techniques. The separation of survey data from archaeological deposits by 15 cm of ploughsoil would appear to represent the borderline between reliability and residuality. Why should this be so? Such problems are hardly specific to field survey and they do not constitute an insurmountable problem when encountered within traditional spheres of research. The literature abounds with instances of inference from indirect evidence. When we excavate and interpret sites we do so knowing that a series of activities and functional areas may be represented within the excavation. All positive and negative evidence is incorporated within the interpretative scheme. This scheme does not collapse when we realise that a number of post-depositional processes are also at work on site. Part of the challenge of archaeology is to isolate such biases and compensate for them. In-

Bowden, Ford, Gaffney and Tingle

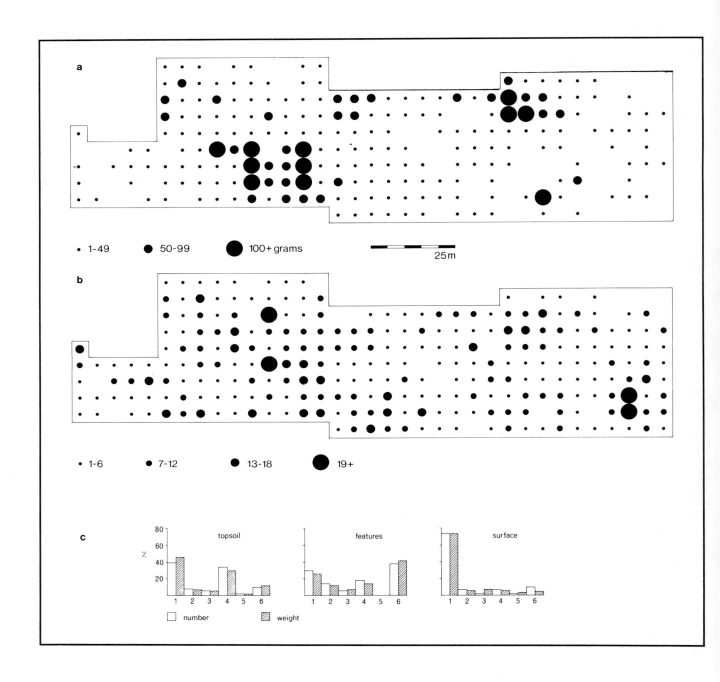

Figure 9.1 Weathercock Hill: a) surface pottery distribution. b) surface flint distribution. c) vertical pottery fabric distribution.

deed the results from research into cultural and non-cultural transformations from excavation evidence have been common in the literature ever since Schiffer's seminal volume *Behavioural Archaeology* was published in 1976. Why we should regard ploughing as qualitatively different from, for example, the sweeping clean of habitation areas (Rathje 1979) is not clear. Such processes simply confirm the continuing dynamism of archaeological sites.

Highland zone archaeology in Britain has suffered similar problems in cases where subsequent ploughing is not a factor. Decades of excavation in the interiors of prehistoric hut circles, for example, have revealed a paucity of artefacts which has generally been regarded as evidence of poverty but which might be better interpreted as evidence of behaviour. For instance, abandonment behaviour, such as that observed by van Gijn (1986,177-8) in West Africa, if more widely applicable, might explain this phenomenon in an area where more recent, post- depositional, processes have been minimal.

The discovery of a "Pompeii" is a rare event and virtually all archaeological data is both fragmentary and indirect. Such differences that do exist between survey and other recovery techniques, therefore, tend to be distinctions of scale rather than essence. Instead of separating the two data sets as incompatible, it is surely more important to emphasise the potential of both for complementary evidence of related behaviour patterns, and the need to integrate surface and topsoil data as part of a general interpretative scheme.

Case studies

The value of incorporating so-called residual data within such a framework can be demonstrated through two case studies in which surface and topsoil data have been incorporated within the context of excavation. The first example is a late Bronze Age lithic and pottery scatter at Weathercock Hill, near Lambourn on the Berkshire Downs, excavated by the Berkshire Archaeological Society Field Research Group (Bowden *et al* forthcoming) and the second, also from Berkshire, is an excavation of a Roman villa undertaken by the Maddle Farm Project team (Gaffney and Tingle forthcoming).

At Weathercock Hill total surface collection, phosphate and metal detector survey was carried out with reference to a 5 m intensive collection grid. Although all man-made material was collected the principal artefact types present on the site were lithics and pottery. Both material groups were tentatively dated to the late Bronze Age, although the presence of a number of fragments of collared urn and a barbed-and-tanged arrowhead indicated some earlier activity. The distribution of the two artefact types

differed radically. The pottery clustered significantly, whilst the lithics tended towards a more general distribution (Figures 9.1a and 9.1b). Peaks in the phosphate survey tended to lie to one side of the pottery concentrations (see Bowden *et al* forthcoming).

Excavation followed survey in order to verify the results and to ascertain the relevance of positive and negative artefact scatters to sub-surface archaeology. In order to achieve such a match all excavation was carried out within the same 5 m total collection grid. Within this grid a series of 5 x 5 m squares above positive and negative scatters were totally excavated and a series of sample 2 x 2 m squares were systematically excavated outside these areas in order to maximise the available data. The topsoil was sample-sieved in an attempt to quantify objectively topsoil artefact content.

Excavation confirmed the overall pottery distribution. However, it also indicated that the most substantial sub-surface features, a group of pits containing considerable amounts of settlement debris, lay adjacent to, rather than beneath, the densest patches of topsoil and surface pottery. The area containing rubbish pits was also coincident with the highest phosphate levels.

A further facet of the discard system that produced this relationship between surface and sub-surface artefact density may be isolated in the composition of the pottery assemblage. The vertical pottery fabric distribution (Figure 9.1c) suggests a number of points. The primacy of coarse fabrics (1) on the surface probably indicates differential destruction of fabric types. It may be significant, however, that some finer and presumably more fragile fabrics (4) are more frequent in the topsoil than in the better protected sub-surface features. This may be the result of a disposal practice in which the larger, coarser pots are more often removed into formal disposal areas. Finer vessels may remain *in situ* because of their function or because they fragment into smaller pieces. Only the incorporation of surface and topsoil data into an excavation framework can test such a hypothesis.

The combined evidence from surface, topsoil and sub-surface features suggests a formal structuring of the archaeological record at Weathercock Hill. It would seem a logical inference that the topsoil concentrations would appear to relate to superficial deposits whose position made them more prone to agricultural damage. Although one cannot be certain, it is probable that such concentrations reflect the positions of floor deposits or structure-related activities. The negative relationship between these topsoil artefact features and rubbish pits and phosphate densities suggests that formal rubbish disposal

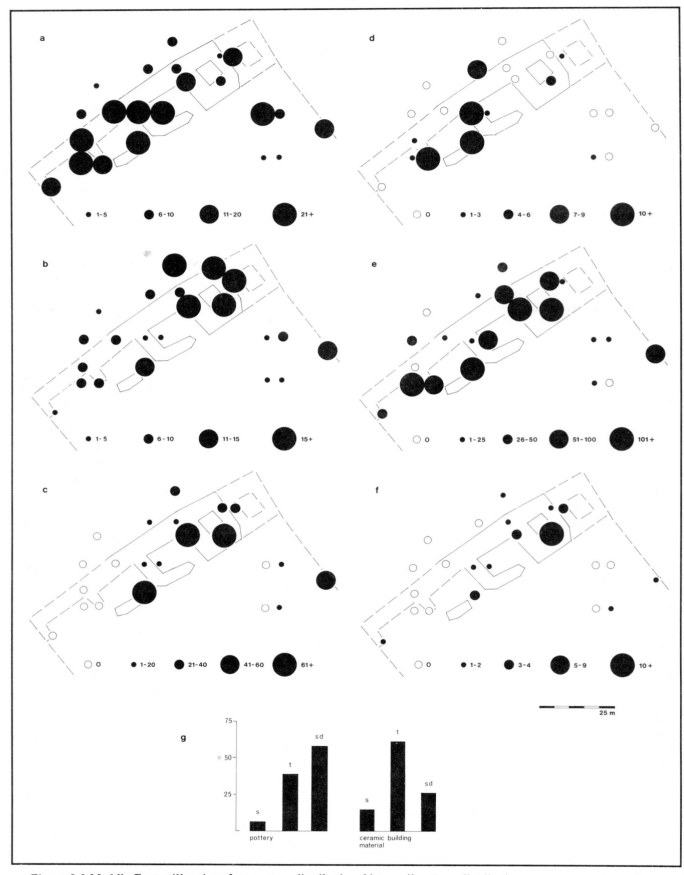

Figure 9.2 Maddle Farm villa: a) surface pottery distribution. b) topsoil pottery distribution over excavated trenches. c) stratified pottery distribution. d) surface ceramic building material distribution over excavated trenches. e) topsoil ceramic building material distribution bover excavated trenches. f) stratified ceramic building material distribution. g) vertical distribution of artefacts through surface, topsoil and stratified deposits.

arrangements, represented by pits, were positioned with reference to such areas.

The significant point to be made from this case study is that the final interpretation of the evidence for a formal relationship between postulated habitation areas and rubbish disposal zones could not have been made without reference to both traditional sub-surface archaeological data and artefactual data contained within the topsoil and on the surface. Artefact distributions, although removed totally from their original cultural deposits by modern ploughing, still retained a spatial relationship to sub-surface archaeological features through the distributions of topsoil and surface material. The removal of the topsoil without suitable recording would have revealed a pit group without any evidence for associated activities. Under such conditions the *status quo* of chalkland archaeology a decade ago would have remained a situation in which many excavations simply recovered data from deeply cut negative features and bemoaned the irretrievable loss of data related to surface deposits (Richards 1985,28).

Although the flint data recovered from survey and excavation at Weathercock Hill did not provide such clear patterning, several interesting points can be made. The flint itself, although contemporary with the settlement, was almost totally a topsoil feature. This is hardly surprising given the nature of late Bronze Age flint exploitation on the Downs. *Ad hoc* flint preparation, in many situations, prevents lithics entering formal refuse deposits in quantity, whilst few people wish to have large quantities of sharp flint fragments lying around their domestic living surfaces. The study of such material under these circumstances is unlikely to be successful, therefore, without reference to so-called residual topsoil material, as stratified deposits will either contain insignificant quantities of lithics or will be biased as a result of clearance activities.

This is not to suggest that lithic topsoil data does not have its problems. The topsoil represents a palimpsest of activities, and separating out different periods of deposition is far more difficult for flint than for pottery. Earlier periods of flint use are certainly represented at Weathercock Hill. The presence of an early Bronze Age barbed-and-tanged arrowhead has already been mentioned. Consequently, the poor patterning in the data may simply reflect multi-period occupation and the nature of flint use. Such problems have also been noted in ethnographic situations (Yellen 1977).

Nevertheless, those instances in which lithic chronological patterning is discernible may be highly significant. K-means analysis of the surface collection at Weathercock Hill isolated a series of blade clusters within the lithic data (see Bowden *et al* forth-

coming). Tentatively it may be suggested that these represent small foci of earlier activity swamped within the larger late Bronze Age data set. Whilst one cannot ignore the possibility that such concentrations are fortuitous, their existence is provocative. Mesolithic and Neolithic settlement is notoriously rare over most of the Downs (Richards 1978,71). It is possible that the only way to locate activity related to these periods is through very intensive survey. Certainly it may be significant that one of the few examples of Mesolithic activity located through survey carried out by the Maddle Farm Project was found during intensive survey of a Romano-British settlement at Knighton Bushes, a site *c* 1 km from Weathercock Hill (Gaffney and Tingle 1989). The formulation of research strategies designed to locate such ephemeral landscape traces would be one step towards the elimination of the settlement vacuum associated with these periods.

The second case study, that of excavation carried out by the Maddle Farm Project team, provides an example of the integration of surface and excavated data from a relatively more substantial and definable archaeological entity, a Roman villa. The villa site at Maddle Farm was also subject to intensive surface collection using a 5 m grid, and then to sample excavation. A total of twenty-four 2 x 3 m trenches were excavated. Each trench was located with reference to a 5 m collection unit for comparative purposes. Although a number of classes of material were recovered during this work, the most common were pottery and ceramic building material, namely tile and brick.

Of the artefacts recovered, pottery was the most numerous. When we consider density from the collection unit above each trench and plot it against the villa as revealed through aerial photography, it appears that density peaks within the western half of the soil mark (Figure 9.2a). However, this situation is reversed when we consider the pottery from excavation and illustrate densities per excavated metre square. Topsoil pottery densities peak within the eastern half of the building (Figure 9.2b) and are closely related to those areas containing extensive surviving stratified deposits (Figure 9.2c).

Ceramic building material, however, provides a very different distribution. The survey distribution of this artefact class, although relatively sparse, provides a scatter of material across the building with a slight peak in the western half (Figure 9.2d). Sub-surface distributions contrast with those displayed by pottery. Within the topsoil, ceramic building materials are distributed evenly across the building (Figure 9.2e), while stratified deposits are represented by very low densities (Figure 9.2f).

The contrasting distributions of pottery and ceramic building material is emphasised when the vertical distribution of the two are compared. In Figure 9.2g this data is illustrated in the form of a histogram. Pottery declines in density from stratified deposits through the topsoil, the lowest densities occurring within the survey data. Ceramic building material, however, peaks within the topsoil and exhibits relatively low densities within surface or stratified deposits. This distribution is reflected in the statistical relationship between survey and sub-surface data for the two artefact groups. When considered using regression analysis ceramic building material provides a strong correlation coefficient of 0.84 for the two variables, whilst pottery is negatively correlated with a significant coefficient of -0.67.

Whilst part of the explanation for the artefact distribution illustrated above must relate to differential destruction of archaeological deposits by modern agricultural practices, this cannot be the total explanation. All things being equal, we would expect the two artefact groups to be equally affected by such processes. The fact that the two artefact groups are being differentially affected suggests that any interpretation of the distribution of these materials must consider the different functions of the two artefact groups, and the probable path taken by each into the survey record.

Tiles and bricks have a specific structural role within any building, either in walls or roofs, although other uses must be envisaged. Except in specific circumstances we need not expect large quantities of such materials to be incorporated within negative features. In entering the archaeological record such materials tend to be incorporated within superficial deposits caused by the collapse or destruction of a building. As such, these deposits are the first that will be affected by post-depositional processes, including ploughing. If the deposit and the ploughing process are uniform such material is likely to enter the topsoil and, eventually, the survey record in a uniform manner. In such a situation we might expect a strong correlation between survey and sub-surface data as the two data sets will be intimately linked. This appears to have been the case at the Maddle villa.

Pottery, however, will be expected to display a more complex route from use to the survey record. Initially, it may have a wide variety of functions other than simply as a vessel. These functions will obviously demand a variety of discard situations, many of which will include formal waste disposal practices including cleaning and disposal, perhaps within pits and middens or incorporation within other stratified deposits. For instance, the Maddle villa provided some evidence for pottery sherds being used in a "tessellated" floor. In such situations pottery will be more likely to enter the topsoil, and the surface rec-

ord, only through the obliteration of stratified deposits contemporary with habitation activity. In such cases, unless a site has been completely destroyed, we might expect surface pottery to vary considerably, and often negatively, in its relationship to sub-surface data. Again the results from Maddle Farm suggest this to be the case.

Other published works indicate that a certain degree of caution is required under such circumstances. One example is the results of combined geophysical and surface survey carried out at the PP17 site in Boeotia (Heron and Gaffney 1987). Here, whilst tile concentrated over the structures located through resistivity survey, pottery tended to avoid them. By analogy with excavated sites, similar adjacent pottery concentrations have been interpreted as resulting from the ploughing of farmyard deposits. Consequently, when dealing with surface and topsoil distributions of functionally different materials, a more sophisticated and cautious approach to interpretation is necessary. Simply taking one artefact, pottery for instance, as a guide to excavation decisions is unwise. If the Maddle Farm Project team had decided simply to excavate those areas with the highest densities of surface pottery, they would have recovered a considerable amount of topsoil pottery, and little else.

Conclusion

The two case studies presented above indicate that in some situations it does not make sense to view survey results in a simplistic way. Both the data from Weathercock Hill and the Maddle Villa indicate that susceptibility to destruction may carry behavioural and functional implications which may be relevant to the final interpretation of the archaeology of a site. This is by no means a new revelation. Work at the Hatchery West in America (Binford 1972) and at Bishops Cannings Down (Gingell and Schadla Hall 1980) are examples of early work carried out within such a context. However, it is to be hoped that this paper builds upon such work and helps to define the potential and limitations of ploughzone archaeology more closely. British archaeology as a whole has been slow to formalise such work. There is still a tendency to regard surface survey as, "the last refuge of the desperate", a convenient guide to the best place to dig, and the topsoil as, "an opencast quarry for durable artefacts" (Richards 1985,29). Such opinions can only continue to the detriment of the sites under investigation, many of which, if agricultural practices are maintained at their present level, will eventually only exist as topsoil features (Groube and Bowden 1982,15-23). How future archaeologists react to this situation will depend largely upon the results of work carried out now.

References

Binford L.R., 1972. Hatchery West: site definition - surface distribution of cultural items, in Binford L.R., *An Archaeological Perspective,* 163-181. Seminar Press, London.

Bowden M.C.B., Ford S. and Gaffney V.L., Forthcoming. The excavation of a late Bronze Age artefact scatter at Weathercock Hill, Berkshire. *Berkshire Archaeological Journal.*

Foley R., 1981. *Off-site archaeology and human adaptation in Eastern Africa: an analysis of regional artefact density in the Amboseli, southern Kenya.* BAR (International Series) 97. Oxford.

Gaffney V.L. and Tingle M., 1984. The tyranny of the site: method and theory in field survey. *Scottish Archaeological Review,* 3, 134-140.

Gaffney V.L. and Tingle M., 1989. *The Maddle Farm Project: an integrated survey of Prehistoric and Roman Landscapes on the Berkshire Downs.* BAR (British Series) 200. Oxford.

van Gijn A., 1986. Habitation in Djenne, Mali: use of space in a west African town, in Fokkens H., Banga P. and Bierma M., editors, *Op zook naar mens en materiele cultuur,* 163-83.

Gingell C.J. and Schadla Hall R.T., 1980. Excavations at Bishops Cannings Down, 1976, in Hinchliffe J. and Schadla Hall R.T., editors, *The past under the plough.* DoE, Occasional Paper 3, 109- 113. HMSO, London.

Groube L.M. and Bowden M.C.B., 1982. *The archaeology of rural Dorset: past, present and future.* Dorset Natural History and Archaeological Society Monograph No. 4.

Heron C. and Gaffney V.L., 1987. Archaeogeophysics and the site: ohm sweet ohm, in Gaffney C.F. and Gaffney V.L., editors, *Pragmatic archaeology: theory in crisis?* 71-82. BAR (British Series) 167. Oxford.

Rathje W.L., 1979. Modern material culture studies, in Schiffer M.B., editor, *Advances in Archaeological Method and Theory* 2, 1- 37. Academic Press, London.

Richards J., 1978. *The archaeology of the Berkshire Downs.* Berkshire Archaeological Committee, Reading.

Richards J., 1985. Scouring the surface: approaches to the ploughzone in the Stonehenge environs. *Archaeological Review from Cambridge* 4, 27-41.

Schiffer M.B., 1976. *Behavioural Archaeology.* Academic Press, London.

Yellen J.E., 1977. *Archaeological Approaches to the past.* Academic Press, London.

Section 4

Presentation and Interpretation of Survey Data: Regional Perspectives

Two aspects of surface collection are most susceptible to investigation: the density of artefacts and the type of artefact classes and associations with which they most commonly occur. Often high density scatters are considered to represent areas of habitation while the remainder of the surface collection, until quite recently, attracted little attention. As the papers in the previous sections have demonstrated, to exclude any aspect of the surface collection in the final analysis is to seriously discredit final interpretation. If all is required is the presentation of a settlement *pattern* then, in some cases, such an approach may be justified. If, however, the intention is to investigate the settlement *system,* then low density scatters form an integral component in final interpretation. As Keay and Millett observe, density may vary both with time in a specific area or, as Schofield and Stoddart and Whitehead suggest, in terms of function and environmental setting. Areas attractive for settlement are more likely to produce larger quantities of material remains than an area unsuitable for habitation.

Schofield's paper demonstrates the use of correlation in evaluating the extent of association between artefact groups. By highlighting those cases where strong positive or negative correlation may be observed, distinctions can be made between activity areas. Indeed the point that high density is more a feature of industrial than domestic activity is of significance when the traditional equation of high density = site = settlement is considered.

Keay and Millett's paper demonstrates the extent to which field survey in the western Mediterranean has developed over the past 10 years, progressing from what was a "site-hunt" to the more critical evaluation of land-use and exploitation. One example, the Ager Tarraconensis survey, is presented as an illustration of the extent to which this transition has occurred. Interpretation in this case begins not simply with the distinction between presence and absence but with the premise that density variation among specific artefact groups will fluctuate through time as a consequence of supply and demand. Where more pottery is in circulation, high densities will more frequently occur. Thus to interpret density variation both in time and space, the effects of circulation must be withdrawn from the equation. This is achieved in the context of the Ager Tarraconensis survey by use of the median, quartile and octile values, producing maps of density variation for individual periods independent of the quantity of pottery present within the social system. Thus "sites" or ADABS (Abnormal Density Above Background Scatter) may be represented by a single sherd per hectare for one period and 100 for another.

The development of field survey in the Mediterranean, described by Gaffney *et al* and Keay and Millett, is given a further dimension by Stoddart and Whitehead. Their discussion of the central Mediterranean and specifically the Gubbio valley demonstrates again the range of human behaviour which surface distributions may represent and the extent to which that may vary both through time (adopting perhaps the evolutionary perspective apparent in the models presented in Chapter 7) and in terms of topography and the cultural landscape.

The use of land-use models may, as Stoddart and Whitehead suggest, provide a valuable insight into the dynamic behaviour behind surface distributions while both the previous papers demonstrate the need for quantitative "proof" in judging the level of variation apparent within the data. All three papers again reflect the point made in Section 1 and echo those made in subsequent sections, that 1) we must have clear objectives and an awareness of the problems in hand, and 2) that many aspects of human behaviour, not just settlement, generate surface remains and may appear through surface collection. Without an understanding of these underlying principles, full interpretation will remain elusive.

Chapter 10

Artefact Distributions as Activity Areas: Examples from South-East Hampshire

A J Schofield

The identification of settlements on the surface of ploughed fields is a major concern. Flint artefacts provide little more than a broad date, certainly not sufficient to argue for true contemporeneity, while intensive arable farming over many areas of southern England has dispersed artefacts to the extent that scatters no longer represent discrete spatial units. It is argued that a combination of theory and practice can offer a solution.

*By looking at the relationship between artefact **density** and the nature or **composition** of the artefact scatter, variations between, for example domestic and industrial waste may be discerned.*

In this paper it is argued that such an opportunity may be enhanced by adopting a predictive approach to surface scatters. If density and assemblage composition can be established for prehistoric settlements and industrial zones, this may enhance our ability to attribute domestic or industrial status to material recovered by surface collection.

An example is presented from the upper Meon valley, south-east Hampshire. The aim is not to present a settlement history of the area, but rather to demonstrate, first, that clear distinctions are apparent between domestic and industrial zones, and second, that specific aspects of the core-reduction sequence are visible on a regional scale.

Introduction

The interpretation of artefact scatters recovered by surface collection has often been considered in terms of *sites*; specific, discrete units generally considered to represent settlement locations. Under certain conditions this may be true. In the majority of cases, however, it is not. To define something as a *site* is to suggest that it is a bounded unit, clearly defined and isolated from its surroundings, in physical or behavioural terms. Where human behaviour has occurred continuously across the landscape (Foley 1981,2) or where disturbance has been considerable, either in terms of physical displacement or natural processes (Allen this volume), such discrete units cannot possibly occur.

To say something must be a *site* because density is higher than the surrounding scatter, assumes that a distinction can be made between what lies within the site, and what occurs outside it. As numerous authors have suggested, this is not an observation but an archaeological decision (Dunnell and Dancey 1983; Cherry 1984). Such decisions will vary between individuals, thus making comparison of site distributions between survey areas all the more improbable. If survey results are to be compared between regions, whether on the basis of period distributions or the relationship between specific types of activity, some form of compatibility in the presentation and interpretation of results is necessary.

A second assumption often made is that the majority of artefact discard will occur within

settlements and that it is those settlements or "loci of habitation" that are recovered by surface collection. This apparently is not the case, at least if we believe the ethnographic literature. As Gallagher (1977) has suggested, archaeologists often presume that the *site* is where the greatest density of tools and other debris will be located. Another hypothesis suggests, however, that this was the area *least* likely to maintain a locus of discard activities. As Gould (1980) has observed, less than 1% of debris may be discarded within a habitation area, while numerous authors have observed cases where refuse deposition is divorced from the focus of cultural activity (for example Binford 1978; Murray 1980; O'Connell 1987 and Simms 1988). Indeed in the case of Bayt Quablan, a Bedouin camp described by Simms (1988,207), refuse location was a reliable indicator of where activities were *not* carried out. In contrast, analysis by Cribb of a nomad campsite produced close and highly structured discard patterns adjacent to the siting of tents (1983,11).

It would seem, therefore, that the *site* or locus of habitation, as a discrete unit, is inappropriate at this level of analysis. Not only is it unlikely to survive as a spatial phenomenon but it may not represent habitation at all.

In this paper, results are presented from one survey area, the upper Meon valley in south-east Hampshire. It is suggested that by dividing the region into ecological zones on the basis of geological or topographical variation, artefact scatters may be considered on a more objective basis. Rather than looking for *sites,* emphasis is towards variation at three levels:

1 between collection units (fields) within each zone,
2 between zones, and
3 between regions. (This level of enquiry has been discussed elsewhere (Schofield 1988) and will not be considered further in this paper).

The remainder of the paper will be divided into three sections, looking first at ways in which areas of settlement and industrial activity may be located, and second, at the types of assemblage associated with them. A case study will then be presented.

Looking for patterns: contributions from geography

Human geography has provided a wealth of information regarding settlement location and the various decisions responsible for generating patterns in the landscape. Until recently this was an area largely ignored in relation to regional artefact distributions (but *cf* Hayes this volume). It is true to say, however, for whatever period, that some areas will be suitable for settlement and some will not. Similarly, areas may be considered either to provide an attractive resource package, including for example water, lithic source areas, timber, pasture and arable land, or only a limited combination of resources.

Although this represents only a simple set of principles, their value for the investigation of activity areas is considerable. Two examples may be cited.

Chisholm (1962) considered the establishment of a new agricultural settlement in an area previously uninhabited. Such a settlement would, he suggested, maintain two sets of space relationships, one with its land, one with the outside world, for example, lines of communication. In the first set of relationships, settlers would have to consider the availability of arable and grazing land, the supply of water, fuel resources and building materials. In addition there would be local considerations such as defence, the need to avoid flooding and natural shelter.

Chisholm suggested that to quantify these variables, hypothetical values should be assigned to each of the resources, showing the relative disadvantage of distance. These were presented in terms of units of cost to the community. The transport of water over 1 km for example, is equivalent to 10 units of cost. If the source of building material were the same distance away, it would represent only one-tenth the cost.

The suggestion is, therefore, that in choosing a settlement location, one is exercising preferences in terms of least-cost location, assuming the economic

aims of a community are paramount. For the prehistoric period this need not be the case. What this does suggest, however, is that some areas would be unsuitable for habitation, at least on a permanent basis, whatever the main locational factor. This is a useful starting point for any regional survey (*cf* Shennan 1985, 105-112).

On a similar theme, Roberts (1977; 1987) has presented a number of criteria relevant to the location of settlement areas. He makes the distinction, for example, between intrinsic site qualities, ie the desirable site characteristics, and extrinsic site qualities, ie the advantages of a specific situation (1987,106). Each settlement location represents a complex balance of all these factors. In terms of drainage, for example, it is considered desirable not only to have a slight slope beneath the settlement, but also to have an area of freely draining soils with high infiltration capacity. As these are generally less nutrient-rich and hence less attractive to agriculture, at least in the long-term, a compromise situation with the settlement on the boundary is considered ideal.

In terms of shelter and aspect, a similar set of requirements can be suggested. South-facing slopes receive more solar radiation than north-facing slopes while the diurnal movement of air in valleys is such that on balance, south-facing slopes are more attractive to settlement. In addition, a southern aspect provides shelter from the north, north-east and north-west from which direction winter winds tend to predominate (Roberts 1987,118). An index established by Lacy (1976) confirmed these observations. A site orientated south and sheltered would score 0 (0+0) while an exposed site, orientated north, would score 10 (6+4). Although derived from modern principles, this simple weighting index does give an idea of the decisions behind settlement location.

It may be suggested, therefore, both from the theoretical ideas of Chisholm (1962) and Lacy (1976) and the more practical issues raised by Roberts (1977;1987), that settlements of a specific period will tend to occur and recur in specific types of location. The concept of "land-cunning" (Roberts 1977), a detailed knowledge of the land, is as relevant in prehistory as it is today. Settlement was not a random process but was directed by specific reasons and decisions. If this is the case, areas of domestic activity will not appear as a general blur across the landscape, but will appear concentrated within specific zones (the extent to which this is true will depend largely upon the strength and nature of the constraints). The association of particular artefact groups, generally associated with domestic activity, may be expected to display strong associations, while the distinction between domestic and industrial activity, which should be equally constrained by ecological factors, should be apparent.

It is with such patterns of continuity and accumulation that regional survey should be concerned. Surface collection cannot be expected to produce the residue of specific moments in time. We should instead concentrate our efforts on understanding variation on a scale appropriate to the methodology we have chosen to adopt and one which affords comparison on a variety of scales. This may now be considered in terms of the upper Meon valley survey, south-east Hampshire.

Looking for patterns: contributions from archaeology

For the purpose of this investigation, two types of location may be considered in terms of stone tool production and resource use:

1 What may be described as "home-range production" in which the raw material is acquired locally, reduced and worked on-site and tools used in a home-range context. Density will in this case be variable, depending on the scale of occupation, although we may suggest that a higher density may be expected for Neolithic occupation than for Mesolithic. Primary and tertiary waste and cores will appear in variable proportions, though high in relation to other areas, while scrapers and retouched artefacts may be present in relatively high numbers. Another aspect and perhaps the clearest indication of on-site knapping will be the predominance of raw material from a local source, in the case of the Meon valley, chalk derived.
2 "Extra-home-range production" in which nodules are imported from a source area some distance away, to the home range for further reduction. Here we must consider where the flint was coming from, for example chalk or gravel. If a home-range is situated on the gravels and much of the flint is chalk-derived, then the source area may be reasonably predicted. In the source area we may expect to see a high proportion of primary waste, but little

in the way of tertiary waste and retouch. In the target area, tertiary waste should be predominant, combined with all the features of a home-range (retouch, scrapers) and a high proportion of cores.

Table 10.1 provides a summary of the "expected" assemblage characteristics where industrial and domestic areas are segregated. Where home-range production has occurred, no clear trends may be apparent:

Activity areas: examples from the upper Meon valley

For the Meon valley, three specific areas within the study area may be considered. Area 1 is situated on upper chalk containing large quantities of good quality flint. The topography may be described as "naturally monotonous" with the absence of any distinct breaks in slope once beyond the river terrace. Areas 2 and 3 by contrast lie on lower chalk in a zone of moderate topographical variation. The floodplain is up to 1 km wide on the east side of the river, rising sharply to an east-west scarp which continues across the survey area. Figure 10.1 illustrates the location of the upper Meon valley survey area while Figure 10.2 shows the location of the three zones and their relationship to the topography of the region

The results of surface collection are considered in terms of individual fields within these zones. The aim is to adopt the results of calibration from the previous section and consider at what scale the line between industrial and domestic may be drawn. Although the lithic collection represents activity between the Mesolithic and Bronze Age periods, the majority appears to be Neolithic in date.

The results of surface collection suggest a number of points: First that areas 2 and 3 situated on the lower chalk, have a mean density of 15.9 and 12.9 flints per hectare respectively, while area 1 on the upper chalk has a mean density of 49.6 flints per hectare. For primary and tertiary waste there is little variation

Table 10.1 Expected assemblage characteristics for domestic and industrial areas assuming a policy of extra home-range production.

	Density	Primary waste	Tools	Cores
Settlement	Low	Low	High	High
Industrial	High	High	Low	Low

Table 10.2a Correlation matrix for variables in zone 1

	flint	%ret	%prim	%tert	%core	%scra
flint	1.000					
%ret	−0.484	1.000				
%prim	0.136	−0.057	1.000			
%tert	−0.375	−0.002	−0.544	1.000		
%core	−0.063	0.647	0.244	−0.125	1.000	
%scra	0.174	−0.100	0.166	−0.145	0.039	1.000

Table 10.2b Correlation matrix for variables in zone 2

	flint	%ret	%prim	%tert	%core	%scra
flint	1.000					
%ret	0.398	1.000				
%prim	−0.255	−0.338	1.000			
%tert	−0.148	−0.641	0.285	1.000		
%core	−0.391	−0.173	−0.017	−0.066	1.000	
%scra	0.364	0.608	−0.313	−0.227	−0.130	1.000

Table 10.3a Correlation matrix for variables in zone 3

	flint	%ret	%prim	%tert	%core	%scra
flint	1.000					
%ret	−0.396	1.000				
%prim	−0.001	0.061	1.000			
%tert	0.267	−0.307	0.094	1.000		
%core	−0.272	0.335	0.011	−0.854	1.000	
%scra	0.001	0.045	0.158	0.431	−0.299	1.000

Table 10.3b Correlation matrix for variables in zones 1 to 3

	flint	%ret	%prim	%tert	%core	%scra
flint	1.000					
%ret	−0.425	1.000				
%prim	−0.103	−0.040	1.000			
%tert	0.070	−0.446	0.110	1.000		
%core	−0.489	0.362	0.099	−0.432	1.000	
%scra	−0.086	0.451	−0.038	0.030	−0.031	1.000

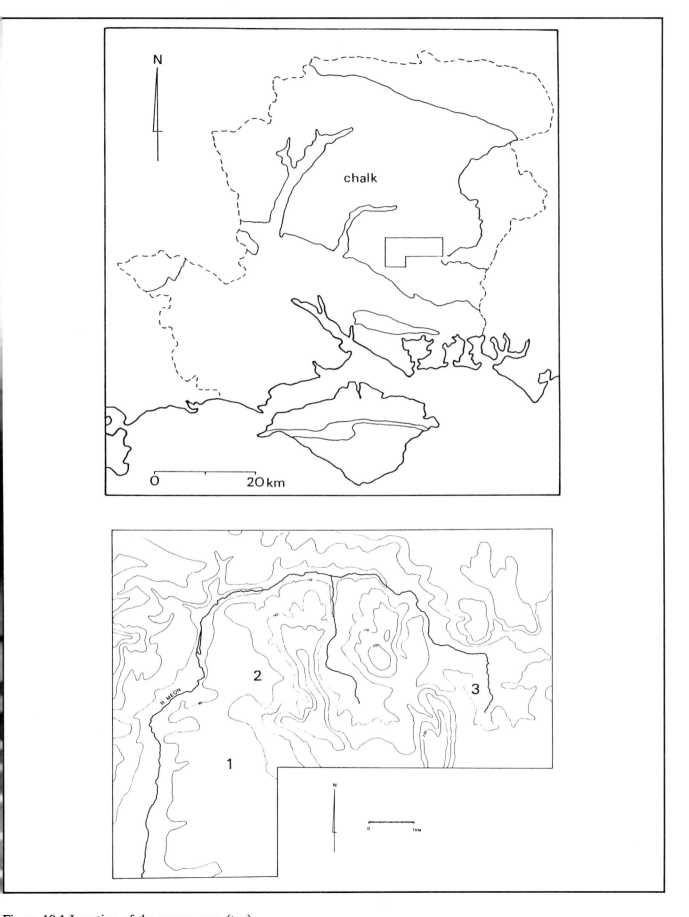

Figure 10.1 Location of the survey area (top).
Figure 10.2 Topography of the upper Meon valley survey area showing the three zones described in the text (bottom).

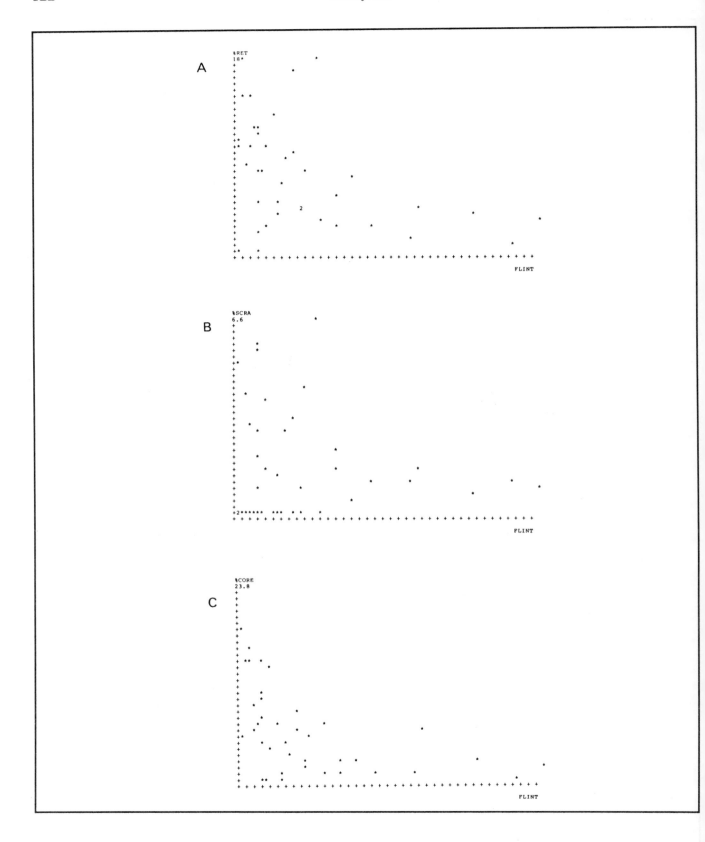

Figure 10.3 Scatterplots relating aspects of assemblages composition to density per hectare (maximum density for each graph is 110.6 flints per hectare). A: density vs % of retouched artefacts (r^2=0.18); B: density vs % of scrapers (r^2=0.01); C: density vs % of cores (r^2=0.24).

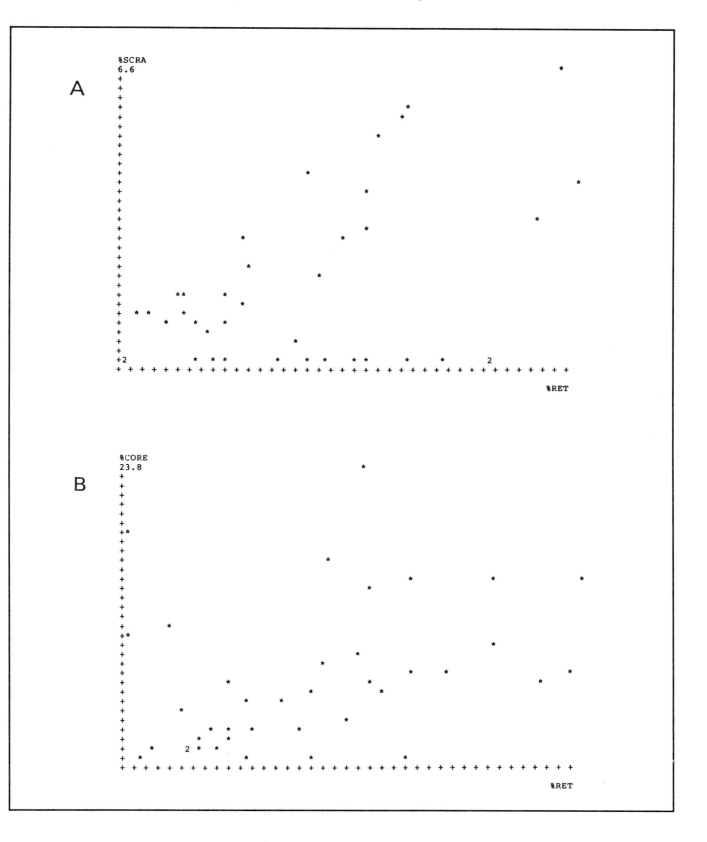

Figure 10.4 Scatterplots relating aspects of assemblage composition to the percentage of retouched artefacts (maximum percentage of retouched artefacts for each graph is 18.0%). A: % of retouched artefacts vs % of scrapers (r^2=0.20); B: % of retouched artefacts vs % of cores (r^2=0.13).

while cores represent 7.5% of the assemblage in area 2, 9.8% in area 3 and only 1.2% in area 1. Both results proved statistically significant through analysis of variance to a level of .005, suggesting that in neither case were they derived from a single population. This is as would be expected if prepared nodules were being removed from industrial to domestic zones for final reduction. That quality flint is naturally occurring on the upper chalk of area 1 and is less prolific and of inferior quality on the lower chalk of area 2 may confirm this. Tools appear to follow the same pattern making up 2.3% of the total collection in area 2, 1.6% in area 3 and 1.2% in area 1 while retouched flakes comprise 9.4% of the total collection from area 2, 8.2% from area 3 and 3.2% from area 1. Although tool frequency did not prove significant through analysis of variance, the proportion of retouch did, at a significance level of .005.

How does the co-association of artefact types considered representative of industrial and domestic activity fit into this pattern? (Tables 10.2 and 10.3, Figures 10.3 and 10.4). First, the relationship between density and the proportion of retouch across the study area displays a negative correlation of -0.425 (Table 10.3b) suggesting that the frequency of retouched items tends to decrease as scatters increase in density. Area 1, by contrast, produced very few retouched items suggesting a positive correlation for areas 2 and 3, a feature expected perhaps for a settle-

ment location. This was partly the case with a correlation in area 2 of 0.398 (Table 10.2b) and a negative correlation in area 1 of -0.484 (Table 10.2a). A negative correlation also appeared in area 3, an area possibly exploited as a general foraging territory rather than for permanent habitation (Schofield 1988).

These associations are confirmed by the nature of relationship between density and scrapers on the one hand and retouch and scrapers on the other. Density and scrapers display no correlation in zones 1 and 3 (Tables 10.2a and 10.3a) and a positive correlation of 0.364 in zone 2 (Table 10.2b), while a strong positive correlation between retouch and scrapers exists in the latter and not the former. Scraper frequency accounts for 20.31% of variation in the proportion of retouch and only 0.75% of variation in artefact density over the entire area.

Another interesting relationship is that between cores on the one hand and retouch and density on the other. Cores display a strong negative correlation with flint density (-0.489) and a positive relationship with the proportion of retouched artefacts (0.362) across the area as a whole (Table 10.3b). In area 1 the correlation between cores and retouched artefacts is 0.647 (Table 10.2a), in area 2 the correlation is -0.173 (Table 10.2b) and in area 3, 0.335 (Table 10.3a). As density is a feature of the industrial zone and retouch a feature of the domestic, the fact that

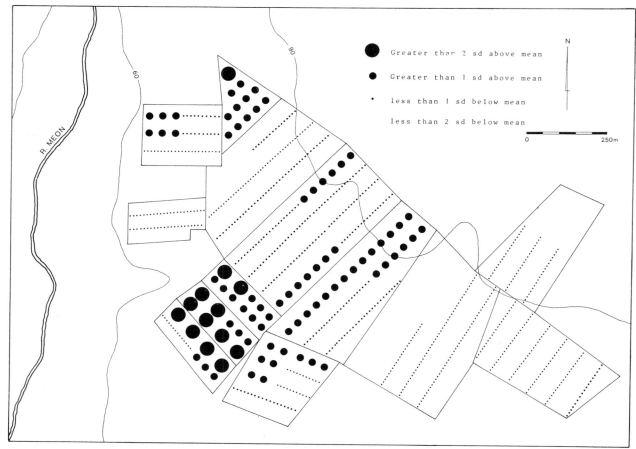

Figure 10.5 Density variation in area 1 (values expressed as standard deviations above and below the mean).

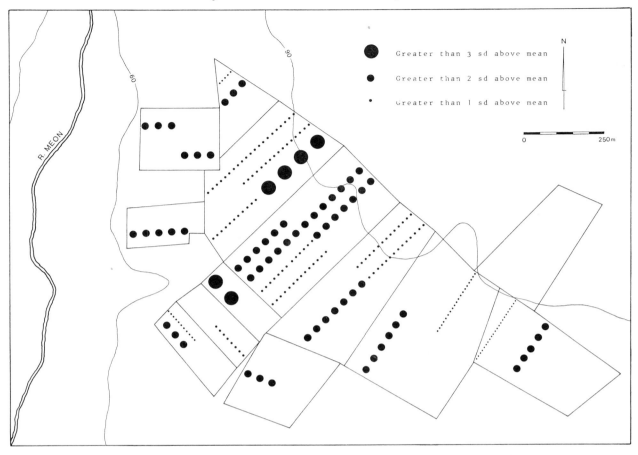

Figure 10.6 Proportion of primary waste in area 1 (values expressed as for Figure 10.5).

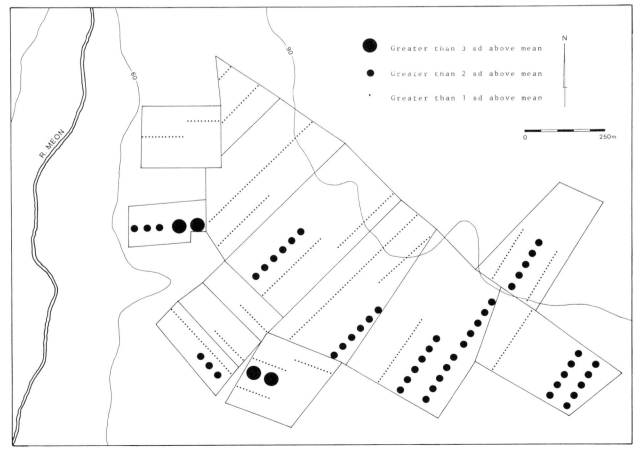

Figure 10.7 Proportion of tertiary waste in area 1 (values expressed as for Figure 10.5).

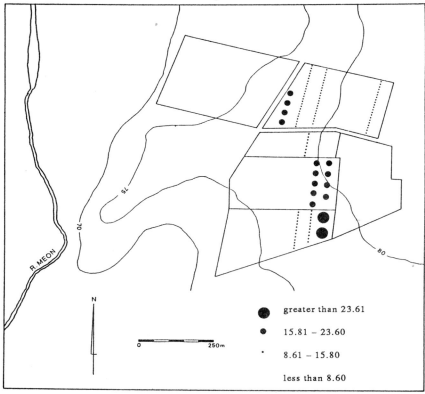

Figure 10.8 Density variation in area 2 (number per 100m). The values are expressed in different format for area 2 because figures from only selected fields are included. Values above and below the mean would have been misleading under such circumstances.

cores appear to be associated with the latter conforms to the suggested pattern of extra-home-range production.

One problem with trying to distinguish between activity areas on such a broad scale is that variation within zones may be masked, and this may be suggested for area 1, the industrial zone. No clear predominance of any particular waste category could be defined, suggesting perhaps that primary and later reduction were occurring within the same zone, but in different areas. In other words some of the variation occurring within zones was not being picked up at this level of analysis.

The pattern which emerges within area 1 may suggest two stages of the core-reduction process (Figures 10.5 to 10.7). Both primary waste and high density are concentrated on the river terrace and at the front of the adjoining plateau or interfluve. This goes against the general trend which points to a low correlation of - 0.103. The distribution of tertiary waste on the other hand appears to be mutually exclusive, located some distance away on the interfluve, separated from the primary industrial zone by perhaps only a few hundred metres. This corresponds to the proposed correlation values between primary and tertiary waste of -0.544 suggesting that in area 1 we are seeing an organised industrial complex in which primary and tertiary reduction were spatially segre-

gated. That cores are more closely associated with tertiary than with primary reduction may confirm this.

A similar argument may be suggested for area 2. Within this zone clear concentrations of domestic activity occur in the form of higher density scatters, combined with high proportions of retouch and quantities of burnt flint. These occur on a slight terrace of the river Meon and display a strong correlation (above). The distributions are illustrated in Figures 10.8 to 10.10.

In summary then, for area 2 the lower overall density and higher proportion of tools suggests domestic activity. Again they fit the expected results with the mean proportion of tools and density for every field analogous to the expected surface frequency suggested by excavated sites in the region (Clark and Schofield this volume). No fields within this area maintain a combination of artefact categories suggestive of industrial activity, just as the opposite was the case in area 1.

In terms of geographical location, the expectations are upheld. Area 1 would be the least cost-effective of the three zones for domestic activity, with Lacy's (1976) exposure index ranking high on the scale. In terms of lithic extraction however, area 1 provides the ideal location. Areas 2 and 3 provide greater natural protection as well as a greater variety of

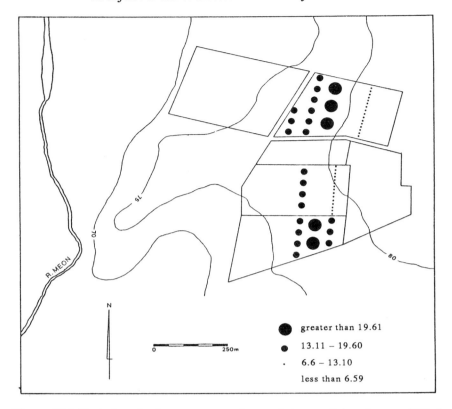

Figure 10.9 Variations in the percentage of retouch in area 2 (number per 100m).

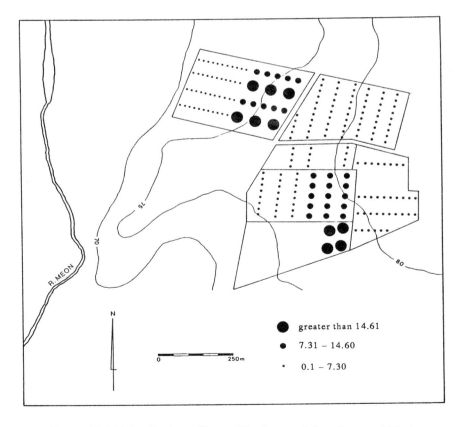

Figure 10.10 Distribution of burnt flint in area 2 (number per 100m).

resource habitats. That the higher ground was used for hunting and timber acquisition is suggested by the distribution of leaf-shaped arrowheads and flint-axes within this zone. That these areas appear mutually exclusive with only limited blurring, and that 11.7% of the collection units produced Mesolithic and early Neolithic artefact groups, does imply early occupation of the area. That few artefacts characteristic of other periods were represented may confirm this.

Conclusion

Sites may occur under certain circumstances while in the majority of cases, and especially in the context of southern England, their definition is based more on interpretation than on observation. If the results of surface collection are to be useful in terms of adaptation across the region as a whole, data from surface collection *must* be compatible. A *site* to one person may be background noise to another.

One possibility is explored in this paper. By presenting data in terms of either density per hectare or as a percentage of the total collection, either from individual fields or collection cells, or between ecological zones, comparisons may be drawn on a variety of scales. By looking at their potential for either industrial or domestic activity, combined with the strength and nature of relationship between artefact classes, the extent to which a specific area was inhabited may be ascertained. Where geographical

probability and archaeological observations do not coincide, other factors may be seen to have influenced the nature of the settlement pattern; colluviation and erosion, for example, being particularly significant in downland contexts (Allen this volume). Where correlation is strong, least-cost location may be considered a possibility. This appears to have been the case in the upper Meon valley.

A final point: If the "high density = site" formula were adopted for the Meon valley, the fields in area 1 would have been described as "sites" at the expense of the majority in area 2. By looking more at the "make-up" of the artefact collections rather than merely their size, fields in area 1 proved to be representative of an industrial zone while it was area 2 which yielded evidence for domestic activity ("sites" in the traditional sense).

Acknowledgements

I am grateful to Clive Gamble and Stephen Shennan for commenting on earlier drafts of this paper. I must also thank participants at both the IFA Conference, Birmingham 1988 and the Neolithic Studies Group/Lithic Studies Society Conference, Cardiff 1988 for comments and debate. I hope the final paper has succeeded in incorporating many of the points raised.

References

Binford L.R., 1978. Dimensional analysis of behaviour and site structure: learning from an eskimo hunting stand. *American Antiquity* 43, 330-361.

Cherry J., 1984. Common sense in Mediterranean archaeology? *Journal of Field Archaeology* 11, 117-120.

Chisholm M., 1962. *Rural settlement and land-use: an essay in location*. Hutchinson, London.

Cribb R., 1983. On-site ethnoarchaeology. *Archaeological Review from Cambridge* 2, 4-16.

Dunnell R.C. and Dancey W.S., 1983. The siteless survey: a regional scale data collection strategy, in Schiffer M. B. editor, *Advances in Archaeological Method and Theory* 6, 267-287. Academic Press, New York.

Foley R., 1981. A model of regional archaeological structure. *Proceedings of the Prehistoric Society* 47, 1-18.

Gallagher J.P., 1977. Contemporary stone tools in Ethiopia: implications for archaeology. *Journal of Field Archaeology* 4, 407-414.

Gould R., 1980. *Living Archaeology*. Cambridge University Press.

Lacy R.E., 1976. *Driving rain index*. DoE, Building Research Establishment, HMSO.

Murray P., 1980. Discard location: the ethnographic evidence. *American Antiquity* 45, 490-502.

O'Connell J.F., 1987. Alyawara site structure and its archaeological implications. *American Antiquity* 52, 74-108.

Roberts B.K., 1977. *Rural settlement in Britain*. Hutchinson, London.

Roberts B.K., 1987. *The making of the English village: a study in historical geography*. Longman, Singapore.

Schofield A.J., 1988. *The interpretation of surface lithic collections: case studies from southern England*. Unpublished PhD thesis, University of Southampton.

Shennan S.J., 1985. *Experiments in the collection and interpretation of archaeological survey data: the East Hampshire survey*. Sheffield University Press.

Simms S.R., 1988. The archaeological structure of a Bedouin camp. *Journal of Archaeological Science* 15, 197-211.

Chapter 11

Surface Survey and Site Recognition in Spain:
the Ager Tarraconensis Survey and its Background

S J Keay and M Millett

A traveller lost in Dublin asked a local the way to the Station. He replied, "to be sure;
if I were going to the Station, I wouldn't be starting from here".

Introduction

Field walking as a method of discovery has a long and honourable history. Surface finds and standing structures attracted the attention of the earliest antiquaries before a spade was ever lifted to disinter the past. This origin betrays the main bias and principal reason for the slow development of a methodology appropriate to surface-survey. If something is obvious, it does not need to be explained or sought further. Thus archaeologists working in places and within periods rich in material evidence have often been victims of the quality of their data. This is especially true for those involved with Roman archaeology. Much of their data is monumental in scale and this has blinded them to its limitations, leaving gaps in the archaeological record which remain unrecognised or explained. This is particularly true in the Mediterranean where the volume and quality of the surviving evidence is so good. By contrast, archaeologists in areas of the Roman Empire with a more limited archaeological record, like their Prehistorian colleagues, tend to concentrate more on methodological refinements in order to optimise results from the data.

As a result of this pattern of development much effort has been expended on the evolution of new methods for understanding small quantities of data; this is particularly true of British and North American archaeology. In contrast, much of Classical archaeology in the Mediterranean has been concerned with coping with the enormous quantities of data which often threaten to overwhelm its practitioners. The contention of this paper, which has been developed in the Ager Tarraconensis survey, is that methods developed for survey since the 1960s can enhance our understanding of the Classical world, whilst the problems and potential of the Classical archaeological data have a major contribution to make to the development of the methodologies themselves.

Systematic surface collection has developed through the divergence of two branches or trends over the past few decades. The first developed during the agricultural revolution stimulated by the mechanisa-tion of farming after the Second World War. This resulted in the introduction of widespread deep-ploughing, especially in Italy where it generated substantial surface-scatters, the recognition of which led to the initiation of the South Etruria survey, under the direction of John Ward-Perkins at the British School at Rome. In South Etruria, the huge quantities of surface material seemed to represent a lost landscape. Thus the finds were interpreted empirically as the result of changes in the character and intensity of rural settlement through time (summarised in Potter 1979). It is hard to overestimate the importance of this work since, for the first time, it showed that the countryside was intensively settled during Classical antiquity and that the data could be collected with relative ease. It also revolutionised theories about the urban nature of Classical social organisation. Because of its success it became the example which many Mediterranean surveys were to follow (*cf* Macready and Thompson 1985; Keller and Rupp 1983). The weakness of its approach lies in the uncritical acceptance of first, that surface evidence is a direct reflection of buried "sites", and second, that "site" numbers equate with population levels (*cf* Haselgrove 1985; Millett, in press).

The second branch of systematic surface collection grew from the theoretical developments in archaeology, largely in the USA, during the 1960s and 1970s. In both the USA and Britain there was an increasing awareness that the past could be interpreted as a series of social and economic systems, using the natural world both as a resource and a framework within which to exist (eg Cherry *et al* 1978). Thus, human populations did not simply live in discrete "sites" but left a series of behaviour patterns in the archaeological record, some of which could be seen as "off-site" activities (Foley 1981) while others were found in areas of habitation. Although these concepts were drawn largely from hunter-gatherer societies, their application to sedentary communities generated new interpretative insights. Thus the material traces left by farming

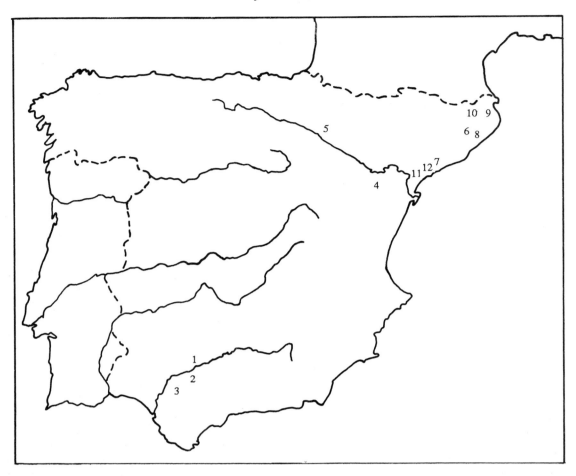

Figure 11.1 Map of the Iberian peninsula showing the surveys mentioned in the text. Numbers refer to the individual surveys as follows. 1. Lower Guadalquivir valley (Ponsich 1974, 1979, 1987). 2. Region of Los Alcores (Amores 1982). 3. Campiña de Sevilla, in the vicinity of ancient Salpensa (Ruiz M., 1985). 4. Mora de Rubielos (Burillo *et al* 1984). 5. Ribera de Navarra (Oña González 1984). 6. Surveys carried out by Estrada (1955, 1969). 7. Coast of the Penedès (Miret, Sanmartí and Santacana 1984, Sanmartí and Santacana 1986, Sanmartí, Santacana and Serra 1984). 8. Maresme (Prevosti 1981). 9. Province of Girona (Nolla and Casas 1984). 10. Banyoles (Jones *et al* 1985). 11. Reus (Vilaseca 1973, Massò 1978). 12. Ager Tarraconensis.

communities varied according to the nature of their activities, whether ploughing, manuring, ditch-digging or habitation (Haselgrove 1985; Gaffney *et al* 1985).

This realisation led directly to two developments. First that field-survey, which was stimulated by the "New Archaeology" of the 1960s, has gradually begun to be integrated with the British tradition of landscape archaeology. This form of field archaeology has concentrated on the examination of field-monuments in their context and has remained lively since the days of Crawford (1953), Williams-Freeman (1915) and others, being best exemplified by the work of the Royal Commission on Historical Monuments. The new integration may be exemplified by developments of air-photographic interpretation (Bewley 1984). Such work has re-vitalised the concept of the archaeology of whole landscapes so rather than simply focusing upon palimpsests of individual

sites, the emphasis is now on the social and economic context of the region.

The second development concerns a growing awareness of the processes which generate surface distributions of artefacts. This is largely derived from research into "site formation processes", developed in the United States during the 1970s (Schiffer 1976). This arose from a desire to understand the relationship between archaeological data and the societies which created them and sought to investigate processes underlying the creation of the archaeological record. Recent work by Haselgrove (1985) has contributed to the subject by investigating the relationship between data and ancient societies in terms of ploughsoil scatters alone, whilst Millett has studied pottery from the ploughsoil in relation to changes in the overall pattern of supply (1985; in press).

These advances in archaeological thinking have led to a much more self-critical approach to the collection and interpretation of material from the ploughsoil, engendering approaches akin to those used in the criticism of written historical sources. There is, however, a danger that this will lead to the situation where either, "it's so complex that we can't understand it", or, "the formation process is all we can ever understand", both of which are views afflicting contemporary British archaeology.

Field survey in Spain

Most of these conceptual and methodological developments have passed Spain by, although this is not to say that the importance of site recognition has been lost on scholars working in Iberia. The antiquity of Iberia is a palimpsest of cultural contact, confrontation and assimilation which has generated an especially rich archaeological heritage. This is of such a high quality that there has been less impetus towards the collection of the less obvious data. However, the ceramic sequences for many of the important prehistoric, protohistoric and Roman horizons in the peninsula have been defined and make site-recognition by survey a very attractive prospect. As a result important site-surveys and distribution studies have been undertaken in the last 30 years. A selective review of these demonstrates their tendency to concentrate upon the archaeologically rich and better known areas of southern Spain, eastern Spain and the Ebro valley (Figure 11.1). Moreover they have been mostly concerned with the consolidation and enhancement of the existing record rather than starting afresh. This is exemplified by the unfinished series *Carta Arqueológica de España,* each volume of which deals with a different province in Spain. This kind of work is in the same tradition as the Royal Commissions in Britain, or the *Forma Italiae* series in Italy.

Southern Spain, especially the lower Guadalquivir valley, has been a focus of antiquarian and archaeological interest since the beginning of this century. It was the heartland of the rich proto-historic culture of Tartessos and the later, Roman, province of Baetica. One of the earliest surveys was undertaken by Bonsor (1931) who mapped all the visible Roman finds along the river Guadalquivir between Seville and Córdoba. This is an immense area and includes some of the richest archaeological remains in Spain. Although taking a particular interest in Dressel 20 amphora stamps, he also built upon his earlier work (*cf* Bonsor 1899), describing prehistoric and protohistoric finds in addition to Roman material. In many cases the sites to which he refers were self-evident standing structures. His interest in Dressel 20 amphorae, however, meant that he was aware of the relationship between

ancient sites and pottery scatters. As a result of his survey, Bonsor was able to produce a distribution map of the Lower Guadalquivir valley, showing the distribution of major ancient settlements as well as lesser sites indicated by the location of pottery, coins or inscriptions.

Bonsor's work was to remain the principal source of reference for the area after the 1930s when known sites in the province of Seville began to be listed in an attempt to compile a dossier on its archaeological heritage (Collantes de Terán 1939; 1943; 1951; 1955): this remains unfinished. In the 1970s, the same area was subject to a systematic and more intensive survey by Ponsich (Ponsich 1974; 1979; 1987). The first two volumes of Ponsich's results examined the area between Seville (ancient Hispalis) and Córdoba (ancient Corduba), while the third looked at the area between Córdoba and Andújar (ancient Isturgi). The survey took place at a time when mechanised agriculture in the area was taking hold and threatening the archaeological heritage. This vast survey was undertaken by one individual with the aid of 1:50,000 military maps and aerial photographs. The aim of the survey was very broad, attempting to look at human settlement in the area throughout antiquity. All ancient finds were identified as "sites" and Ponsich developed a site-hierarchy consisting of towns, villas, farms and shelters based on the density or quality of the finds at a given location. The latter category was an important departure from the usual conception of a rural site, recognising the existence of ephemeral traces not readily identifiable on sites of continuous occupation. In effect, Ponsich was recognising the existence of some "off-site" archaeology by analogy with contemporary agricultural practice (Ponsich 1974,17,281), an area of human activity not generally recognised by archaeologists in other parts of Spain. A very broad chronology for most sites was proposed on the basis of an *ad hoc* collection of pottery, coins and inscriptions. As a result, Ponsich produced a series of important site-distribution maps, showing a remarkable density of ancient settlement. These have been used as the basis for many analyses of the agricultural economy of Roman Baetica down to the present day.

Recently, however, the Departamento de Prehistoria y Arqueología de la Universidad de Sevilla has begun a programme of much more detailed multi-period surveys (Cartas Arqueológicas) of the province of Seville, beginning with a restricted region already covered by Ponsich (Amores 1982). The work is intensive and has resulted in the discovery of an even greater density of sites, although disqualifying some of those claimed by Ponsich. This author is more explicit about the chronology of the sites but, at the same time, makes little attempt to establish a site hierarchy. Work to a similar standard has been undertaken in the vicinity of the Roman town of Salpensa (El Casar) to the south- east of Seville (Ruiz 1985).

Comparable work has been undertaken in the Ebro valley. This was another important avenue of cultural contact in antiquity and shares a similarly dry climate. The richness of the archaeological heritage, especially for the late pre-Roman and early Roman Iron Age had given rise to a number of hypotheses for the development of Iberian and Celtiberian urbanism and the development of rural settlement systems focused upon Roman towns (Bosch Gimpera P. 1929,19ff; Burillo 1986). Survey work, however, has started to broaden the data-base available to archaeologists. One important project, begun in 1979, aims at the intensive and systematic survey of a small parish in the province of Teruel (Mora de Rubielos: Burillo F. *et al* 1984). The importance of this project is that it explicitly recognised the need for field-survey, as opposed to occasional week-end excursions, as a prerequisite to further detailed regional studies and the excavation of particular sites. It also recognised the influence of agricultural disturbance, erosion and colluviation/alluviation in burying ancient landscapes and potentially distorting site-distribution maps. No site-hierarchy was developed and the chronology of sites appears to have been achieved in a succint manner. The author has used work of this kind to elaborate hypotheses about the emergence of urbanism during the second and first centuries BC.

This approach was taken one stage further by another survey, further up the Ebro valley, in the Ega valley (Oña González 1984). This was a "one-person" survey and, although not systematic, is important as different environmental aspects of the area are taken into account in the analysis of Roman settlement over a relatively small geographical area. Geomorphology, topography, lithography, water resources, vegetation, soils and communications are all used as constraints in the analysis. Moreover the difficulties of classifying archaeological finds into site-hierarchies are recognised and that used by Ponsich was rejected in favour of one which was felt to be more appropriate to the region in question. Thus sites were classified on the basis of their extent, while their function was directly related to their geographical situation. Like Ponsich, Oña González also recognised the existence of sites of ephemeral character related to transhumance routes.

The other main area of survey in Spain has been in the north-east, modern Catalunya, where local rambling associations have hunted for, and published, sites on a casual basis since the later nineteenth century. Many local archaeological groups and archaeologists in the Empordà, Vallès, Penedès and Tarragonès built up substantial lists of all classes of ancient monument and displayed the finds in local museums. Despite various attempts by the Generalitat de Catalunya during the 1930s, and the Comisarias Provinciales de Excavaciones Arqueológicas during the 1950s, none of this work was ever co-ordinated and is not susceptible to full interpretation. A first attempt to provide a regional picture was undertaken by Serra Ràfols (1928) and amplified by Almagro (Almagro *et al* 1945).

Without doubt, the greatest contribution to site survey was that of Estrada i Garriga who began the large scale coverage of the central Vallès in 1946, and who has subsequently amassed finds from hundreds of Iberian and Roman sites in the Museu de Granollers (Estrada 1955; 1969). This research has revealed an intensely settled landscape, although details of its chronological development are still obscure. Giro Romeu gradually built up a list of sites in the Penedès in a similar way, publishing summaries of his discoveries in the journal *Ampurias* (eg Romeu 1959). More intensive work, and much broader in scope, has been undertaken in the same area by Sanmartí, Miret and Santacana (Miret, Sanmartí and Santacana 1984; Sanmartí and Santacana 1986). Although not on a large scale, the survey did focus on the spatial relationship between Iberian settlements of different sizes along the coast to the north of Tarragona. The results of this and attempts to refine the chronology of different sized settlements have been calibrated by excavation (Sanmartí, Santacana and Serra 1984).

The coastal Maresme in the province of Barcelona has benefited from the work of several archaeologists, for example, Ribas and Cuyas Tolosa, both of whom have produced summaries of rural settlement in the vicinity of the coastal towns of Iluro and Baetulo (Ribas 1952; 1975; Cuyas 1977). Recently, however, all this work, together with new material and the results of recent excavations was incorporated into two immense and detailed site lists published by Prevosti (1981a; 1981b). In the province of Girona, the archaeologist M. Oliva was similarly assiduous, accumulating finds of all periods from throughout the province and publishing short notes in local journals and the Journal *Ampurias*. Following the death of Oliva in 1974, this work was brought up to date and published along with much new material by Nolla and Casas (Nolla and Casas 1984). This was an important step, as the authors working through the accumulated finds were able to construct a series of chronological maps for the province, and attempted an interpretation of the results produced. In the work, the finds are listed as sites in the manner of the *Carta Arqueológica de España* series.

The Ager Tarraconensis survey

Background
The characteristics of all the valuable studies outlined above show that they fall into the category of record enhancement, complemented by selective fieldwork. As such they clearly provide an invaluable source of information about what is known, fulfilling the same function as county sites and monuments records in Britain. Such a role contrasts with that of field survey in its present sense, where research is directed towards testing the actual distribution of past settlement as objectively as possible and thereby revealing the limitations of existing knowledge.

All of these studies, and others besides, are laudable for the work that they represent and in terms of their implicit objective of widening the archaeological data-base as a tool to understand ancient rural settlement. However, the isolation of many archaeologists from contemporary methodological developments in the United States, United Kingdom, Italy and Greece, means that their investigations suffer from a number of limitations which hinder our understanding of the character of rural settlement in antiquity and the dynamics of its development.

The first of these is that they are methodologically varied, and hence their results are not readily comparable. This problem has its roots in the immense geographical and cultural variety of Iberia. Each archaeologist has employed their own, frequently *ad hoc*, method with little fore-thought or cross consultation with other archaeologists. Until the "language" of field-survey and an appropriate methodology are developed, the results of surveys such as those considered above cannot be optimised.

Secondly, most studies have suffered from a lack of problem orientation. It is probably fair to say that most have followed the co-ordinators of the *Carta Arqueológica de España* series, who compile details of all known sites within modern political boundaries, and see data collection as preceding analysis without fully appreciating that the two processes are related.

Surviving landscapes are so large and available manpower so small that, like excavations, surface-surveys must examine samples which are designed to answer specific questions. In doing so, archaeologists invariably have to make methodological refinements appropriate to the cultural and geographical character of the area in which they are working.

When many of the Spanish surveys are used to measure the development and distribution of ancient settlement, one becomes aware of a lack of explicitness in the presentation of the data. As a result it is difficult to estimate, for example, whether blanks on a distribution map indicate areas where there was no settlement in antiquity, or merely those areas which, for various reasons, could not be visited during the survey. Additionally, it is possible that a huge regional survey, like that of Ponsich in the lower Guadalquivir valley, might have yielded a far greater density of sites if a large team of 10-15 people walked the area systematically. Factors such as these, however, are rarely discussed.

All surveys are dominated by the concept of "site" and the assumption that human activity is invariably defined in terms of fixed, residential, settlements in the landscape (see, however, Ponsich 1974,281). Furthermore, for the Roman period, it is usually assumed that these can be readily identified on a size/scale hierarchy with the "villa" at its head. Such simple definitions exclude a whole range of "off-site" agricultural activities which do leave archaeological traces and which, if recognised, can alter our understanding of the settlement pattern under study (see above). Once this is accepted, a survey methodology should be employed which is sufficiently sensitive to allow full interpretation of surface scatters as evidence of different types of activity, whether "on-" or "off-site".

Finally, there is the problem of site-chronology. Most survey sites have been dated using non-random selection of a very small proportion of the more recognisable/readily datable surface pottery (principally fine-wares). This means that the dating of a particular site, where given, is biased in favour of the greater visibility of better known pottery, not on an assessment of relative quantities of all pottery present on the surface. Moreover, many sites are dated merely by the presence or absence of different varieties of finewares. This assumes, first, that there was a regular supply of these ceramics to every kind of site, in whichever location or region, throughout their period of production. It must be appreciated that the material collected on the surface has arrived through a whole series of processes (Haselgrove 1985). Account must be taken of these before it can be assumed that the surface finds are representative of the whole history of any particular scatter, whether a habitation site or not. Second, it cannot be assumed that the supply of different finewares to areas in Spain or anywhere else in the Mediterranean was constant through, or between, different periods of time. Indeed the evidence presently available suggests that there were considerable fluctuations in supply (Millett, in press; Keay, in press a).

It was against this background that the Ager Tarraconensis Survey was conceived. In the first

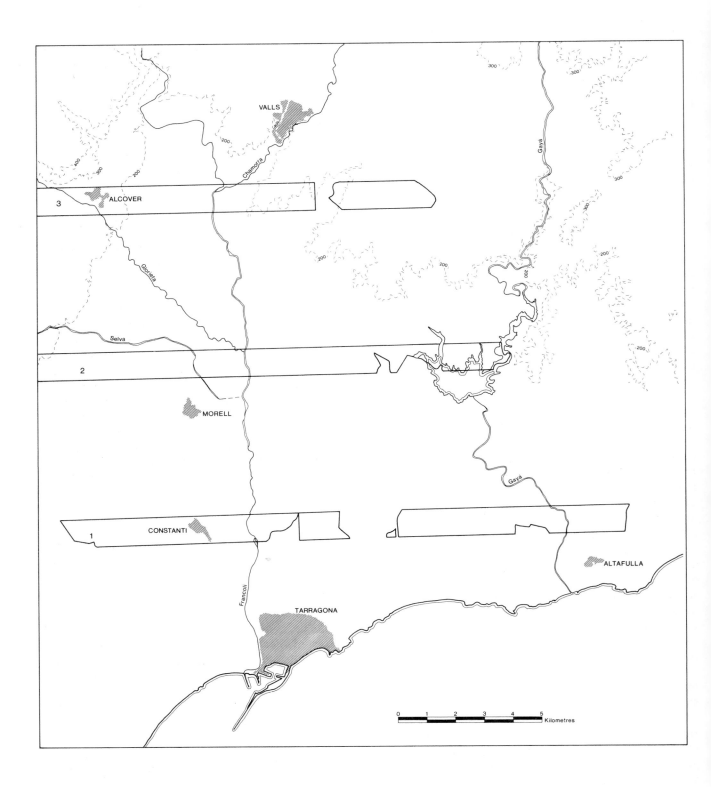

Figure 11.2 Map showing the sample transects walked within the Ager Tarraconensis survey, 1985-86.

instance, survey was adopted as the most appropriate way of studying one of the most momentous episodes of culture contact and culture change in the history of the Iberian peninsula: namely, the impact of Rome upon indigenous settlement patterns between the late third century BC and the fifth and sixth centuries AD (Keay 1987). Much scholarly attention has been paid to the development of Roman towns and the evolution of villae (Gorges 1979; Fernández Castro 1982) during the later Republican and early Imperial periods. Virtually no systematic study, however, has been undertaken on the subject and our understanding of the impact of Roman towns upon native settlement patterns, and their subsequent development within a Provincial framework, is still in its infancy. In view of recent advances in techniques and methods of interpretation (above), it was felt that field-survey was the most efficient way of studying this problem, provided appropriate questions were asked of the data collected. Similarly it was felt that methods originally developed for the examination of less culturally rich areas would benefit from being tested in a culturally central area where larger volumes of material were likely to be recovered.

The survey area

The hinterland of the Roman town of Tarraco (modern Tarragona), the Ager Tarraconensis, was chosen for a number of reasons. By comparison to other parts of Catalunya, the province of Tarragona has been neglected, and until recently, virtually nothing was known about rural settlement distribution during antiquity. During the 1930s, Salvador Vilaseca had built up an important inventory of prehistoric sites in the Baix Camp (Vilaseca 1973), to some degree augmented by Massò's work on the Roman settlement in the vicinity of the modern town of Reus (Massò 1978). In addition, a limited and non-systematic survey was undertaken within the confines of the municipal boundary of Constantí (Papiol 1973-1974). Together with excavations of one or two large villa sites, this represented the totality of work carried out in the hinterland of Tarraco, one of the most important towns in Iberia during antiquity.

In cultural terms, the town itself had been an important settlement during the pre-Roman Iberian period (late 5th to late 3rd centuries BC), drawing upon the resources of a very rich agricultural hinterland. The great strategic and political importance of Tarraco during the Roman period was partly a recognition of its advantageous geographical position. The town lay on the coast adjacent to the river Francolí, whose source lay at a considerable distance inland, in the Conca de Barbera, and relatively close to the mouth of the river Ebro. As a result, it rapidly became an important focus of land and sea-borne communications. During the Republican period (late 3rd to 1st centuries BC), Tarraco became a major strategic centre and, from the end of the 1st century BC onwards, was designated as the capital of the province of Hispania Tarraconensis (Keay in press a). As such, the town could be expected to be a more sensitive indicator of political and economic change than any other town along the east coast of Spain, except perhaps Emporion (Empúries) or Carthago-Nova (Cartagena). The results of a new series of rescue and research excavations at Tarragona are starting to exploit this potential. Indeed, good relations with the excavation unit in Tarragona (TED'A) promised to allow our Survey the chance to exchange data and relate economic change in the town to that in the country.

Despite the great potential for the discovery of ancient settlements that one might expect in the hinterland of a town like Tarraco, very little was known about ancient settlement in the Ager Tarraconensis. This was especially true of the eastern sector (the Alt Camp and Tarragonès). Moreover, preliminary investigation of the area in 1984 suggested that, unlike certain parts of north-eastern Spain (the Ebro valley, the Banyoles area: Jones *et al* 1985) much of the lower lying hinterland of Tarragona was unaffected by major post-Roman geomorphological change, either colluviation, alluviation or erosion. There was, therefore, a good chance that much of the ancient landscape could still be discovered by surface collection. At the same time large tracts of the area were being rapidly destroyed by urbanisation, industrialisation and the use of the deep plough.

As a result, therefore, the eastern sector of the Ager Tarraconensis was selected in an attempt to answer the following questions in the context of systematic field-survey:

1 What was the impact of the foundation of the Roman town of Tarraco upon the indigenous settlement pattern of the region?
2 What was the character of the subsequent town-country relationship and how did it develop through classical and later antiquity?

The answers to these questions could then be used to develop a model for the development of Roman rural settlement in Mediterranean coastal Spain, against which later area studies might be profitably compared (Keay 1987; in press b). The methodology of the survey built upon the experience of other surveys in Spain (above) as well as Britain, Italy and Greece, and attempted to further develop certain aspects in terms of analysis and interpretation. This may now be discussed in more detail.

Keay and Millett

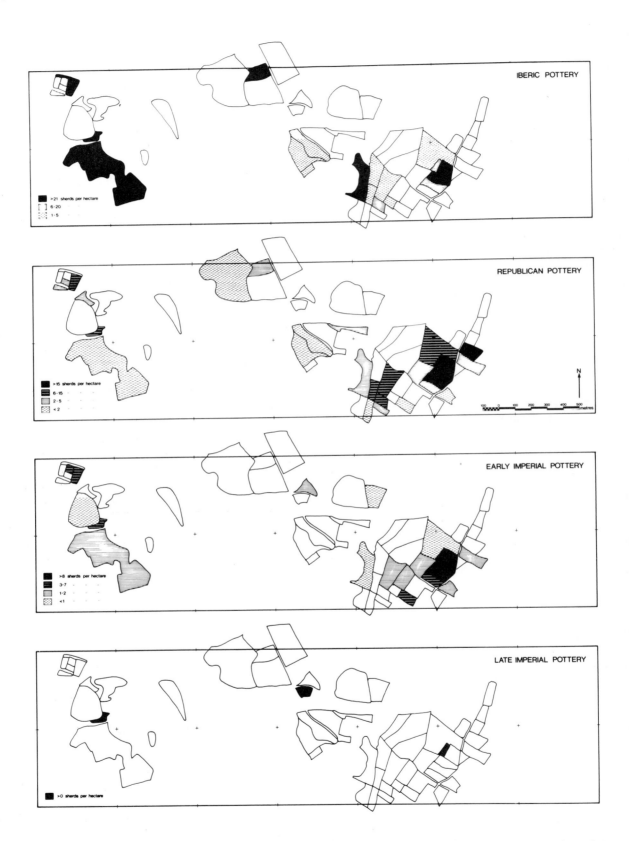

Figure 11.3 Maps of part of the Ager Tarraconensis survey 1986, showing changes in the density of pottery per hectare through time. The scales used are based on the range of values established in 1985-86. The divisions used are the top octile, second highest octile etc for each period.

Methodology: quantifying variation and defining "sites"

The methodology was selected with the aim of obtaining a high level of intensive field-coverage within a sample of the region from which all surface artefacts would be recovered. The justification for this intensive sample approach was two-fold. First, we accepted the contention of Shennan (1985) and others that a properly constructed sample of the landscape, cutting across the different ecological zones, would provide a sufficiently reliable population from which to make generalisations about the remainder of the region. To this end, we defined four evenly spaced one-kilometre wide transects, which ran from east to west across the geological zones of the countryside (Figure 11.2). The progression of these transects inland from the coast provided the opportunity for an evaluation of the town's impact on its territory with distance from the central place.

Secondly, we believe that the material collected from the surface could provide a sufficiently large sample to enable us to examine questions of trade as well as chronology (Millett 1982). Thus, our aim from the outset was to look at the pottery in detail and to evaluate changing patterns of supply through time. This optimisation of information from the survey required the collection of as much material from the surface as possible, rather than selecting the "diagnostic" sherds as has been customary on many other surveys in the Mediterranean. To this end, we decided to walk available fields at 5m intervals with a team experienced in surface collection.

The availability of detailed 1:5000 maps, together with the small scale of the land-parcels in the area, allowed us to use fields as our collection units. Thus, material is collected by the lines of walkers from each available field. It is then processed as if from an excavation, with the material from each field quantified and the figures presented as numbers/weights per hectare in order to facilitate comparison between fields. Whilst each diagnostic sherd is identified as closely as possible and assigned to the narrowest possible chronological period, the data for each field is also summarised into broader horizons, for example, "Republic", "Early Empire", "Late Empire" to enable more general comparisons to be made.

These broad period divisions are used for the definition of "sites". The average amount of pottery per field is calculated for each period division in terms of comparable scales, so that deviation from the normally expected quantity of pottery in a field will be identifiable, irrespective of absolute quantity. A relative scale is, therefore, presented.

Comparable scales are provided by dividing the range of values of quantity of pottery per hectare into quartiles and octiles. Thus if we have data from 79

fields we first find the middle or median value (in this case the 40th value from lowest). This is a more useful value for our purpose than the mean as it is not invalidated by the skewed graphical distribution which is often a feature of this type of data. The scale is subsequently divided into quartiles (the 20th and 60th values in this case) and further into eighths or octiles (the 10th, 30th, 50th and 70th values). By this method the same part of two distributions can be compared without concern for the absolute value. The advantages of this approach are best illustrated by the example from the 1986 season (Figure 11.3) where concentrations of pottery appear and disappear through time.

If values, and hence supply (Millett in press), remain constant through time, the values of the median, quartiles and octiles will remain the same. This does not appear to have been the case with data from the 1986 and 1987 seasons; instead there is a regular decline in the quantity of pottery found from the Iberian period to the Late Empire. In this example our definition of "site" (or Abnormal Densities Above Background Scatter = ADABS) relates to the top eighth of values. Thus a threshold density of 21 sherds per hectare is used for the definition of Iberian ADABS, against only between 0 and 1 sherd per hectare for the Late Empire.

Despite having been "tried and tested" in the context of the Ager Tarraconensis survey, there remain problems in defining the archaeological significance of ADABS. The method only ensures that peaks of the pottery distribution are of equal magnitude for the different periods. To distinguish "site" from "non-site" is really only a function of the desire to define settlement nodes or *places* rather than looking at the *space* between those places, leading to a clearer understanding of the settlement pattern as a whole.

Summary

By the methods described in this paper, we hope to provide a valuable insight into the changing dynamics of the Ager Tarraconensis in antiquity, whilst also developing a survey methodology, appropriate to culturally rich areas, which does not rely on a pre-conceived notion of what constitutes a "site".

Acknowledgements

The authors would like to thank those bodies which have generously funded the Ager Tarraconensis survey, including the British Academy, the Generalitat de Catalunya, the Society of Antiquaries of London, the University of Southampton and the University of Durham. They would also like to thank their Catalan colleagues and all those who have participated in the survey between 1985 and 1987.

References

Almagro M., *et al* 1945. *Carta Arqueológica de España I: Barcelona*. Barcelona.

Amores F., 1982. *Carta Arqueológica de Los Alcores (Sevilla)*. Sevilla.

Bewley R., 1984. *Prehistoric and Romano-British settlement: the Solway Plain, Cumbria*. Unpublished PhD thesis. Cambridge University.

Bonsor G., 1899. Les Colonies Agricoles Pré-Romaines De La Vallée du Bétis. *Révue Archeologique* T XXXV, 1-143.

Bonsor G., 1931. *The Archaeological Expedition Along The Guadalquivir 1899-1901*. New York.

Bosch Gimpera P., 1929. *La Cultura Ibérica Del Bajo Aragón*. IV Congreso Internacional de Arqueología. Barcelona.

Burillo F., 1986. *Aproximación diacrónica a las ciudades antiguas del valle medio del Ebro*. Teruel.

Burillo F., *et al* 1984. Un estudio sincrónico y diacrónico del poblamiento y el territorio: El proyecto interdisciplinar de Mora de Rubielos (Teruel). *Arqueología Espacial* I, 187-205.

Cherry J., Gamble C. and Shennan S., 1978. *Sampling in contemporary British Archaeology*. BAR (British Series) 50. Oxford.

Collantes de Terán F., 1939. *Catálogo Arqueológico y Artístico De La Provincia de Sevilla, Tomo I*. Sevilla.

Collantes de Terán F., 1943. *Catálogo Arqueológico y Artistico De La Provincia de Sevilla, Tomo II*. Sevilla.

Collantes de Terán F., 1951. *Catálogo Arqueológico y Artistico De La Provincia de Sevilla, Tomo III*. Sevilla.

Collantes de Terán F., 1955. *Catálogo Arqueológico y Artistico De La Provincia de Sevilla, Tomo IV*. Sevilla.

Crawford O.G.S., 1953. *Archaeology in the Field*. London. Phoenix House.

Cuyas J.M., 1977. *Historia de Badalona: Badalona Romana i Visigótica. Vol.III*. Badalona.

Estrada J., 1955. *Síntesis Arqueológica de Granollers y sus alrededores*. Granollers.

Estrada J., 1969. Vías y Poblamiento en el territorio del area metropolitana del urbanismo de Barcelona. *Comisión Técnica Revision PC-53, y para uso interno*. Barcelona.

Fernandez Castro M.C., 1982. *Villas Romanas En España*. Madrid.

Foley R., 1981. Off-site Archaeology: an alternative approach for the short-sighted, in Hodder I., Isaac G. and Hammond N., editors, *Pattern of the Past: essays in honour of David Clarke*, 157-182. Cambridge University Press.

Gaffney V., Gaffney C. and Tingle M., 1985. Settlement, economy or behaviour? Micro-regional land-use models and the interpretation of surface artefact patterns, in Haselgrove C., Millett M. and Smith I., editors, *Archaeology from the Ploughsoil: studies in the collection and interpretation of field survey data*, 95-108. Sheffield University Press.

Gorges J.G., 1979. *Les Villae Hispano-Romaines*. Paris.

Haselgrove C., 1985. Inference from ploughsoil artefact samples, in Haselgrove C., Millett M. and Smith I, editors, *Archaeology from the Ploughsoil: studies in the collection and interpretation of field survey data*, 7-30. Sheffield University Press.

Jones R.F., Blagg T.F.C., Devereux C.M., Jordan D.W. and Millett M., 1985. Settlement, landscape and survey archaeology in Catalunya, in Macready S. and Thompson F.H., editors, *Field Survey in Britain and Abroad*, 116-128. London. Society of Antiquaries, Occasional Papers No 6.

Keay S., 1987. The impact of the foundation of Tarraco upon the indigenous settlement pattern of the Ager Tarraconensis. *De Les Estructures Indígenes A L'Organitzacio Provincial Romana De La Hispania Citerior. Jornadas Internacionals d'Arqueologia*, 53-58. Granollers.

Keay S., in press a. The impact of the Roman Conquest and processes in the development of the coastal communities of Hispania Citerior during the Republic. In, Millett M. and Blagg T., editors, *The Early Roman Empire in The West*.

Keay S., in press b. The Ager Tarraconensis In The Late Empire: A Model For The Economic Relationship Of Town And Country In Eastern Spain? In, Barker G., editor, *Roman Agrarian Structure: Archaeological Survey In The Mediterranean*. British School at Rome Supplementary Publication.

Keller D.R. and Rupp D.W., 1983. *Archaeological Field Survey in the Mediterranean Area*. BAR (International Series) 155. Oxford.

Macready S. and Thompson F.H., editors, 1985. *Field survey in Britain and Abroad*. London. Society of Antiquaries, Occasional Papers No 6.

Massò J., 1978. *Reus. Prehistoria i Antiguitat*. Reus.

Millett M., 1982. Town and Country: a review of some material evidence, in Miles D., editor, *The Romano-British Countryside*, 421-431. BAR (British Series) 103. Oxford.

Millett M., 1985. Field Survey Calibration: a contribution, in Haselgrove C., Millett M. and Smith I., editors, *Archaeology from the Ploughsoil: studies in the collection and interpretation of field survey data*, 31-38. Sheffield University Press.

Millett M., in press. Pottery: population or supply patterns?, in Barker G., editor, *Roman Agrarian Structure: archaeological survey in the Mediterranean*. British School at Rome, Supplementary Publication.

Miret M., Sanmartí J. and Santacana J., 1984. Distribución espacial de núcleos Ibéricos: un ejemplo en el litoral Catalan. *Arqueología Espacial* 4, 173-186.

Nolla J.M. and Casas J., 1984. *Carta Arqueológica de les comarques de Girona. El poblament d'època Romana al N.E. de Catalunya*. Girona.

Oña González J., 1984. El Poblamiento rural de epoca Romana en una zona de la ribera de Navarra. *Arqueología Espacial* 5, 71-93.

Papiol L., 1973-1974. Noticias sobre hallazgos Romanos en el término de Constantí. *Boletín Arqueológico de Tarragona*, 121-128.

Ponsich M., 1974. *Implantation Rurale Antique Sur Le Bas-Guadalquivir, I*. Paris.

Ponsich M., 1979. *Implantation Rurale Antique Sur Le Bas-Guadalquivir, II*. Paris.

Ponsich M., 1987. *Implantation Rurale Antique Sur Le Bas-Guadalquivir, III*. Paris.

Potter T., 1979. *The Changing Landscape of South Etruria*. London. Paul Elek.

Prevosti M., 1981a. *Cronologia i Poblament A L'Àrea Rural De Baetulo*. Badalona.

Prevosti M., 1981b. *Cronologia i Poblament A L'Àrea Rural De Iluro*. Mataró.

Ribas M., 1952. *El Poblament D'Iluro*. Barcelona.

Ribas M., 1975. *El Maresme En Els Primers Segles Del Cristianisme*. Mataró.

Romeu G., 1959. Una lápida Romana en Sant Pere Molenta. *Ampurias* XX, 302.

Ruiz M., 1985. *Carta Arqueológica de la Campiña Sevillana*. Zona Sureste I. Sevilla.

Sanmartí J., Santacana J. and Serra R., 1984. El Jaciment Ibèric De L'Argilera I El Poblament Protohistòric Al Baix Penedès. *Quaderns De Treball* No. 6. Barcelona.

Sanmartí J. and Santacana J., 1986. La jerarquia de nuclis en el Poblament Ibèric de la costa del Penedès. *Protohistoria Catalana. 6e Col.loqui Internacional D'Arqueologia De Puigcerdà*, 227-243.

Serra Ràfols J. de C., 1928. *Forma Conventus Tarraconensis I: Baetulo-Blanda*. Barcelona.

Schiffer M.B., 1976. *Behavioural Archaeology*. Academic Press. London and New York.

Shennan S., 1985. *Experiments in the collection and interpretation of archaeological survey data: the East Hampshire survey*. Sheffield University Press.

Vilaseca S., 1973. *Reus y Su Entorno En La Prehistoria*. Reus.

Williams-Freeman J.P., 1915. *An Introduction to Field Archaeology as illustrated by Hampshire*. London. MacMillan and Co.

Chapter 12

Cleaning the Iguvine Stables: Site and Off-site Analysis from a Central Mediterranean Perspective

S K F Stoddart and N Whitehead

"Quae segetem stercorent. Stercus columbinum spargere oportet in pratum vel in hortum vel in segetem. Caprinum, ovillum,
bubulum, item ceterum stercus omne sedulo conservato".
Cato. De Agri Cultura. XXXVI
"Quae segetem stercorent fruges: lupinum, faba, vicia".
Cato. De Agri Cultura XXXVII, 2.

Introduction

The analysis of off-site distributions has received relatively scant attention in the central Mediterranean. The major Italian tradition of research, the *Forma Italiae,* has concentrated more on bounded sites and their distribution within artificially defined regional units (Celuzza and Regoli 1981). Many important regional surveys have not concentrated explicitly on the problem of off-site archaeology, since the sites of complex societies were considered well defined and finds occurring between sites regarded as sporadic and without context. It is suggested that this site-orientated approach has had negative implications for the accurate identification of prehistoric and protohistoric activity in the central Mediterranean (di Gennaro and Stoddart 1982).

A brief review of the recent survey literature, however, reveals that there is now a much greater awareness of the need to analyse "scatters and patches" of artefacts and to adopt a continuous as opposed to discrete approach. This paper aims to assess the implications of this new trend by reviewing different regions of the central Mediterranean where survey work, acknowledging the importance of the off-site approach, has been implemented. The main case study will be the intermontane valley of Gubbio.

Underlying principles

The study of off-site archaeology runs the risk of becoming simply an empirical analysis of artefact distributions. A theoretical framework needs to be established by which the nature and intensity of land-use responsible for artefact distributions may be investigated. Work on hunter-gatherer communities is more advanced in this respect (Binford 1980) while parallel studies of more complex societies are only now beginning to emerge. Examples to date, following the work of Chisholm (1962), have tended to assume a simple relationship between land-use in-tensity and the distance from settlements (Wilkinson 1982). More recent work has correctly criticised this assumption, one example illustrating the complexity of land use around the villa site at Maddle Farm, Berkshire (Gaffney *et al*, 1985).

The successful implementation of an off-site investigation requires an integration of theory and practice. In particular, three points need to be investigated:

1 The nature of post depositional distortion.
2 The nature of cultural deposition. In particular there is demand for a clear methodology for the recovery of off-site information suitable for understanding different levels of economic organisation. The identification of Land Utilisation Types (FAO 1976) is suggested here as one possibility.
3 Although survey data can stand alone, excavation is useful, especially for testing hypotheses suggested by survey data. Excavation may be introduced, for example, to test assumptions about the nature of local ecology, resource utilisation and the cultural practices of refuse disposal (Bowden *et al*, this volume).

The central Mediterranean landscape

Prime areas of the central Mediterranean landscape have been heavily utilised since the fifth millennium BC (Malone 1986). Activity in central Italy and particularly in the Gubbio basin was more restricted until *c* 1200 BC, but this was followed by a rapid intensification that in some areas led to state formation. Rather than a simple case of intensification through time, in common with areas of the eastern Mediterranean (Van Andel *et al*, 1986), the situation is one of complex cycles of intensified and reduced utilisation. In the territories of the Etruscan coastal polities, for example, even where only site-orientated survey has been practised, cycles of occupation have been identified (summarised in Stoddart 1988). The recovery of the subtleties of these cycles of utilisation is one potential target for off-site archaeology. The nature of those cycles, however, makes the recovery of such information rather more difficult.

In addition, the central Mediterranean landscape is extremely delicate. Erosion and deposition are complex phenomena that cannot be reduced to the bipartite climatic model originally proposed by Vita Finzi (1969). Local effects, dependent on human activity and tectonic conditions, have been as important as the more general climatic fluctuations. In the extreme conditions of the tectonic valleys of inland central Italy, for example, the steep limestone escarpments are particularly unstable.

There is, therefore, in areas of the central Mediterranean, a complex system of colluvial and alluvial processes. These processes are clearly an important factor in considering the distribution of artefacts at a regional scale (Allen this volume).

Off-site archaeology in the central Mediterranean: a review

Current research in the central Mediterranean is beginning to turn its attention to the issue of off-site archaeology (Barker 1986). Some of the earliest published work is that of the Agro Pontino project (Kammermans *et al* 1985). This has been concerned largely with a geographically well-defined open plain to the north of the famous Neanderthal site of Monte Circeo. The work is orientated towards testing models of land evaluation as perceived by early prehistoric populations (the land evaluation technique has been developed for modern populations by the FAO and is discussed below in the context of the Gubbio project). The suggestion was that an ecologically predictive framework could be tested directly by implementing intensive survey which cross-cuts the predicted zones of land use variation. The Montarrenti project has also addressed the off-site issue (Barker *et al* 1986) by resurveying the same geographical area over several seasons. This has allowed the reconstruction of artefact density by field units under different recovery conditions, with important implications for the replication of off-site survey results.

Work in the Alto Polesine of northern Italy (Balista *et al* 1987) has concentrated initially on investigating the relationship between surface and sub-surface material prior to intensive survey. In particular "surface contexts" were defined on the basis of colour, texture and composition in order to elucidate cultural and natural processes.

After classic extensive surveys in the tradition of the British School at Rome's South Etruria survey, a new direction can be perceived in the organisation

and aims of field survey. To date, however, research aims which emphasise the study of hunter- gatherer communities have tended to operate a more detailed off-site approach than work directed at more complex societies.

An example from the Italian Apennines

Since 1983, a multi-period survey has been underway in the well- defined tectonic basin of Gubbio, northeast Umbria. The conditions of this upland basin throw into relief many of the key problems for the implementation of an off-site approach to archaeological distributions. First, tectonic and geomorphological forces have produced a complex pattern of eroded relict surfaces on upland landforms and complex drainage and alluviation in lowland areas. Integrated geomorphological and pedological work was, therefore, essential. Second, the relatively high altitude (between 350 and 1000 m) most probably favoured the presence of extensive rather than intensive economic systems in many periods. This does not preclude the application of off-site analysis, but requires explicit modelling of economic organisation suited to the local context and not one simply transferred from elsewhere. Third, the upland area was removed from the centres of social complexity, only entering the wider system of central Italy on a cyclic basis. The late Bronze Age was the first period of intensified land-use while the Roman period was the first in which the landscape was extensively occupied. Even at this period, the position of the city of Gubbio, at some distance from the *Via Flaminia*, did not encourage such intensive economic activity as in other areas of central Italy.

A major consequence for the research design in this area was, therefore, that the quantities of artefacts within the region were not as overwhelming as was generally the case for Mediterranean landscapes (Bintliff and Snodgrass 1985; Keay and Millett this volume).

In terms of temporal diversity, there are clearly period biases in the recovery of off-site information. Recorded human occupation of the valley began in the Middle Palaeolithic. Lithic material of this period has only been recovered on badly dissected fluvio-lacustrine terraces while only a small proportion of the original landscape is available for analysis. In this state of preservation, natural rather than cultural processes will almost certainly predominate with the result that only a small proportion of the artefact distribution can be interpreted in terms of prehistoric behaviour.

For the Neolithic period, a different preservation bias is apparent. Flint material displays considerable density variation suggesting that land-use intensity was by no means uniform. Pottery is generally of poor quality and includes none of the well-fired painted wares found on the Adriatic coast or in the south of Italy. Pottery survival is, therefore, subject to severe post-depositional distortion. At a more general level, Neolithic sites tend to occur on a complex of centrally placed alluvial fans, although the location of high density scatters do not necessarily correspond with stable pedological and geomorphological surfaces. Instead they often appear on buried surfaces subject to active erosion. The excavation of one Neolithic site revealed the complexity of the site-formation process and demonstrated that differential survival of cultural material, brought to the surface in this manner, raises severe problems for the analysis of off-site distributions. The site of San Marco was discovered as a dense scatter of flint, pottery, daub and dark cultural sediment across a field while the artefacts recovered did not display any degree of correlation. The stratigraphy of the site - revealed by deep ploughing in the 1970s - showed a single, short phase of modern land-use that dismantled the surviving Neolithic surface. This single ploughing event produced a mantle of cultural material which was the product of the one detectable disturbance since Neolithic times. The surface artefacts were the product of the active modern disturbance by ploughing of this mantle. Underneath it, the sealed deposits include ditches and a pit which represented secondary cultural deposits with excellent preservation of environmental and cultural material. In quantitative terms the results show a decreasing density of finds with depth.

Evidence from the Bronze Age and early Iron Age raises further problems for the investigation of artefact distributions. Excavation has shown that at least until the late Bronze Age, flint material was still employed in small quantities. Unfortunately such artefacts are difficult to distinguish from those types that would generally be attributed an earlier date when recovered by surface collection. The traditional dating of pottery requires the presence of particular diagnostic types which, in a typical sample, are only present in small quantities. Pottery was still relatively poorly fired and easily destroyed by post-depositional processes. The more closely dated metalwork was a recycled and relatively precious commodity rarely found in a surface sample. So-called sporadic finds do, however, take on renewed significance if interpreted in terms of off-site analysis. Excavation has shown that the Bronze Age sites only survived when covered by later cultural deposits on the uplands and natural sedimentary deposits in the lower parts of the valley. This has major implications for the recovery of off-site distributions.

By contrast, the Roman period has clearly datable artefacts that occur with relative frequency (some more detailed comments are made on the preliminary analysis of this material below). This represents the first period (with the possible exception of the Neolithic) where land-use can potentially be measured through artefact density. Few of the artefacts, however, are temporally specific, to the extent that cycles of economic organisation, expected even within the relatively short period of Roman occupation, may be identified. Tile cannot be readily distinguished into temporal categories. Even in certain parts of coastal central Italy, present knowledge allows only a broad temporal subdivision, while coarse wares depend on tightly stratified local sequences. As a result, the implementation of an off-site approach requires a methodology that goes beyond surface survey. Excavation confirmed that the formation processes acting on Roman cultural material were strikingly different to those of preceding periods. Excavation of one small agricultural building showed that the density of artefacts distributed vertically was the opposite to that of the Neolithic site, in this case an *increasing* quantity of artefactual material with depth. The Neolithic surface remains were the product of a truncated sub-surface deposit. The Roman surface remains were the product of a collapsed structure. This differential preservation is not merely the product of a difference in time-scale. Cultural and natural processes have differentially affected the surviving residues of two different economic systems.

Traditionally Roman field workers, perhaps affected by the Roman ideology of ritually bounded space, have emphasised the concept of the bounded site: the city and its villas. Although the state and imperial societies may emphasise boundaries, these may not be so well defined at a behavioural level. Instead a more complex pattern of land-use may be suggested, offering a major challenge to the successful implementation of an off-site strategy.

Towards a methodology

The methodological approach to the survey and concurrent excavation followed a common framework despite a flexible response to current research problems:

1 The survey programme was multi-period, although excavation concentrated on the first millennium BC. During surface survey, complete recovery of all artefactual material was undertaken, with the exception of modern pottery and tile (which was counted in the second phase of the survey). The absence of quantified information on modern pottery precludes direct comparison with modern land-use or ethnoarchaeological studies.

2 Analysis was at a regional scale. The basin of Gubbio is well defined geographically and forms

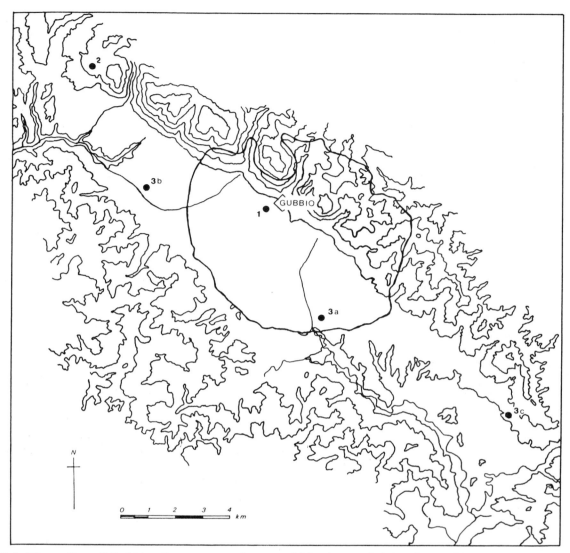

Figure 12.1. The valley of Gubbio. Contours are drawn at 100m interval rising from 400m. (Drawn by Caroline Gait).

a natural study region, approximately 25 km long and 7 km wide (Figure 12.1). Geomorphological, pedological, botanical and archaeological studies were confined to sampling within this region.

3 The fragmented modern land-use of the valley made the field (or sub-sections of the field) the most convenient sampling unit. Artificial units would have taken much longer to implement.

4 Recovery was by line-walking at 5 to 10 m intervals. Standard forms were completed to record land use, weather conditions, time of day and general information on finds. Locations were plotted on 1:10,000 maps. After the first season, aerial photographs with superimposed contours were made available by the local authorities.

5 Areas of optimum visibility were examined. This was to allow comparison of artefact density between collection units. A relatively full coverage of lowland areas has been achieved by revisiting

over several seasons. Sections were also examined wherever possible.

Within these principal guide-lines, the survey developed an increasingly intensive strategy to investigate the off-site problem. The first season in 1983 concentrated on well defined land forms and selected sample areas. Three principal areas were investigated: watersheds, the ancient Pleistocene landscape and the immediate environs of the Umbrian, Roman and Medieval city of Gubbio. In 1984, once a more detailed 1:50,000 pedological map (Schomaker and Van Wavaren 1984) was available, the remaining terrace landscape was examined. In 1985, after completion of a geomorphological map at a scale of 1:25,000 (Coltorti 1985), experimental work was undertaken to select an appropriate method by which continuous artefact distributions could be measured (Tucker and Stoddart 1985; Milliken

1986). In the final two seasons of 1986 and 1987, a more intensive strategy was adopted, compatible with pre-existing work. For this, the field was maintained as a maximal sampling unit. Scale diagrams on the reverse of each form were constructed for each field (regardless of the quantity of finds) to record the position and direction of walkers. The form was also modified to include a record of the quantity of finds made by individuals. Mechanical counters were introduced for the control of tile quantities. This technique proved to be a practical approach to tackling fragmented land-use in the valley and, at the same time, rapidly collect information on the density of artefacts across the terrain. This approach was implemented in four distinct areas of the valley. Two transects were placed at the extreme ends of the tectonic valley cross-cutting the local ecological diversity and the major geological fault-line. Two further transects were placed across the the central part of valley; this analysis coincided with a more detailed environmental study (including further pedological work by Finke and Sewuster 1988) of the territory (Harding 1985), of the excavated sites and of the major centre of population from the end of the first millennium, the city of Gubbio itself. Finally, an extensive area of the valley bottom with relatively favourable modern land use was examined some distance from modern urban centres.

Research in other similar tectonic valleys has, in the past, emphasised the importance of natural transforms in the implementation of field survey (Stoddart 1981). In this case only limited geomorphological and pedological information was available when the project began. A programme of work was, therefore, required to refine and increase available knowledge. The first stage, by Dutch and Italian colleagues, aimed to stratify the landscape into zones that were the product of different combinations of natural processes and transforms. In this respect the different traditions of research represented by the Dutch and Italian work have proved complementary in elucidating the complexity of the natural landscape. The Dutch have emphasised soil formation as a distinguishing variable. In particular, their work has identified the relative stability of sectors of the landscape. The Italian geomorphologist, on the other hand, has emphasised stratigraphic relationships in a more explicitly temporal framework.

Although the final complex sub-division of the landscape still remains to be compared with the archaeology, it is clear that the evidence provided by one direction of research would have been largely inadequate.

After initial screening for the distortion of natural transforms, the pedological evidence can also be used for the reconstruction of land-use patterns. In the territories of excavated sites, defined by site-catchment, information was collected on soil characteristics considered important for early agriculture, for example, moisture, oxygen availability and workability. These data, following the FAO evaluation technique (FAO 1976), make it possible to predict land-use by communities characterised by a particular level of technology. With the appropriate controls on environmental change, this can make an important contribution to the modelling of the local economy that is so essential for the interpretation of off-site distributions.

In the central area of the Gubbio valley, a series of controls have been implemented for the interpretation of off-site material. A territory related to the main excavated sites of the Bronze Age, but also incorporating the excavated sites of the Neolithic and Roman periods, has been defined by site-catchment analysis for intensive study. For this specific area information on the local environment from excavated sites and geological sections can be integrated with the results of pedological work. Furthermore, a direct comparison can be made between the evidence for landscape utilisation, refuse disposal and site formation from the five excavated sites, and the nature of artefact distributions across the territory as a whole. In a study region on this scale, it may be possible to distinguish land-use from other natural transforms as a mechanism for producing off-site material.

Modelling land-use: an application

Although analysis is incomplete, it is useful to consider the value of testing land-use models in the interpretation of off-site distributions in the case of Gubbio. For the purpose of this investigation it is essential to consider, not only surface material, but evidence from excavated contexts for site-formation processes, economic organisation and refuse disposal. A more detailed discussion of the Roman material is presented.

Each of the prehistoric periods presents its own unique set of problems. Although modelling discard behaviour among hunter-gatherer populations is relatively advanced, Palaeolithic and Epi-palaeolithic material from the Gubbio valley has been subjected to considerable post-depositional transformation. Conclusions for this period of human activity are therefore more likely to represent an integration between geomorphological and archaeological information. It is also unlikely that excavation, if carried out, would be able to provide any control on site formation processes.

Excavation was carried out for the Neolithic period, providing detailed evidence for the range of resources extracted from the local environment. Given the complementary nature of excavated and surface material, it should be possible to construct a general model of land-use, at least for the valley floor, during the Neolithic period. The distribution of lithic artefacts, for example, should act as a guide for extensive activities. The Bronze Age period, by contrast, lacks well defined, common and well preserved cultural artefacts which could be used for identifying period-specific land-use activities. Interpretation has consequently depended on excavation, since the few surface finds that do exist are difficult to disentangle from geomorphological processes.

In the late Bronze Age (*c* 1000 BC) there is at least a bipartite pattern of artefact discard relating to two topographically distinct site-groups. Upland sites (*c* 900 m) are characterised by large middens, used for the discard of domestic refuse. The altitude presents an ecology suitable for pastoralism, an interpretation that is confirmed by the evidence from the middens themselves. Logistically placed "sites" associated with this pastoral economy can be envisaged, but modern land-use and erosion make detection difficult. The colluvial footslopes below these upland areas (*c* 500 m) most probably comprised the cultivation component of the mixed economy. Indeed late Bronze Age material is distributed across the slopes but is seemingly absent from the valley bottom. In these areas, however, geomorphological forces have intervened so heavily that is it is often difficult to offer a cultural rather than geomorphological interpretation.

Evidence for Roman exploitation is, for two reasons, rather more convincing: 1) land surfaces since the period of deposition have been relatively stable and 2) artefacts are more closely datable. It is also possible to present a model of economic organisation with implications for land-use on a regional scale. This identifies exploitation on three levels:

1 The immediate city area, with encircling cemeteries. Beyond this, an intensively farmed and manured landscape with logistical, but not residential, locations.
2 Upland pastoral sites which would not be expected to show a manuring pattern, but perhaps small logistical locations.
3 Agricultural sites in the lowland landscape not directly exploited from the town. These would create a less continuous but densely manured landscape, probably more in the form of "haloes" around the sites concerned.

The testing of this model shows a much more complex pattern of land-use than that encompassed by the model itself. This is particularly the case in the valley bottom, an area favourable to research but where a great range of cultural and natural processes were in operation. Greater methodological promise is often confronted by greater theoretical complexity in economic modelling.

A crucial element in exploring this complexity is establishing a bridging argument between economic models of land-use, such as that presented above, and cultural mechanisms of artefact dispersal from concentrated activity areas. The two opening quotations from *Cato* illustrate the range of complexity for Roman agricultural practice. It is also apparent that the Roman authors only presented certain idealised types of behaviour. A particular dimension of this complexity is found in a marginal region such as the Gubbio basin where intensive manuring, incorporating cultural material, from a farmstead was probably only practised at times of peak economic activity and then only in certain culturally and politically specific areas of the landscape. In the preceding model and the following discussion, however, it is assumed as a

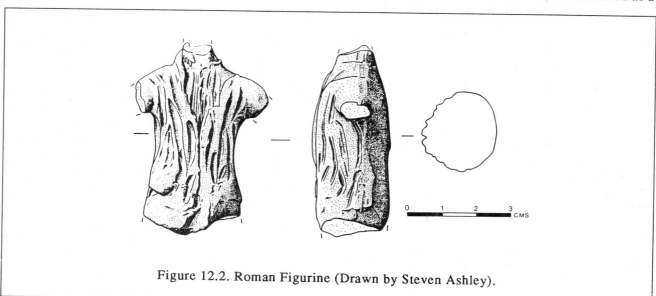

Figure 12.2. Roman Figurine (Drawn by Steven Ashley).

Table 12.1. Provisional densities (per 600 m²) of Roman material
for five arbitrary sample areas (for locations see Figure 12.1).

Area	Minimum Density		Maximum density	
	Coarse	Tile	Coarse	Tile
1. Town Periphery	10	2	79	3
2. Upland	0	0	116	537
3A. Lowland	< 1	< 1	185	757
3B. Lowland	0	0	1	10
3C. Lowland	< 1	< 1	60	75

working hypothesis that cultural debris was incorporated in manure discard.

The local environment of the town appears much as expected (Table 12.1, 1), although recent expansion of the modern town outside the medieval walls does not allow as complete an investigation as might be hoped. Beyond the cemeteries and away from the principal roads, dense scatters of off-site material have been registered. In these scatters, fine and coarse wares occur more frequently than tile, suggesting an intensively manured and farmed area. Within these relatively dense scatters it is difficult to assess the significance of local density variations that would be considered highly significant in more remote parts of the valley. The upland "pastoral" pattern (Table 12.1, 2) is difficult to test effectively because of the modern abandonment of many upland areas by intensive agriculture. It appears, however, that those areas which have been ploughed conform to the expected pattern. Where erosion has not intervened, sites "stand-out" from the more general background scatter.

The pattern of the valley floor, however, is considerably more complex (Table 12.1, 3A-C). Some "sites" stand out fairly clearly from sparse scatters of cultural debris (Table 12.1, 3A). This includes the excavated site (and other surface sites with dark soil marks and abundant pottery) where large quantities of refuse had not been redistributed, but left *in situ*. In this case manuring was apparently extensive rather than intensive while small logistical locations have also been observed, generally some distance from dense artefact scatters. Other lowland sites appear to stand out starkly from a landscape devoid of surface material. This is particularly true of the more remote areas of the valley bottom. Small variations in density appear, in this part of the landscape, to be highly significant, although they would not be interpreted as such for areas close to major urban centres.

Further work needs to be carried out if the possibility of geomorphological distortion is to be excluded and mechanisms for investigating the variable density of tile and pottery are to be established. It is already clear, however, that in the Roman period, land-use is not related simply to distance from settlements. Instead we must consider the full complexity of Roman economic organisation at a local logistical scale and at a regional scale with the complex cross-cutting factors of the market economy and ecological potential. Under these conditions, many categories of discard are apparent, most of which are difficult to unravel. One of these categories is ritual; clay figurines, for example, have been discovered across the lowland landscape, unassociated with other material (Figure 12.2).

The medieval period raises a further complication. Documentary sources have demonstrated clearly the complexity of land-use cycles which are difficult to tackle archaeologically for two reasons (Allegrucci nd): first, there has been considerable continuity of site occupation and second, datable artefacts are rarely recovered in the field; the most prominent datable off-site activity can be detected around the richer Renaissance villas on the slopes overlooking the valley. Unfortunately, this is only one aspect of economic activity and can hardly be considered representative.

Conclusion

The analysis of off-site distributions is dependent on an integrated study of artefact patterning and economic and cultural modelling. Surface survey can be greatly aided by excavation to establish the nature of discard patterns and the supporting economy in the local area (Bintliff *et al* this volume). However, even this may be insufficient. Many processes, cultural and natural, have combined to make interpretation difficult. A clear signal may be impossible to interpret when the level of cultural and natural interference increases.

As a final note of caution, Malta represents an extreme example of the problems described in this paper. The islands have been intensively cultivated since the Neolithic and considerable erosion has taken place. Geomorphological distortion, however, is not the most serious problem. Prehistoric pottery was, until recently, used as a roofing material while there are legal codes encouraging the movement of large blocks of soil around the islands. This is the manuring theory taken to its logical conclusion. It does, however, raise the important problem that the palimpsest effect of repeated land-use makes the interpretation of off-site patterns very difficult to attain in increasingly complex economic contexts. In the case of Malta, "intact" discard may only be fully verified where it is stratified. Interpretation becomes a Herculean task.

Acknowledgements

The Gubbio project is very grateful to the Azienda di Soggiorno e Turismo per l'Eugubino, the Comune of Gubbio, the Comunità montana dell'Alto Chiascio, the Provincia di Perugia, the Regione dell'Umbria and the Soprintendenza archeologica per l'Umbria for assistance.

The following British and American funding bodies have supported the project: British Academy, the British School at Rome, Crowther Beynon Fund (University Museum of Archaeology and Anthropology, Cambridge), Emslie Horniman Fund of the Royal Anthropological Institute, Magdalene College, Cambridge, National Geographic Society of America, Washington, D.C., Prehistoric Society, and the Society of Antiquaries of London.

Olivetti, S.P.A. and British Olivetti have kindly provided computer support.

References

Allegrucci F., nd. *L'economia agraria dell'eugubino tra l'XI secolo e la fine dell'autonomia del governo roveresco.*

Balista C., Blake H., De Guio A., Davis C., Howard P., Whitehouse R. and Wilkins J.. 1987. Alto Polesine Project. *Lancaster in Italy. (Archaeological research undertaken in Italy by the Department of Classics and Archaeology in 1986)* 1987, 6-12.

Barker G., 1986. L'archeologia del paesaggio italiano: nuovi orientamenti e recenti esperienze. *Archeologia Medievale* 13,7-30.

Barker G., Coccia S., Jones B. and Sitzia J., 1986. The Montarrenti survey 1985: integrating archaeological, environmental and historical data. *Archeologia Medievale* 13, 291-320.

Binford L., 1980. Willow smoke and dog's tails: hunter gatherer settlement systems and archaeological site formation. *American Antiquity* 45, 4-20.

Bintliff J.L. and Snodgrass A.M., 1985. The Cambridge/Bradford Boeotian Expedition. *Journal of Field Archaeology* 12, 123-63.

Celuzza M. and Regoli E., 1981. Alla ricerca di passaggi, in Carandini A., editor, *Storie dalla Terra*. Bari, De Donato, 301-316.

Chisholm M., 1962. *Rural settlement and land use*. London, Hutchinson.

Coltorti M., 1985. *Geomorphological map of the Valley of Gubbio*. Unpublished.

di Gennaro F. and Stoddart S.K.F., 1982. A review of the evidence for prehistoric activity in part of South Etruria. *Papers of the British School at Rome* 50, 1-21.

FAO, 1976. A framework for land evaluation. *FAO Soils Bulletin* 52.

Finke P. and Sewuster R.J.E., 1988. *A soil survey and land evaluation in a Bronze Age context for the central Gubbio basin, Italy*. Amsterdam, Laboratory for Physical Geography and Soil Science.

Gaffney C., Gaffney V. and Tingle M., 1985. Settlement, economy or behaviour? Micro-regional land use models and the interpretation of surface artefact patterns, in Haselgrove C., Millett M. and Smith I., editors, *Archaeology from the ploughsoil: studies in the collection and interpretation of field survey data*, 95-107. University of Sheffield.

Harding J., 1985. *Site territories in the Gubbio Area*. Unpublished Provisional report of the Gubbio Project.

Kammermans H., Loving S. and Voorrips A., 1985. Changing patterns of prehistoric landuse in the Agro Pontino, in Malone C. and Stoddart S.F.K., editors, *Papers in Italian Archaeology IV. Part i. The Human Landscape*, 53-68. BAR (International Series) 243. Oxford.

Malone C., 1986. *Exchange systems and Style in the Central Mediterranean 4500-1700 bc*. Unpublished Ph.D. thesis. Cambridge University.

Milliken S., 1986. *The Palaeolithic of the Gubbio valley, Central Italy*. Unpublished B.A. dissertation. University of London.

Schomaker M. and Van Wavaren E., 1984. *A physiographic soil map of the Gubbio basin, Umbria, Italy*. Amsterdam, Laboratory for Physical Geography and Soil Science.

Stoddart S.K.F., 1988. An archaeological survey in the Casentino: per una storia archeologica del Casentino. *Archeologia Medievale* 8, 503-526.

Stoddart S.K.F., 1988. Divergent trajectories in central Italy, 1200-500 BC, in Champion T.C., editor, *Centre and Periphery*, 88-101. London. Allen and Unwin.

Tucker D. and Stoddart S.F.K., 1985. *Gubbio Survey 1985*. Unpublished provisional report of the Gubbio Project.

Van Andel T.H., Runnels C.N. and Pope K.D., 1986. Five thousand years of land use and abuse in the southern Argolid. *Hesperia* 55 (1), 103-128.

Vita-Finzi C., 1969. *The Mediterranean valleys: geological changes in historical times*. Cambridge, Cambridge University Press.

Wilkinson T.J., 1982. The definition of ancient manured zones by means of extensive sherd sampling techniques. *Journal of Field Archaeology* 9, 323-333.

Index